Raymond's Checklist for His Personal Bucket List

Raymond's Checklist for His Personal Bucket List

By
Raymond Greenlaw

Roxy Publishing
Savannah, Georgia
United States of America

Copy Editor—Marjorie Roxburgh
Cover Design—Robert Greenlaw
Text Design—Raymond Greenlaw
Typesetting—WORD – Garamond 11

Roxy Publishing
Savannah, Georgia 31419
United States of America

http://drraymondgreenlaw.com

Second edition, paperback.

Book 4 in *Raymond's Checklist Series*.

© By Raymond Greenlaw, 2020. All rights reserved.

No portion of this work may be reproduced, stored in a retrieval system, or transmitted in any form or by any means—electronic, mechanical, photocopying, recording, or otherwise—without prior written permission of the publisher. All readers of this book are responsible for their own actions and decisions.

ISBN 978-1-947467-17-0 (Paperback)

Dedication

To the servicemen and women of the United States of America. Your willingness to serve and sacrifice has given me the opportunity to fulfill my dreams. I appreciate my freedom every single day. Thanks from the bottom of my heart.

Table of Contents

1. Dedication 5
2. Preface 9
3. Acknowledgments 11
4. Chapter 1 Introduction 13
5. Part I General Categories 20
6. Chapter 2 Adventure 21
7. Chapter 3 Travel 32
8. Chapter 4 Nature and Animals 39
9. Chapter 5 Sports 46
10. Chapter 6 Culture 57
11. Chapter 7 Entertainment 67
12. Chapter 8 Music 72
13. Chapter 9 History 80
14. Chapter 10 Education 92
15. Chapter 11 Personal Writing 96
16. Chapter 12 Self 106
17. Part II Specific Travel 114
18. Chapter 13 UN Countries 115
19. Chapter 14 Capitals of UN Countries 132
20. Chapter 15 World Territories 143
21. Chapter 16 World Islands 148
22. Chapter 17 USA's States 162
23. Chapter 18 USA's State Capitals 166
24. Chapter 19 USA's Second Cities 170

25. Chapter 20 USA's National Parks, Seashores, and Lakeshores 176
26. Chapter 21 USA's National Forests and Grasslands 182
27. Chapter 22 USA's National Monuments 193
28. Chapter 23 USA's Territories 203
29. Chapter 24 USA's Extreme Points 206
30. Chapter 25 Thailand's Provinces 210
31. Chapter 26 Thailand's National and Marine Parks 216
32. Chapter 27 Thailand's Extreme Points 226
33. Chapter 28 Thailand's Mountains 228
34. Chapter 29 Thailand's Scuba-Diving Sites ... 230
35. Part III Sporting Competitions and Activities 234
36. Chapter 30 Marathon Running 235
37. Chapter 31 Ultra-Marathon Running 252
38. Chapter 32 Road/Shorter Trail Races 264
39. Chapter 33 Multi-Sport and Triathlon 272
40. Chapter 34 Cycling 288
41. Chapter 35 Scuba Diving 310
42. Chapter 36 Mountaineering 320
43. Chapter 37 Hiking 326
44. Part IV Professional Activities 337
45. Chapter 38 Career 338
46. Chapter 39 Computing Books 349
47. Chapter 40 Speaking Engagements 357

48. Chapter 41 Journal Papers 394
49. Chapter 42 Conference Papers 405
50. Chapter 43 Conclusions 415
51. Books by Raymond Greenlaw 418
52. About the Author 420

Preface

During the COVID-19 pandemic, I'm writing a book series titled: *Raymond's Checklists*. This is the fourth book. The others written are: *Traveling in the USA* (Book 1), *Traveling in Thailand* (Book 2), *Traveling the World* (Book 3), *Gear for a Long Hike* (Book 5), and *Cycling Gear* (Book 6). A few additional books are in the works. I prefer to be engaged in exploits rather exposing about them. These are strange times.

The Cambridge Dictionary defines the phrase *bucket list* as a collection of things a person would like to do or achieve before they die. Throughout my life, I set goals for myself. I kept records of things—a palmarès containing athletic achievements, UN countries visited, a curriculum vitae, scuba-dive sites explored, and so on. Creating, maintaining, and updating this information served as a compass, providing my life direction. I saw what I was missing. My curiosity piqued. To fill in gaps, I took on new challenges. Those in turn snowballed into other dreams.

On many occasions I received solicitations for information about my various pursuits. To satisfy those requests, I decided to organize and publish my materials in the form of a bucket list. It evolves. I include a broad range of categories. I provide anecdotes, but for the most part, I let the bucket list itself do the talking. Many items are self-explanatory.

I hope my bucket list provides inspiration. It has motivated me. My list grows and takes me in unanticipated directions. I follow my nose. I keep chasing dreams. Based on what's here, maybe you can add new items to your bucket list. I hope you achieve items that I couldn't. I hope your opportunities grow.

Although I tried to be as careful as possible in my writing, a few grammatical errors and typos may remain. I apologize in advance. I would like to eliminate any errors in future editions of this work. I appreciate any corrections.

Enjoy!

Raymond Greenlaw
May 10, 2020
Revised: November 29, 2021

Acknowledgments

A special thanks to Wongduean "Kig" Bohthong for her endless support.

Thanks to my best friends Geir Agnarsson, Theresa Araneta, Glenn Fleagle, Barry Fussell, Paul Göransson, Sanpawat Kantabutra, Shigeki Makino, Patrick Messer, Mirna Morrison, Andrew Phillips, Adrian Plante, Marjorie Roxburgh, Peter Solomon, Linda Spring-Andrews, James Wogulis, and Nuj Wongprapas for sharing and proposing many adventures over the years. Thanks for opening my eyes wider than I could have ever done without you. Thanks for adding items to my bucket list. Sincere apologies to anyone whom I accidentally omitted.

Thanks to my other friends, colleagues, training partners, and students who helped make everything special and worthwhile. Sharing good times has been very meaningful to my life.

A warm thanks to Marjorie for her careful reading and comments on the manuscript.

A special thanks to Adrian for providing me with a number of helpful suggestions and edits. Thanks for holding me to the highest standards.

A sincere thanks to reviewers and to those who provided me with constructive criticisms on early drafts of this work. Your suggestions helped me to improve this book. I'm indebted to you. Many others contributed to this project. A sincere thanks to everyone involved.

Chapter 1
Introduction

The reader who wants to jump to my bucket list immediately may skip to Chapter 2. Here I provide some personal background and introductory remarks.

I grew up in Riverside, Rhode Island in the US in a middle-class family in a home in the suburbs. I'm the youngest of four children born to Roxy and Bob. I attended public schools. My high school's mascot is the Townies. Starting from age 12, I worked mowing lawns, raking leaves and pulling weeds, cleaning homes, filing metal shards from the insides of improperly cast mood rings, shoveling snow, polishing whales' teeth, and cleaning tennis courts. I didn't spend much time contemplating destinations beyond my backyard. I didn't dream.

During my sophomore, junior, and senior years of high school, I worked full-time as a dishwasher at the exclusive Agawam Hunt Country Club (AHCC) in Rumford, RI. I lied about my age to secure the job. My girlfriend waitressed there. She dumped me for a cook who had a salary. I earned the minimum hourly wage— $2.75. I had a time card. I punched it 50+ hours during school weeks. My take-home pay exceeded $100, but it wasn't enough.

I commuted ten miles per day to AHCC by bicycle. The riding helped me heal. I focused on the busy roads.

I studied hard. I didn't quit my job. I lettered in four sports. I worked hard. I started to dream. I saved for a trip to Europe. I saved for college. I spent the summer of 1979 in Europe. I paid for the trip. It broadened my horizons and was an eye opener. Few people I knew went to Europe. It was a dream I made come true. That trip is the first item on my (original) bucket list. I didn't know it at the time. The phrase *bucket list* was coined 35+ years later.

I kept dreaming. I traveled to California. Another bucket-list item checked. I attended Pomona College and worked 20 hours per week. The move out West further opened my eyes. I graduated. Check. I had no savings. I was in debt. I went to graduate school in Washington State and worked 20 hours per week. The move to the Pacific Northwest showed me another part of the country. Check. Because of my scholarship and higher rate of pay, I was able to save money. I bought a house. Check. From a young age, people told me I would become a doctor. I graduated with a PhD. Check. I made them proud. I sold my house.

When I was 24, I purchased a car. Check. It was a beater. I paid $400 cash for my *second* car—a Toyota Corolla with 190,000+ miles. A cruel Texas summer had baked its poor dashboard, forcing me to vacuum crumbling pieces on a weekly basis. After driving it 40,000+ miles, I sold the Corolla for $500. I purchased my first new vehicle at age 32. Check. I traded it in for an SUV. Check. I gave it to my brother. Check. I haven't owned a vehicle for many years. I get around on foot and by bicycle.

I needed to repay college loans. I became a university professor (check) and a researcher (check) in New Hampshire (check). My responsibilities involved teaching and publishing. I developed many new courses, including one of the first ever about the Internet and World Wide Web. I wrote a textbook for my course. Check. I set my own research agenda. Check. To a large extent, I worked independently. Check. I continued to work hard.

My nine-month contract allowed me summers off, but instead I conducted research during that time. I won National Science Foundation grants. Checks. The advantage of working in academia was I could do my research wherever and whenever I wanted. I didn't need to sit in an office. This gave me flexibility. While sitting in airports and while in flight, I disciplined myself to work. I got a lot done. I finished paying off my college loans.[1] Check.

I love the New England area. When I hiked the Appalachian Trail (check), I fell in love with the South. Eventually, I accepted a full professorship (check) and department-chair position (check) at a university in Georgia (check). I formed my own school. Check. I became a Dean. Check. I published more books. Checks. I continued to dream. I traveled to South America, Africa, Asia, Antarctica, and Australia. Check times five. I was offered a Distinguished Professorship at the United States Naval Academy (USNA). Check. I served my country. Check. I won Fulbright fellowships. Checks. I helped develop accreditation standards for the emerging field of cyber security. Check.

My work paid well. I began investing and accumulating resources. They provided me freedom to follow my dreams. With each new trip, more items were added to my bucket list. My interests branched out. I honed my organizational skills. I took up many different sports: marathon running, swimming, cycling, triathlons, ultra-marathon running, scuba diving, mountaineering, rock climbing, and hiking. Check times nine. When I participated in competitions, I met like-minded people. Their stories fueled my bucket list.

---

[1] I *never* considered otherwise. It was *my* responsibility. I would be deeply embarrassed and ashamed not to repay a loan.

As I traveled, I learned about other destinations and opportunities. Places, which I heard were dangerous, seemed safe: Thailand, Columbia, Croatia, Malta, Kazakhstan, Oman, Argentina, Romania, Tajikistan, and Albania. Check times ten. Many destinations seemed safer than the US. I traveled to places that no one whom I knew had ever been. Frankly, few had even heard of them: Encarnación, Vanuatu, Chuuk, Andijan, Yap, Pilar, Palau, Aitutaki, Rarotonga, Le Réunion, Viti Levu, and the Heritage Range. Check times 12. Uniformly, I enjoyed my experiences—the people, history, culture, cuisine, and activities. I became fascinated with the world. The more I saw, the more I wanted to see. My bucket list mushroomed.

Due to endurance-sport activities, I had tremendous energy. It helped me tackle my dreams. I went farther afield. I branched out. I took on new challenges. My bucket list expanded even faster. I couldn't keep up with the growing list. I became selective in choosing activities and travel destinations. There are so many wonderful things to do and see. I won't be able to do them all. I continue to fulfill dreams. I continue to enjoy my journey. I continue to build precious memories. The road is long. I'll travel on ...

You may wonder why a kid from Riverside, Rhode Island built this bucket list. I never really thought about it. When opportunities presented themselves, I took them. I created opportunities. I took chances. My life seems natural to me. I simply do things that I want to do—the things my evolving bucket list puts in front of me. I'm a curious person. I like to see and experience things for myself.

Reviewing my bucket list stirs wonderful memories. The most beautiful ones remain in the forefront of my mind. When I visit places now, I create experiences that add volumes catalogued near the front entrance to my internal library. It's a great feeling to be able to recall happy places and experiences to satisfy my mood. This ability, more so than checking off boxes, motivates me to create additional wonderful memories. They make me smile; they provide me security and comfort. In good and bad times, I draw on them at will.

In my bucket list, you'll find items that I've already checked off (↑), things I realize I won't ever be able to accomplish (↓), and items I still hope to achieve (❑). The list is a work in progress—items come and go. For example, although purchasing a first car and home were once on my (original) bucket list, I achieved and removed them. I deleted other basic elements as well. For example, the bucket-list item of going to Africa got replaced by visiting all seven continents and living in Africa for a year. Items that were important to me, but I never attained, remain on my list marked (↓). As I grow older, I make adjustments to the list.

I don't list everything that I've done in each city, park, country, or place where I traveled. For well-known or iconic spots, I highlight certain items that many readers may recognize. In all places which I visited, I tried to see the main sights, meet the local people, sample the local culture and cuisine, learn the history, dabble in the language, and wander around the streets, both during the day and at night. I include a sufficient sampling of activities to give a flavor of what I experienced. If you're familiar with a place, it's easy to guess what else I did.

My bucket-list items aren't of equal weight in any dimension that you can imagine—time commitment, danger, cost, fun factor, preparation, expertise, fitness level required, value, and so forth. They aren't ranked or ordered. They can't be quantified or compared via a simple metric. To check off one box might require a Herculean effort and great skill, whereas checking off another may be trivial. I participated in a diverse range of activities, including some that challenged me and some that were as easy as pie. Each holds a special meaning for me. Although I provide a lot of information about my life, the material isn't comprehensive, as some things are private.

This book is organized into four main parts. Part I contains bucket-list items for broad-subject areas: adventure, travel, nature and animals, sports, culture, entertainment, music, history, education, personal writing, and self. These chapters contain general goals. Some items belong in more than one category. I put them where they fit best for me.

Part II includes bucket-list items for specific destinations: UN countries; capitals of UN countries; world territories; world islands; USA's states; USA's state capitals; USA's second cities; USA's national parks, seashores, and lakeshores; USA's national forests and grasslands; USA's national monuments; USA's territories; USA's extreme points; Thailand's provinces; Thailand's national and marine parks; Thailand's extreme points; Thailand's mountains; and Thailand's scuba-diving sites. The bucket-list items regarding Thailand emerged gradually, as I spent a number of years residing in the country. If I live in another country for several years, I envision a similar set of bucket-list items developing there.

Part III includes bucket-list items for sporting competitions and activities: marathon running, ultra-marathon running, road and trail races, multi-sport and triathlon, cycling, scuba diving, mountaineering, and hiking. These items vary widely in risk factor, commitment required, cost, skill level, and duration.

Part IV includes bucket-list items for professional activities: career, computing books, speaking engagements, journal papers, and conference papers. I worked as a professor. I taught students and conducted research. I formed my own consulting and publishing companies. Although my bucket-list items in Part IV may not directly relate to your career, I hope that you'll find the breadth of items interesting.

I don't anticipate you'll read every word in every entry. You can select the items of strong interest and skim the others. If the book sits around on a coffee table, you can glance through it from time-to-time. You may find humor in unexpected places. I do. The last chapter presents conclusions and final thoughts. Without further ado, let's turn to Part I.

Part I
General Categories

This part of the book contains bucket-list items for broad-subject areas: adventure, travel, nature and animals, sports, culture, entertainment, music, history, education, personal writing, and self.

Chapter 2
Adventure

I begin with a host of adventurous things. They add challenges and excitement to my life.

(↑) Complete the coveted Triple Crown of hiking—the Appalachian Trail (2,169 miles), Pacific Crest Trail (2,659 miles), and the Continental Divide Trail (2,800 miles).

(↑) Search for dinosaur footprints on Cable Beach near Broome in Western Australia.

❑ Climb the Seven Summits—the highest peak on each of the seven continents.

I climbed the following six of the Seven Summits:

1. Mount Elbrus: the highest mountain in Europe at 18,481 feet on July 24, 2001.
2. Aconcagua: the highest mountain in South America at 22,840 feet on July 9, 2002.
3. Mount Kilimanjaro: the highest mountain in Africa at 19,339 feet on August 3, 2002.
4. Mount Kosciusko: the highest mountain in Australia at 7,310 feet on March 17, 2003.

5. Vinson Massif: the highest mountain in Antarctica at 16,067 feet on January 10, 2005.
6. Mount McKinley: the highest mountain in North America at 20,320 feet on May 26, 2009.

I reached my sixth of the Seven Summits in 2009. I haven't attempted Mount Everest. On several occasions I almost joined an expedition to the 29,032-foot high peak. I communicate with Sherpas and climbing expeditions. My gear is ready. However, I never made the mental and financial commitments necessary. Achieving a bucket-list item is about commitment. It's about taking that first (big) step; it's about assuming risks, costs, and responsibilities.

I can't achieve my prior fitness level. If I attempt Everest, I won't be at my best. I'm wiser and a better decision maker though. I wish I climbed the mountain before it became popular. A congested mountain, my age, the $80,000 price tag for a slot on an expedition, and the possibility of dying are chipping away at my motivation. Recent disasters on Everest (involving terrible avalanches), its closure for a season, and the COVID-19 outbreak at base camp aren't pushing me in the right direction. These are excuses.

(↑) **Raft down the boiling rapids of the Skykomish River in Washington State.**

The crux of a trip down the Skykomish River is Boulder Drop—a class-five rapid.

❑ **Stand at the North Pole of the Earth.**

At age 18 I went beyond the Arctic Circle for the first time on a trip to Narvik, Norway. It's still 1,500 miles to the North Pole.

(↑) Ride a Greyhound Bus from Providence, Rhode Island to San Diego, California.

I completed this 78-hour journey twice. One time, I traveled with my friend Scott Entwistle. The other time, I traveled alone. I rarely ride buses anymore.

(↑) Canoe the mighty Green and Colorado Rivers.

While in college, my friend Jim "Jimbo" Wogulis and I spent a week tackling 150 miles of the Green and Colorado Rivers in a canoe. We were on our own. We ran low on food. Temperatures in the canyons soared. We rationed. Our water evaporated. We were thirsty and hungry. We ran out of food. It was terrible planning on our youthful parts. We lost weight and became weak. Sunstroke afflicted us. Our conversations deteriorated into stupid ramblings. Loading extra supplies into a canoe is a no brainer. They're easy to transport. Jimbo!

Obviously, we survived. While returning to Santa Barbara, California from Moab, Utah, we stopped in Las Vegas, Nevada. After our overexposure to the sun, we continued to make bad decisions. If our lucky stars aligned, we planned to spend the night partying our brains out on the strip. If we lost, we planned to hit the road immediately. Before entering the casinos, we made one good decision. We filled Jimbo's stepfather's two-tank Ford Explorer to the gills. RIP, Russ.

During the 360-mile return drive, we shook our sunburned heads and dreamed what might have been if red had come up on that (word deleted) roulette wheel instead of black. We gambled and lost. Once back in Santa Barbara, we gorged. We applied skin cream. We stowed the gear. We washed Russ's SUV. We went back to class. I took away a few valuable lessons.

(↑) Enter the largest cave system on Earth.

I went into Mammoth Cave in Kentucky.

❏ Cross Canada from south to north.

I traveled in seven of ten Canadian provinces. I want to make a full crossing and get deep into the backwoods. A combination of canoeing, kayaking, hiking, and cycling would be my dream crossing. I would take several liters of Deet and load plenty of food and beverages into the canoe.

(↑) Drive the length of the rugged Baja Peninsula and back from Los Angeles, California to Cabo San Lucas, Mexico.

I made this drive twice with a group of close friends from Pomona College: Timothy "Crewski" Crew, Grant "Minnow" Mason, and Phillip "Phil" Ihinger. Back in the late 1970s and early 1980s, the route was wild and remote with almost no services. The roads were rough. Corona beers were cheap. Montezuma's Revenge was prevalent.

(↑) Along the border between Georgia and Florida, canoe through the cypress-lined, alligator-infested Okefenokee Swamp.

I went to the beautiful Okefenokee a handful of times. The flora and fauna are amazing.

(↑) Travel through the Stan countries via the northern Silk Road, including the section of the Pamir Highway from Dushanbe, Tajikistan to Osh, Kyrgyzstan.

I traveled through the rough roads of Kazakhstan, Kyrgyzstan, Tajikistan, Uzbekistan, and Turkmenistan.

(↑) Raft down the huge whitewater of the Kicking Horse River in British Columbia, Canada.

(↑) Jumar to the top of the vertigo-inducing Brazilian Rainforest's canopy and traverse through the monkey-infested treetops via dangling rope bridges.

❏ Cross Canada from the Atlantic to the Pacific Ocean.

Terry Fox has been my hero since his courageous effort to run across Canada in 1980 to raise money for cancer research. After his amputation he ran on one leg. Let me say that again: He ran on one leg! Terry's cancer spread. The amazingly courageous young man stopped running after 143 days, *having averaged a marathon per day!* At the tender age of 22, my hero died. I was 19. I felt sick. I wondered why. I cried. Terry planted the dream of crossing Canada in my head.

I love Canada's natural beauty—spectacular mountains, sensory-overloading sunsets, vast open spaces, incredible wildlife, old-growth forests, and pristine waterways. It's the second largest country in the world, while ranking only 39th in population. There are only four people per square kilometer. It's peaceful. I researched the Great Trail. While following it across Canada, I'll think of Terry. RIP, my hero. Your inspiration lives. You give me great strength!

(↑) Scuba dive and penetrate deep into ship and plane wrecks in the Bermuda Triangle.

I went deep underwater into dark, eerie, confined spaces in the mysterious Bermuda Triangle, where many have perished.

❏ Drive the epic Mongol Rally from Europe to Russia.

The Mongol Rally formerly ended in Ulaanbaatar, Mongolia, hence its name. It now ends in Ulan-Ude, Russia. The change was made so drivers can avoid taxes and costs associated with vehicle import and disposal in Mongolia. Drivers whom I met in Uzbekistan planted this idea in my head.

(↑) Drive the perimeter of vast Australia in the middle of summer.

I drove 10,000-miles of Heaven and Hell—pristine beaches, crashing waves, untouched forests, mountains, moonscapes, cliffs, Indigenous peoples, endless wildlife, deserts, desolate landscapes, dry-lake beds, dead kangaroos, fires, and temperatures soaring above 120°F.

(↑) Go to the top of the Leaning Tower of Pisa.

In 1979 I went to the top of the Leaning Tower. Back then, there were no railings. I returned many years later. The tower was closed. In 2019 I returned for a third time. They reopened the tower, installed banisters, and charged a hefty admission fee. I went to the top again, 40 years after my first ascent. The feeling of the tower's sway remained the same.

(↑) Pet a giant crocodile.

During this experience, I wore my running shoes.

(↑) Try the flying trapeze.

Words flew at me, as much as I flew: "Hang on! Swing! Flip! Twist! Let go! Good job!"

(↑) Witness an avalanche exploding down a mountainside.

I saw massive rock and snow avalanches in Switzerland, a snow avalanche in Washington State, and a rock avalanche in Argentina. The power of these events induce intense fear.

(↑) Search for and find meteorites on Antarctica's glaciers.

The interior of Antarctica is completely white. On the ice it's not hard to spot anything that's dark.

(↑) Ride the Tianmen Shan cable car out of Zhangjiajie, China.

The Tianmen Shan cable car is reputed to be the "longest passenger cableway of high mountains in the world." It's 4.5+ miles long, ascends 4,000+ feet, and reaches gradients of 35+%. The views are spectacular. My friend Yongfeng Wei kept her head down for much of the journey.

❑ Raft the churning, swift-moving Colorado River through the Grand Canyon in Arizona.

(↑) Go downhill skiing in the soaring Andes Mountains of Chile.

❑ Cross the desolate Gobi Desert in Mongolia on foot.

(↑) Skydive.

While in graduate school, I drove past a skyport in Washington State on a regular basis. After a dozen times seeing colorful parachutes floating down to Earth, I thought: "That looks like fun!" I went skydiving with my friend Ed Shepard. It took some nerve to jump out of a perfectly good airplane. We high-fived after flaring and rolling, bursting with adrenaline. I returned for more jumps.

(↑) Float across the dramatic cones, towers, and caves of Cappadocia, Turkey in a hot-air balloon.

(↑) Take a bird watching and pink-dolphin viewing canoe trip through the jungle on a remote stretch of the Amazon River in Brazil.

The departure point was in a dangerous "red zone" on the border of Columbia and Brazil. On my arrival I was offered cocaine. The scenery is fantastic, as is the wildlife.

❑ Dive with great white sharks.

I plan to be inside a (strong) cage.

(↑) Canoe the fast-flowing Zambezi River among the African wildlife.

A hippopotamus attacked the canoe. We paddled away full gas. Giant crocodiles lined the shore. I'm glad we didn't capsize. Bird species galore flew overhead. Even with the crocs around, I felt relieved to return to shore.

(↑) Bicycle across the US between the Atlantic and Pacific Oceans.

I rode across the US four times.

(↑) Witness the violence of a glacier calving.

I saw the awesome spectacle of glacier calving on several occasions in Alaska and Patagonia. I remember the frightening sound of ice cracking, then giant waves emerging from where ice chunks crashed violently into the water.

(↑) Go whitewater rafting through the jungles of wild Costa Rica.

My friend Peter Solomon and I fulfilled this bucket-list item together.

❑ Cross the immense Sahara Desert with camels.

(↑) Cross the brutally hot Mojave Desert in Southern California.

I walked across the Mojave Desert during daylight hours. I bicycled across it three times. It lived up to its reputation for absurd heat.

(↑) Hike to the top of the towering Singing Dunes in Kazakhstan's Altyn-Emel National Park.

For every two steps forward on the dunes, you slide one step backwards. The beauty and sound of the Singing Dunes allows you to enjoy the slow slog to the top. Running down creates even more interesting sounds.

(↑) Mud wrestle the darling, bikini-clad Little Red Riding Hood in Los Angeles, California.

In front of a wild, drunken crowd, I pinned the gorgeous redhead in round three. My buddies enjoyed rinsing the dirty beauty clean.

(↑) Fly a Boeing 747 in a life-size flight simulator.

An urgent voice shouted: "Pull up! Pull up!" I started sweating. My co-pilot stood up. I panicked and crashed the 747. We received a heavy jolt on simulated impact, as the plane fell a substantial physical distance via its enormous supporting jacks.

(↑) Sled down an icy, steep bobsled track.

I took several speedy runs in the frigid temperatures of Quebec City, Montreal, Canada.

❑ Cruise around the world on a private yacht.

Readers of this book owning yachts are at liberty to contact me.

(↑) Paddleboard in the South Pacific off the coast of Vanuatu's tree-lined shore.

(↑) Climb the Sydney Harbor Bridge in Australia.

(↑) Take an airboat ride through the vast Everglades in Florida.

(↑) Zip line in the wild mountains of Jamaica.

❑ Stand at the South Pole of the Earth.

When I was at Patriot Hills in Antarctica at a latitude of 80°S, I missed a golden opportunity to reach the South Pole. I was only 550 miles away. I should have flown to the 89°S and done the "last degree" ski trip. From there, the South Pole was only 70 miles. I was in top condition. I needed to drop $40,000 to join the trip. At the time it seemed prohibitive. Arghhh!

(↑) Take a one-week, private rafting trip with friends down a wild river in the Alaskan wilderness.

(↑) Fly an ultra-light over Victoria Falls on the Zambezi River between the border of Zambia and Zimbabwe.

From an ultra-light, the view of Victoria Falls is amazing. The buffeting winds add to the excitement, as the ultra-light gets tossed around in the updrafts. During my flight, there was a giant herd of elephants migrating below. I craned and grinned. I felt relieved to land safely. I high-fived my friends. We backslapped.

(↑) Go canyoning in the Swiss Alps.

At the last possible moment on a giant swing across a deep canyon, like a monkey being chased by a big cat, I shimmied up a rope to avoid a horrible impact with a log that I was meant to grab. While swinging back, I caught it. I blew out massive volumes of air from my cheeks. The remote area wasn't a good place to break my hips and legs. I learned about several previous clients who were airlifted to hospitals by helicopters.

(↑) Snorkel with colorful marine iguanas and fast-moving seals in the Galapagos Islands.

The sea life in the Galapagos is stunningly beautiful and unique.

(↑) Sled down a mountainside on an alpine slide.

I sped down a harrowing alpine slide in the mountains of northern New Hampshire. While racing full gas, a friend of mine went over the edge of the track and broke her arm.

Chapter 3
Travel

This chapter contains a variety of general travel goals. As usual, they vary widely in their difficulty, cost, and level of commitment. Their meaning to me is often proportional to their duration. Comparable trips undertaken earlier in life felt more adventurous and rewarding. In numerous other categories, destinations I traveled to are mentioned. In the history category, for example, I discuss many historical sites. Specific travel destinations are contained in Part III. To the extent possible, I don't duplicate bucket-list items.

(↑) Visit all seven continents.

(↑) Stand at the Equator, Tropic of Cancer, and Tropic of Capricorn, and go north of the Arctic Circle and south of the Antarctic Circle.

❏ Spend at least one year living in Africa.

I spent four months in Africa. In February 2022, I plan to move to Namibia for ten months.

(↑) Visit all 51 UN countries in Europe.

(↑) Cruise to Cuba, meet the people, and walk around the island.

(↑) Travel in the interior of desolate and frigid Antarctica.

(↑) As a teenager, travel independently through Europe by rail.

I visited 18 countries on my first trip to Europe. My eyes were the size of saucers. My excitement enough to power a home. I added many more things to my bucket list.

(↑) Cruise the River Seine in France.

❑ Take the epic Trans-Siberian Railroad from Moscow to Vladivostok.

(↑) Spend at least five years living in Asia.

❑ Take a train trip to explore the capital cities of Eastern Europe.

Contrary to what I was led to believe, the capital cities of Eastern Europe—Prague, Budapest, Sofia, Bucharest, and Bratislava among others—are amazing: the people delightful, the food delicious, and the architecture stunning.

(↑) Visit all 50 US states and the District of Columbia.

I lived in the four corners of the US: Lee, New Hampshire; Savannah, Georgia; Claremont, California; and Seattle, Washington. I walked across the US via three different routes: East Coast, Continental Divide, and West Coast. I bicycled across the US four times via northern and southern routes. I went to Hawaii and

Alaska three times each. The only state I specifically went out of my way to visit to check this box was North Dakota. I visited all other states via "regular" plans.

(↑) Spend at least two years in Europe.

(↑) Take a one-year around-the-world trip visiting 50+ countries.

(↑) Visit the Rock of Gibraltar.

(↑) Take a gondola ride in the canals of Venice, Italy.

(↑) Cruise the mighty Mississippi River.

❏ Take a train trip across America from coast to coast.

(↑) Drive across the US from coast to coast via southern, central, and northern routes.

(↑) Cruise the Caribbean.

❏ Visit Ha Long Bay in Vietnam.

(↑) Take a train trip across America from south to north.

❏ Spend at least one year in South America.

I spent eight months there so far.

(↑) Take a train trip through Western Europe.

I did this with my friend Adrian Plante, and we covered 10,000+ miles.

(↑) Visit Shangri-La in China.

❏ Take a multi-day cruise on the Mekong River.

(↑) Cruise Alaska's Inside Passage.

(↑) Visit the Palm Islands in Dubai, United Arab Emirates.

❏ Visit all 50 UN countries in Asia.

I traveled to 37 so far.

(↑) Visit the Christ the Redeemer statue in Rio de Janeiro, Brazil.

(↑) Visit the USA's great lakes.

❏ Visit the capital cities of all UN countries in the world.

I traveled to about two thirds of the capital cities of UN countries so far.

(↑) Travel along the Danube River.

I traveled along the Danube in the following countries: Germany, Austria, Hungary, Croatia, Serbia, Romania, and Bulgaria.

❏ Visit all 24 UN countries in North America.

I traveled to 21 so far.

(↑) Visit Venice Beach in Southern California.

I visited many beaches along the West Coast in California, Oregon, and Washington. Venice Beach was a crazy place back in the late 1970s and 1980s. I loved it.

(↑) Become a member of the M-Club.

Roman M is 1,000. An M-Club member is a person who has visited 1,000+ destinations of the 3,600+ listed in my book *Traveling the World,* Book 3 of *Raymond's Checklist Series*.

(↑) Visit all 14 countries in South America.

❑ Spend at least one year living in Oceania.

I spent four months there so far.

(↑) Visit the Dettifoss Waterfall in Vatnajökull National Park in Iceland.

I visited both sides of Dettifoss. There's no bridge. They're an hour apart. When at high water, the ground vibrates and rumbles. At the time of my visit, there was *no one* else there. The area was pristine. I heard it has become touristy now. I'm sure it's still spectacular.

(↑) Ride the bullet trains (Shinkansen) in Japan and visit Shinjuku Station in Tokyo.

At the busiest rail station in the world, Shinjuku, it seems that the majority of the 2,000,000 passengers riding the trains *daily* are running through the station. To say the place is bustling is a major understatement. It's organized chaos at its finest. To ask for help, you need to stop someone who's running.

❑ Visit all 50 US state capitals.

I'm missing Lansing, Michigan and Madison, Wisconsin.

(↑) Take a canoe trip on stunningly beautiful Lake Louise in Alberta, Canada.

❏ Become a member of the exclusive MM-Club.

An MM-Club member is a person who has visited 2,000+ destinations of the 3,600+ listed in my book *Traveling the World,* Book 3 of *Raymond's Checklist Series.* I'm working toward checking off this bucket-list item. Once the COVID-19 pandemic ends, I can reach this goal after ten more years of steady travel.

(↑) Visit the ancient city of Jerusalem in Israel.

❏ Visit all 14 UN countries in Oceania.

I traveled to only six so far. They each entail long trips from the US. Few flights operate to these island countries.

(↑) Visit all 77 of Thailand's provinces.

The last province for me to visit was Yala, on the southern border of Thailand with Malaysia. I heard Yala was dangerous. I found the people there incredibly friendly. It's one of the cleanest and most beautiful provinces in the country. The province is 80%+ Muslim. The state religion of Thailand is Buddhism and about 95% of Thais are Buddhists. There's some tension between the two religious groups.

(↑) Visit the Uyuni Salt Flats in Bolivia.

❏ Visit Kaieteur Falls in Guyana.

I traveled to Guyana. I made arrangements to visit Kaieteur Falls. One day prior to my flight, the details were confirmed. On the morning of the flight, I received notice my trip had been canceled. It was a huge disappointment. I had little recourse. If I make it to Guyana again, I plan to trek in to see the falls. Flight reservations aren't guaranteed, unless you're traveling with a large group.

(↑) Visit the Golden Gate Bridge in San Francisco, California.

❑ Visit all 54 UN countries in Africa.

When I move to Namibia in 2022 for a year, I plan to make more progress toward this bucket-list item. Of the inhabited continents, I traveled least in Africa. Although I made 10 trips there, I only visited 12 countries.

(↑) Visit Dubrovnik, Croatia.

Walking around on top of the city's old defensive walls provides amazing views. Although touristy and crowded, I enjoyed Dubrovnik.

Chapter 4
Nature and Animals

I love nature and animals. I love to encounter animals in the wild. Such encounters excite me. They make me feel alive. I appreciate the conversation and educational efforts that good zoos make, especially as habitats are reduced and species become endangered. I support these efforts. Here I list a variety of bucket-list items relating to nature and animals. Many of these items fit into the travel chapter, too. Some fit nicely into the adventure chapter.

(↑) Visit the massive, mighty Iguazu Falls on both the Argentine and Brazilian sides.

(↑) Visit the expansive, animal-filled Kruger National Park in South Africa.

My friend Paul Göransson and I drove around Kruger on our own. When I got out to take a leak, nine lions appeared. I held it.

(↑) Visit the blue, green mirror-like Moraine Lake in Banff, Alberta, Canada.

❏ Scuba dive with humpback whales.

(↑) Visit the massive Half Dome rock structure in Yosemite, California.

(↑) Pet a full-grown Siberian tiger.

(↑) Visit the fertile Ngorongoro Crater in the Great Rift Valley of northern Tanzania.

This paradise is a 100 square-mile extinct volcanic caldera full of wild animals—elephants, giraffes, rhinos, hippos, lions, buffaloes, cheetahs, leopards, hyenas, wildebeests, and zebras—and countless species of birds. It's been called the eighth wonder of the world.

(↑) Trek to see mountain gorillas in the wilds of Uganda and meet a giant silverback face-to-face.

While trekking with the gorillas high in the mountains of Uganda with my friend Paul, we got lucky when the troop exited the forest into the open. We spent considerable time with the largest silverback in the world. At one point he charged me to within seven feet and pounded his chest. The armed guard said: "Don't look him in the eye." I responded: "Can I crap my pants?" I don't think the guard understood. I held it. While my hair stood on end, I stared at the ground and prayed.

(↑) Visit the San Diego Wild Animal Park in California.

❑ See a Komodo dragon on the island of Komodo in Indonesia.

After he went to Komodo, my friend Glenn "Fiddlehead" Fleagle added this item to my bucket list.

(↑) Visit the La Brea Tar Pits in Los Angeles, California.

(↑) On foot, track giant rhinoceros in the open African plains.

Walking among black mambas is much different than riding in a jeep, as is meeting a rhino face-to-face from ground level.

(↑) See the Southern Cross.

Although the Crux constellation is best viewed from below the equator, it can be seen from the southernmost parts of the US, including southern Florida, southern Texas, and Hawaii. While in the southern hemisphere, I saw the Southern Cross many times.

(↑) Visit with the giant tortoises in the Galapagos Islands.

(↑) Mingle with giant-racked elk in Banff, Alberta, Canada.

(↑) Hold a (live) shark.

During a shark-feeding dive at Stuart's Cove in the Bahamas, the shark feeder handed me a six-foot long shark. When I held the fish vertically, I thought to myself: "This is crazy." The shark woke up. He wasn't happy. It was crazy. I got thrashed by his tail, as he sped off in a rage. He didn't look back. I'm sure of that.

(↑) Visit the Boston Aquarium.

Before becoming a scuba diver, I went to many of the best aquariums in the world. These experiences added becoming a certified diver to my bucket list. I wanted to get up close to sea life in a natural setting.

(↑) Hold a baby panda bear.

In Chengdu, China, I was asked if I wanted to hold an eight-month-old panda. I responded: "Yes, I do!" The baby already had an adult-size head. While holding him, I thought to myself: "I'm not sure this is smart. I have a bear on my lap." His jaw appeared fully developed.

(↑) Visit the White Cliffs of Dover in the United Kingdom.

(↑) Visit Tāne Mahuta and other giant kauri trees in the Waipoua Forest of New Zealand.

(↑) See black bears in the wild.

I had many encounters with black bears, including some far too close for comfort.

(↑) Visit the incredibly high Yosemite Falls in Yosemite National Park in California.

(↑) Ride an elephant.

I rode elephants in several countries in Asia. If the saddle isn't good, the ride is horribly uncomfortable.

(↑) Visit with a blue-footed booby in the Galapagos Islands.

The blue-footed booby is a strange bird indeed, and appropriately named.

(↑) Visit the terraced rice fields in beautiful North Vietnam.

(↑) Visit Disney's Animal Kingdom in Orlando, Florida.

❑ See a polar bear in the wild.

(↑) Visit the lovely Butchart Gardens in Victoria, British Columbia, Canada.

(↑) See the "big five" animals on an African safari.

I saw buffaloes, elephants, leopards, lions, and rhinos on one trip.

(↑) See a cheetah running in the wild.

Cheetahs are indeed the fastest animals on the planet.

(↑) Visit Raymond Burr's outstanding Sleeping Giant Orchid Garden in Fiji.

I was a big Perry Mason fan. I had a crush on Della Street, played by Barbara Hale. RIP, Raymond and Barbara.

(↑) Hand feed giant crocodiles.

I fed 20-foot-long crocs buckets of whole chickens in Tanzania and in Thailand. I never knew that a crocodile had a ten-foot vertical leap. Next time, I'll be standing farther back.

(↑) While fishing in the wilds of Alaska, catch a king salmon.

(↑) Visit the mud volcanoes in Azerbaijan.

(↑) Visit Niagara Falls in New York State on the Canadian border.

A kid from the neighboring town where I grew up went over Niagara Falls in a "barrel." He added this item to my bucket list. He survived. I visited. His barrel is displayed in one of the museums at the falls. He wanted to become a Hollywood stuntman.

❑ Witness the great wildebeest migration in the Serengeti Plains.

Although I went to the Serengeti in Tanzania, I wasn't there at the right time for the wildebeest migration. My friend Adrian has witnessed it and told me it's marvelous. I credit him with adding this item to my bucket list.

(↑) Catch a giant halibut in the Gulf of Alaska.

As my pole bent and line squealed, I remember one of the older guys saying: "You've got a barn door there!"

(↑) See the breathtaking Northern Lights.

(↑) Walk along the earthquake-prone San Andreas Fault in California.

(↑) Ride a camel.

(↑) Hold a giant King Cobra.

When I handed the heavy King Cobra back to his owner, I noticed that from the second knuckle onward the man's index finger was bent at a right angle. I shook my head and counted my lucky stars. I quickly backed away from the snake.

(↑) Ride Icelandic horses.

(↑) Hold and feed a baby tiger.

A male-cub Siberian tiger can weigh 90+ pounds at six months. The baby tiger who sat on my lap drinking milk wasn't a small animal. Before his milk ran out, I stood up.

(↑) See grizzly bears in the wild.

I watched the scene in the movie The Revenant, where Leonardo DiCaprio gets mauled by a grizzly bear. I rewound. I watched it again. The size and power of a grizzly bear is frightening. I'm glad some of the bears that I saw didn't see me.

(↑) Confront a bull moose.

A bull moose came toward me on the Continental Divide Trail in Glacier National Park in Montana. My finger stayed on the trigger of my bear spray until he sauntered off into the woods.

(↑) Visit many of the world's great zoos.

I have been to the Perth Zoo in Australia, San Diego Zoo in California, Antwerp Zoo in Belgium, Rotterdam Zoo in the Netherlands, Tallinn Zoo in Estonia, Copenhagen Zoo in Denmark, Chiang Mai Zoo in Thailand, and Barcelona Zoo in Spain among others.

(↑) Visit the Lipizzaner Stallions in Lipica, Slovenia.

My friend Shigeki "Shagg" Makino and I visited the beautiful farm where the stallions live. They are big, powerful, and majestic animals.

Chapter 5
Sports

This chapter contains a grab bag of sporting items, including both participation and spectating. Chapters in Part III contain bucket-list items for specific sports: marathon running, ultra-marathon running, road and trail races, multi-sport and triathlon, cycling, scuba diving, mountaineering, and hiking. Many of these sporting items took me to new destinations and led me on new adventures.

(↑) Break a world record in a sporting event.

In 2003 I set the world record for the fastest known time (FKT) of the 2,659-mile long Pacific Crest Trail. I broke both the supported and unsupported FKTs. My records fell many years ago.

❑ Visit all cities that hosted the summer Olympics.

I'm an avid Olympics fan. My earliest memories from the age of seven are of the Olympic Games in Mexico City, Mexico. In chronological order of the summer Olympic Games, I went to: Athens, Paris, St. Louis, London, Stockholm, Antwerp, Amsterdam, Los Angeles, Helsinki, Melbourne, Rome, Tokyo, Mexico City, Munich, Montreal, Moscow, Seoul, Barcelona, Atlanta,

Sydney, Beijing, and Rio de Janeiro. I ran on the track in most Olympic stadiums, envisioning myself going toe-to-toe with the all-time greats. I'm missing Berlin, where the legendary African American Jesse Owens won four gold medals in 1936 in front of a chagrined Adolf Hitler.

(↑) Complete the London-Boston Marathon double on consecutive days.

My friend Paul and I took on this bucket-list item together. When we asked about the cost of flight upgrades to return to Boston, so we could stretch our cramping legs, the British flight attendant replied: "Two thousand pounds." I quipped: "That's a ton of money." We all laughed. Although sore at Boston, Paul and I managed good times at both races. We ticked another box together.

❏ Swim the English Channel.

I tried to add this item to my friend Peter's (nicknamed Fish-out-of-Water) bucket list, but he expressed little interest in joining me.

(↑) Win a mixed-doubles tennis tournament.

I grew up playing tennis several hours per day. In one of the last times I ever played tennis, Jessica Papazian and I won a tournament in Rhode Island. She carried me to attaining this bucket-list item. Thanks, Jessie.

(↑) Run rim-to-rim across the Grand Canyon in Arizona.

Jimbo and I completed this run for Bob "Ultrabuns" Holtel's birthday celebration. RIP, Bob.

(↑) Become a PADI Scuba Dive Instructor.

I dove for many years and wanted to achieve one of the highest possible dive certifications. Although I never plan to work in the scuba-diving industry, achieving this certification with my friend Paul fulfilled another long-term goal. It made me become a better and safer diver.

(↑) Complete a marathon swim race.

Off the coast of Sattahip in a time of just over three hours, I completed a 6.2-mile (10 km) open-water swim in the Gulf of Thailand. I finished 12th out of 146 swimmers.

(↑) Dive the Blue Hole in Belize.

I dove the Blue Hole with my friend Peter.

(↑) Win a bicycle race.

I won the Adirondack 500—a 544-mile race—in the Adirondack Mountains of New York.

❑ Become an age-group world time-trial champion on my bicycle.

In Borrego Springs, California, I finished second in the six-hour world time-trial championships for men 50+.

(↑) Do 1,000 consecutive sit-ups.

As a teenager, I accomplished this feat with my friend Peter. We have the scars to prove it.

(↑) Attend a professional-soccer match in Chile in a seat facing the snow-capped Andes Mountains.

❏ Do 20 consecutive (quality) pullups.

I only managed 18.

(↑) Attend an NBA all-star game to see Larry Bird and Earvin "Magic" Johnson play.

(↑) Hike in the Grand Canyon of China in the Zhangjiajie district.

❏ Learn kite sailing.

(↑) Train with Olympic synchronized-swimming gold medalist Tracie Lehuanani Ruiz-Conforto.

(↑) Win a 26.2-mile road marathon.

❏ Become a black belt in a martial art.

(↑) Visit Churchill Downs in Louisville, Kentucky.

(↑) See the Paavo Nurmi and Lassie Virén statues outside the Helsinki Olympic Stadium in Finland.

Nurmi and Virén are two of the greatest distance runners of all time.

(↑) Attend an Army-Navy football game.

While working at the USNA, I attended a game. It was extra special because I had several players in class.

(↑) Climb a vertical ice wall.

I ice climbed on a Swiss glacier.

(↑) Attend a fight card of Muay Thai (Thai kick boxing) in Bangkok, Thailand.

(↑) Attend the Men's Final Four in college hockey.

❏ Learn to surf.

(↑) Attend a soccer match in Brazil to see Bahia play at home in Salvador.

The crowd at a Bahia soccer game in Salvador is truly wild.

(↑) Attend the US Open Tennis Championship finals.

(↑) Learn archery.

My father was an archer. He added this item to my bucket list.

❏ Skate the Elfstedentocht (11 cities tour) in the Netherlands.

(↑) Attend the Men's Final Four in college basketball.

I attended the Final Four in 1984 in Seattle at the Kingdome with my friend Steve Hudson. We had outstanding seats to see Georgetown, Houston, Kentucky, and Virginia play. We saw all four games: both semifinals, consolation final, and final. We sat in the Hoyas section. Nearly all the starters ended up playing in the NBA, including Patrick Ewing, Akeem Olajuwon, Ralph Sampson, and many others. Ewing was the MVP and the Hoyas won the championship.

❏ Attend the summer Olympic Games.

I planned to go to Tokyo 2020, until fans weren't allowed due to the COVID-19 pandemic.

(↓) Compete against the "big four" in triathlon.

I raced against Scott "The Terminator" Molina and Scott "ST" Tinley, but I never got a chance to race against Mark "The Grip" Allen or Dave "The Man" Scott.

(↑) Throw the javelin for Pomona College's track team.

(↑) Attend the Women's Final Four in college basketball.

I attended the Final Four in 2003 in Atlanta at the Georgia Dome. Connecticut defeated Tennessee in the finals. In a great shootout, the two legendary coaches of women's basketball were up and down the sidelines: Geno Auriemma and Pat Summit.

❑ Do 100 consecutive (perfect) pushups.

(↓) Run a sub-2:40 marathon.

As an avid runner for years, I set a goal of running at near six minutes per mile for 26.2 miles. At age 44 in one of my best attempts, I went through the half marathon in 1:18 at the Tucson Marathon in Arizona. Although on a 2:37 pace through mile 18, I faded. As abdominal cramps set in from pressing the accelerator down too far, my dream slipped away, yet again. I ran a 2:51. The world record for men 60+ is 2:36:30. I let my dream go. My time in Tucson equates to an age-graded time of 2:41:15, which is as close as I ever got to this bucket-list item.

(↑) Complete the Race across America (RAAM) from Oceanside, California to Annapolis, Maryland.

I took on the "World's Toughest Cycling Race." The Race across America covers 3,020 miles and features 160,000+ feet of climbing—30+ vertical miles—and must be completed in less than 12 days. After being declared unofficial in 2013 for finishing just outside the time limit, I planned to return in 2014 with a crew consisting of a group of friends and some of my students from the USNA. The race requires mental and physical strength and dedication.

In training I was hit by a motorcycle and broke my collarbone. I began riding again three days later. The pain was intense. I overcame much adversity. I reached the starting line in Oceanside healthy. The support and love that my crew provided gave me enormous strength. I bonded deeply with them. I completed RAAM again. This time I was an official finisher.

Taking on the ultimate personal challenge, putting myself out there, giving everything, experiencing the kindness and devotion of friends and supporters, these things built my faith in humanity. The depth and meaning of this experience are far greater than a cycling competition or bucket-list item. To test one's willpower, courage, self-worth, values, and identity; to commit fully and have the commitment of friends; to take risks and overcome fears; to push past normal human limits; to endure great pain and suffering; to go up against Mother Nature; to confront one's demons, and the list goes on and on; but, to do all these things and more, and meet the challenges, after coming up just short the previous year, gives me an immense sense of satisfaction and a lifetime of gratification and shared memories. This is one of the most important items on my entire bucket list.

(↑) Participate in a wide range of sports.

I enjoy many different sports—the physical aspects and competition, as well as the camaraderie. The letter 't' after a sport denotes I participated on a team and competed, for example, in high school, college, or somewhere else along the line. A 'c' denotes that I competed in organized events in this activity. I participated in the following sports: tennis (t), golf, ping pong, softball (t), baseball, football (t), ice hockey, bocce, mountaineering, boogie boarding, Wiffle ball, backpacking, street hockey (t), swimming (t), trampoline, sailing, canoeing, abseiling, Pilates, paddleboarding, croquet, archery, trapeze, diving (t), ultra-marathon running (c), skate boarding, downhill skiing, go carting, ballooning, volleyball, racquetball, go-carting, ice golf (c), squash, ATV'ing, boxing, track and field (t), shooting (pistol and rifle), kayaking (c), horseshoes, calisthenics, snorkeling, bodyboarding, racquetball, aerobics, step, yoga, pickle ball, canyoning, ziplining, skating, ultimate Frisbee, paddle ball, badminton, water polo, duathlon (c), rafting, rowing, darts, cross-country running (t), ice climbing, billiards, skydiving, bowling, snowmobiling, freediving, weightlifting, bouldering, handball, gymnastics, cycling (c), juggling, hiking, cross-country skiing, running (c), water skiing, mountain biking, snow shoeing, orienteering (c), Muay Thai, triathlon (c), bobsledding, tabagoning, soccer, basketball (t), fishing (c), scuba diving, skydiving, mixed climbing, body building, marathon running (c), caving, horseback riding, Frisbee golf, and rock climbing.

(↑) Attend the Newport Open Tennis Championships in Rhode Island.

(↑) Swim the 1,650 freestyle in under 20 minutes.

In 1988 I swam a 19:27.

❑ Take up whitewater kayaking.

(↑) Attend a soccer match between FC Barcelona and Real Madrid at Camp Nou in Barcelona, Spain.

I lived closed to Camp Nou in Barcelona. I attended a handful of games. The 100,000-seat stadium was always full of fanatical fans. My street was covered in trash after the matches.

(↑) Hold season tickets for a professional-baseball team.

I had season tickets for the Seattle Mariners.

(↑) In person watch Pelé play a soccer match.

Edson Arantes do Nascimento, known as Pelé, is considered by many to be the greatest soccer player of all time. He was famous for his bicycle kick.

(↑) Complete a swim workout with Jenny Thompson.

Jenny Thompson won more Olympic (12) and gold medals (8) than any other female, American athlete in history. I swam with her in Dover, New Hampshire. The pool has since been renamed in her honor.

(↑) Above Lake Como visit the Our Lady of Ghisallo Cycling Museum in Magreglio, Italy.

The museum is a cycling shrine. Most patrons love cycling deeply. The displays gave me goose bumps.

(↑) Complete the hardest Ironman-distance triathlon in the world.

I entered the Swissman Extreme Triathlon in the Swiss Alps. The race has 17,500+ feet of climbing. Out of respect for the course, I trained exceptionally hard and was in tremendous shape at the start. My crew of Diana, Kig, and Shagg helped me check this epic challenge off my bucket list. The organizers of the Ironman-distance Norseman Triathlon in Norway claim their race is harder. Triathletes who completed both races differ in their opinions. I haven't added the Norseman to my bucket list.

(↑) Dive the Blue Corner in Palau.

The first question I got asked in Palau was: "Do you have a hook?" I shrugged my shoulders. At the Blue Corner, you hook onto the coral, inflate your BCD, and pretend you're flying. Lots of sharks arrive and swim right underneath. If my hook came loose, I would have rocketed to the surface like a Polaris missile. For that and environmental reasons, I didn't enjoy hooking onto the coral. The dive was spectacular though.

❑ Visit all cities that hosted the winter Olympics.

In order of the games, I visited: Chamonix, St. Moritz, Lake Placid, Garmisch-Partenkirchen, Oslo, Cortina d'Ampezzo, Squaw Valley, Innsbruck, Grenoble, Sarajevo, Calgary, Albertville, Salt Lake City, Turin, and Vancouver. I'm missing: Sapporo, Lillehammer, Nagano, Sochi, and Pyeongchang.

(↑) See Michael Phelps compete in a swim meet.

Michael Phelps won more Olympic (28) and gold medals (23) than any other athlete in history. He's considered by many to be the greatest Olympian of all time. I saw him compete in a meet at the Naval Academy. He holds almost all the pool records there.

❑ Ride a cyclocross race.

(↑) While out on a ride meet cycling's Olympic silver and bronze medalist Rebecca Twigg.

(↑) Witness a world record set in track and field.

At the World Track and Field Championships in Doha, Qatar in 2019, I saw three world records set: American Dalilah Muhammad ran a time of 52.16 in the women's 400-meter hurdles, the American 4 by 400-meter mixed-relay team of Tyrell Richard, Jessica Beard, Jasmine Blocker, and Obi Igbokweof ran a 3:12.42, and the team of Wil London, Allyson Felix, Courtney Okolo, and Michael Cherry ran a 3:09.34 to break that record in the finals. It was a dream to see Allyson Felix compete.

(↑) Hold season tickets for a professional-basketball team.

I had season tickets for the Seattle Supersonics.

❑ Attend the cyclocross world championships.

In January 2022, for only the second time in history, the cyclocross world championships are being held in the US. I have tickets to attend in Fayetteville, Arkansas.

Chapter 6
Culture

I list cultural bucket-list items here. Many of them originated in my youth. Some items fit into the travel and/or historical categories as well.

(↑) Visit the Van Gogh Museum in Amsterdam, Netherlands.

Vincent van Gogh is my favorite painter. The Potato Eaters is one of my favorite paintings.

(↑) Visit the Dalí Theatre-Museum in Figueres, Spain.

The surrealist artist Salvador Dalí is another favorite painter of mine. I love the museum in Figueres with its gigantic eggs balancing on top. I went there several times. The Persistence of Memory is a favorite painting. Dalí's moustache always evokes a smile.

(↑) See the Mona Lisa by Leonardo da Vinci in the Louvre Museum in Paris, France.

Whenever I visit the Louvre, I go to see the Mona Lisa.

(↑) Visit the Galleria Borghese in Rome, Italy.

The Galleria Borghese houses some of my favorite sculptures by Lorenzo Bernini and some of my favorite paintings by Michelangelo Merisi da Caravaggio. The Villa Borghese gardens are a wonderful place to take a stroll in Rome. Whenever I go to Rome, I go to the Villa Borghese.

❑ Visit Ancient Mesopotamia in Iraq.

(↑) Attend the musical Rent on Broadway in New York City.

(↑) See the Birth of Venus by Sandro Botticelli in the Uffizi Gallery in Florence, Italy.

❑ See **Leonardo** da Vinci's Salvator Mundi in the Louvre Abu Dhabi in the United Arab Emirates.

In 2017, the Salvator Mundi painting, which depicts Jesus with his fingers making a cross, sold for $450,000,000 dollars.

(↑) See Michangelo's David in Florence, Italy.

(↑) Visit Vigeland Park in Oslo, Norway.

As an 18-year old, the seemingly endless intertwining nude bodies in the outdoor Monolith made a big impression. It changed my way of thinking and opened my mind further.

(↑) Visit the Meiji Jingu Shrine in Tokyo, Japan.

(↑) Visit Balboa Park in San Diego, California.

My friend Adrian lives near Balboa Park. When I visit him, we visit the park. I added it to my bucket-list long before Adrian moved to San Diego though because the annual Footlocker High School Cross-Country Championships were run there since 1979, when I was running high-school cross-country.

(↑) See Diego Velázquez's Las Meninas in the Museo del Prado in Madrid, Spain.

(↑) See the Hope Diamond at the National Museum of Natural History in Washington, DC.

(↑) Visit the Sistine Chapel in the Apostolic Palace in Rome, Italy.

I first saw Michangelo's Sistine Chapel in 1979, before its restoration. It was restored during much of the 1980s. I saw it after the restoration in the late 1990s. The vibrant colors of the restoration were in stark contrast to my original viewing. I had to wonder if something hadn't been lost. Many visitors in modern times aren't aware of the restoration.

(↑) Visit the Rodin Museum in Paris, France.

(↑) Visit the Museum of High Altitude Archaeology in Salta, Argentina with the archaeologist who found the three child mummies.

(↑) Visit the Grand Bazaar in Istanbul, Turkey.

The Grand Bazaar is the largest covered shopping complex in the world. The bright colors of the exotic products and the smells of the perfumes, spices, and herbs overload one's senses. There are an uncountable number of evil eyes for sale.

❑ See Vincent van Gogh's The Starry Night painting in the Museum of Modern Art in New York City, New York.

(↑) Visit Sloppy Joe's Bar in Key West, Florida.

When he lived in Key West, Sloppy Joe's was a favorite place for Ernest Hemingway to go.

(↑) Visit the Picasso Museum in Barcelona, Spain.

I like museums that are dedicated to a single artist. They help one to appreciate how an artist's style developed. The Picasso Museum has 4,000+ of his works. I was amazed at the quality and sophistication of art Pablo Picasso produced as a young boy. He was precocious.

❑ Become a decent salsa dancer.

(↑) See Rembrandt van Rijn's Nightwatch at the Rijksmuseum in Amsterdam, Netherlands.

The Nightwatch is a painting I can stare at for hours. The sheer size of it—more than one third that of my condo—and it's dramatic use of light to create the perception of movement in the soldiers make Rembrandt's artistic skill incomprehensible.

(↑) Visit the Grand Palace in Bangkok, Thailand.

I led tours of the Grand Palace complex for many friends.

(↑) Attend the funeral ceremony for King Bhumibol, Rama IX, of Thailand at Sanam Luang in Bangkok, Thailand.

A $90,000,000 Phra Meru Mas (Golden Mountain) crematorium was constructed for King Bhumibol, Rama IX. After a one-year period of mourning, in which everyone in the country wore black daily and draped black-and-white cloths over practically everything in sight, his cremation took place. Millions and millions of Thais, and some foreigners, including dozens of heads of state, went to Sanam Luang to pay their last respects to King Bhumibol who ruled Thailand for 70 years. It was incredibly moving seeing thousands and thousands of Thais carrying his portrait and weeping uncontrollably. It was heartbreakingly sad to witness. The Thai people lost their guiding light—a God-like figure who many Thais considered to be their father. The country and Thai people haven't been the same without him.

(↑) Take the Star Ferry between Hong Kong Island and Kowloon.

(↑) Visit the French Quarter in New Orleans, Louisiana.

(↑) Visit the Sydney Opera House in Australia.

(↑) See Pablo Picasso's Guernica in the Museo Reina Sofía in Madrid, Spain.

❏ Visit the Guggenheim Museum Bilbao in Spain.

(↑) Attend a performance of William Shakespeare's play Romeo and Juliet.

❏ See the Bolshoi Ballet perform at the Bolshoi Theater in Moscow, Russia.

(↑) Attend a performance of the ballet Sleeping Beauty.

(↑) Attend a tap-dancing show featuring Jimmy Slide.

(↑) Attend a performance of Phantom of the Opera on Broadway.

(↑) Visit Plaza de la Constitución in Mexico City, Mexico.

This enormous concrete-covered square has a gigantic Mexican Flag at its center. It's lined by beautiful buildings with stunning architecture, including the Metropolitan Cathedral and National Palace. The plaza is the heart and soul of the city, and Mariachi bands roam around serenading people among the vendors.

(↑) Visit Times Square in New York City.

Times Square is the heart and soul of New York City. By many, it was/is considered the center of the world. It's one of the biggest tourist attractions in the world—a vibrant area with hundreds of thousands of pedestrians passing through daily.

(↑) Visit Wat Arun (Arun Temple) in Bangkok, Thailand.

(↑) Take ballroom-dancing lessons.

(↑) Attend a performance of Beauty and the Beast on Broadway.

(↑) Visit Faneuil Hall Marketplace in Boston, Massachusetts.

(↑) Attend a performance of William Shakespeare's play Hamlet.

❑ Attend a performance of The Wiz on Broadway.

(↑) Attend a performance of Peter Shaffer's play Equus.

At age 15 I attended this disturbing play alone. I walked seven miles to the theater in downtown Providence from Riverside, RI. After the protagonist Alan blinded six horses with a steel spike and the play concluded, I walked back through Providence late at night. I didn't know the city too well, and of course, back then, there was no GPS. I went by feel.

I encountered drunks and drug addicts in the alleyways. After the play little else troubled me. In the dark it took me two hours to get home. I had plenty of time to mull over the plot. When I got home, my parents were asleep. I didn't talk with anyone. I didn't sleep well that evening. In my life I haven't met any other 15-year olds who walked 14 miles alone through a dark city to watch a play by themselves.

❏ Attend a performance of the ballet Giselle.

(↑) Attend a tango show in Buenos Aires, Argentina.

(↑) Attend a performance of the opera La Fiamma in Rome, Italy.

I saw La Fiamma with my close Italian friends Rossella and Maurizio. The sets were stunning. I watched the scrolling banner whose display was in Italian. My friends explained the plot to me. Silvana is condemned to death for being a witch. RIP, Maurizio.

(↑) See the Crown Jewels in the Tower of London in the United Kingdom, including the 530-carat Cullinan I diamond (the Great Star of Africa).

❏ Attend a performance of Wicked on Broadway.

(↑) Attend a Nang Yai (large shadow puppets) show in Bangkok, Thailand.

When done by experts, the 2-3 people controlling a puppet are invisible. The giant puppets appear to move on their own accord.

❏ Attend a performance of Cats on Broadway.

(↑) See the Little Mermaid sculpture in Copenhagen, Denmark.

(↑) Attend a performance of William Shakespeare's play Macbeth.

(↑) See the most famous of the bronze Thinker sculptures at the Rodin Museum in Paris, France.

(↑) Attend a flamenco performance in Andalusia, Spain.

(↑) See the Manneken Pis sculpture in Brussels, Belgium.

(↑) Visit Gilbert Stuart's birthplace in North Saunderstown, Rhode Island.

Gilbert Stuart is considered one of America's foremost portraitists. He painted portraits of numerous US presidents, including one of George Washington that appeared on the one-dollar bill.

(↑) Attend a Castells event—where human towers are constructed—in Catalonia, Spain.

A small, lightweight child is the one who tops a Castell. The towers can be nine or even ten persons high. The barefoot child scrambles up the tower grabbing onto the loose-fitting garments of those forming the lower levels. The fear in the face of the child is visible. The teams try to build more stories and go higher than the competition.

When the towers collapse, bodies go flying into the crowd. Before the construction of a tower begins, I enjoy watching participants spin around as their wide, black faixas (sashes) are wrapped tightly around their waists for support. The white pants, black faixas, and bright shirts of the team members make for a colorful scene at these traditional Catalan festivals. Rum is consumed in vast quantities.

(↑) Attend a performance of Miss Saigon on Broadway.

(↑) Visit the Kon-Tiki Museum in Oslo, Norway to see the original boats, Kon Tiki and Ra II, which Thor Heyerdahl used on his voyages. Travel to Lake Titicaca in Bolivia to meet Paulino Esteban—the reed-boat builder who assisted Heyerdahl.

(↑) Visit the Museo Nacional del Prado in Madrid, Spain.

(↑) Attend a performance of the ballet Swan Lake.

(↑) Spend several days visiting the Louvre Museum in Paris, France.

(↑) Attend a tap-dancing show with Savion Glover performing.

(↑) Attend a performance of the musical Chicago.

(↑) See the Topkapi Dagger in Istanbul, Turkey.

While a young boy, I saw Melina Mercouri star as the nymphomaniacal thief Elizabeth Lipp in the movie Topkapi. The film added the dagger to my bucket list.

(↑) See a Fabergé egg.

James Bond placed this item on my bucket list. I saw one at the Liechtenstein National Museum in Vaduz.

Chapter 7
Entertainment

I enjoy a variety of shows and performances. This portion of my bucket list isn't comprehensive. I can't recall everything. The list evolves along with my taste. There are still many shows that I would like to see. As usual, some items fit into other categories as well, for example, travel. Most entertainment bucket-list items relating to sporting events are included elsewhere. Most music-related items are included in the music chapter.

(↑) Attend the World's Fair in Vancouver, Canada.

(↑) Attend a Cirque du Soleil show.

I love the Cirque du Soleil's high-energy shows. I attended the following shows: KÀ, Mystère, The Beatles Love, Zumanity, and RUN.

(↑) Visit the Chateau Ste. Michelle Winery in Woodinville, Washington.

(↑) Attend a magic show by Penn and Teller.

(↑) Attend a Monster Truck show.

❏ Attend the Indianapolis 500.

(↑) Attend the Calgary Stampede rodeo.

(↑) Attend the World's Fair in Shanghai, China.

(↑) Visit Monte Carlo's Casino in Monaco.

(↑) Attend a ladyboy cabaret show in Thailand.

I attended shows in the following Thai cities: Bangkok, Phuket, Pattaya, and Chiang Mai.

(↑) Go to the Disneyland Park in Anaheim, California.

I attended college in Southern California. On uneventful weekends, we went to Disneyland. Tickets were cheap. I enjoyed the rides, mascots, food, and people watching.

(↑) Visit Madame Tussauds Wax Museum in London, United Kingdom.

(↑) Attend a magic show by David Copperfield.

(↑) Visit the Blue Lagoon on the Reykjanes Peninsula in Iceland.

❑ Attend the Kentucky Derby in Louisville.

(↑) Visit Atlantic City's casinos.

(↑) Attend a performance by the Flying Karamazov Brothers.

(↑) Visit SeaWorld.

I went to SeaWorld in Orlando and Tampa Bay, Florida and in San Diego, California.

(↑) Visit the largest wine cellar in the world—Milestii Mici in Moldova.

The Milestii Mici wine cellar holds 2,000,000+ bottles in its endless, underground corridors. A tour of a small portion of the cellar requires a 20-mile drive.

(↑) Visit Disney Hollywood Studios near Orlando, Florida.

(↑) Ride a mechanical bull.

I was thrown off the bull after a short ride.

(↑) Attend a show by Siegfried & Roy.

(↑) Visit the Las Vegas Strip in Nevada.

Las Vegas has doubled in size since my first visit. Because I grew up in Rhode Island and most people whom I knew didn't travel by airplane, Las Vegas seemed like it was on the other side of the Earth. For me it was another world. I made 15+ trips there.

(↑) Visit Busch Gardens in Tampa, Florida.

(↑) Attend Carnival in Encarnación, Paraguay.

Although smaller than the more famous carnival in Rio de Janeiro, Brazil, the festival in Encarnación is still entertaining and wild. Everyone has a dozen cans of white-snow spray, and they constantly blast each other.

(↑) Attend a World Wrestling Federation (WWF) program.

Since the matches I attended, the WWF has been renamed the WWE for World Wrestling Entertainment.

I saw André the Giant, Vince McMahon, Fred Blassie, Haystacks Calhoun, and many other professional-wrestling stars.

(↑) Attend a performance of Riverdance.

I like the music and the sound fast feet make at Riverdance.

(↑) Visit MGM Studios in Lake Buena Vista, Florida.

(↑) Attend a performance of Jersey Boys on Broadway.

(↑) Visit the Winchester Mystery House in San Jose, California.

(↑) Attend a burlesque show in Las Vegas.

(↑) Hold season tickets to the Lee Speedway in New Hampshire.

(↑) Visit California's Great America amusement park in Santa Clara.

(↑) Attend a performance of Mamma Mia! Mamma Mia!

(↑) Visit the casinos in Reno, Nevada.

(↑) Visit Disney's Epcot Center in Orlando, Florida.

(↑) Visit the Chimay Brewery at the Scourmont Abbey in Hainaut, Belgium.

(↑) Attend a motocross show.

(↑) Attend a performance of Blue Man Group.

(↑) Ride the Crescent Park Looff Carousel in Riverside, Rhode Island.

(↑) Attend a world-class martial arts demonstration.

(↑) Visit Universal Studios in Universal City, California and Orlando, Florida.

(↑) Visit Walt Disney World in Orlando, Florida.

❏ Visit Macau's casinos.

(↑) Ride the rollercoasters at Cedar Point Amusement Park in Sandusky, Ohio.

(↑) Attend a show by the National Chinese Acrobats troop.

(↑) Attend the Tournament of Kings knight show at the Excalibur in Las Vegas, Nevada.

(↑) Ride the rollercoasters at Six Flags Magic Mountain in Valencia, California.

Chapter 8
Music

Music plays an important role in my life. I listen to it for enjoyment and relaxation. I sing songs while hiking. I listen to many musical genres: classical, rock, pop, punk, Greek Zorbas, luk thung (Thai country), blue grass, folk, blues, dance, African, reggae, rhythm and blues, orchestra, opera, new wave, fusion, techno, piano, and flamenco. I love live shows.

Some music inspires me: the themes from Chariots of Fire and Rocky, Eye of the Tiger, We are the Champions, Angie, Good Morning Starshine, The Star-Spangled Banner, and Bridge over Troubled Water. I dabble with my 1984 Yamaha acoustic, 1988 Fender Stratocaster, and 2000 Martin acoustic. I wrote numerous songs. I list a variety of concerts and music-related items here. This list isn't comprehensive.

(↑) Attend the Unite in Song (US) Festival in San Bernardino, California in 1982.

The co-founder of Apple Computers, Steve Wozniak, put on this show. It was the Woodstock of my generation.

(↓) Attend the Unite in Song (US) Festival in San Bernardino, California in 1983.

The concert was held over Memorial Day weekend. I graduated from college in early May and left the Los Angeles area by the time of the second US Festival. I missed a tremendous lineup of bands.

(↑) Attend a Cars concert.

(↑) Visit The District in Nashville, Tennessee.

(↑) Attend a Black Flag concert.

I saw the show at The Mountaineers club in Seattle, Washington. Henry Rollins got wildly out of control. He went into the crowd. There was a lot of violence.

❑ Attend the Newport Jazz Festival in Rhode Island.

(↓) Attend a Small Faces concert.

RIP, guys.

(↑) Attend a Boston Pops performance.

(↓) Attend a Badfinger concert.

RIP, Pete, Tom, and Mike.

❑ Attend a Mike Dawes concert.

(↑) Attend a Talking Heads concert.

The Talking Heads met at the Rhode Island School of Design (RISD). I sometimes hung out there. While growing up, they were one of my favorite bands. I saw them four times: Los Angeles area twice, Seattle, and at the US Festival in Southern California, when the bass player Tina Weymouth was very pregnant. She didn't want to miss the opportunity of playing in front of hundreds of thousands of spectators.

(↑) Attend a Bob Dylan concert.

(↑) Attend a Turtles concert.

(↓) Attend a Pink Floyd concert.

(↑) Attend a Tom Petty and the Heartbreakers concert.

RIP, Tom.

(↓) Attend a Bread concert.

(↑) Attend a Clash concert.

(↑) Attend a concert by The Buckinghams.

(↑) Attend a Fleetwood Mac concert.

I went to this concert with one of my first true sweethearts—her name was Joanne.

(↑) Attend a Ramones concert.

(↓) Attend a John Lennon concert.

RIP, John.

(↓) Attend an R.E.M. concert.

(↑) Attend a concert by The Grass Roots.

(↑) Attend a Jimmy Buffet concert.

(↑) Attend a Jackson Browne concert.

❑ Attend a Maroon 5 concert.

I somehow missed their concert at the USNA. When they performed, I was working there.

(↑) Attend an Eddie Money concert.

(↑) Visit 25+ Hard Rock Cafes.

(↑) Attend an Oingo Boingo concert.

(↓) Attend a Sex Pistols concert.

(↑) Attend a B52's concert.

(↑) Attend a Kinks concert.

(↑) Attend a Gang of Four concert.

(↑) Attend a Dave Edmonds concert.

(↑) Attend a Pousette-Dart Band concert.

(↑) Attend a Red Hot Chili Peppers concert.

(↑) Attend a concert by the band America.

❑ Attend a concert by Natalie Merchant.

(↑) Attend a Green Day concert.

(↑) Attend a Grateful Dead concert.

(↑) Attend a Psychedelic Furs concert.

The Psychedelic Furs are one of my favorite bands. I saw them in concert four times. My childhood friend Carl Gibbs worked for the band. By coincidence we met at a concert in Seattle. Carl was kind enough to get me backstage passes.

(↓) Attend a Nirvana concert.

RIP, Kurt.

(↑) Attend a Santana concert.

Carlos Santana is one of my favorite guitarists.

(↑) Attend a Neil Young concert.

(↓) Attend a Crosby, Stills, Nash, and Young concert.

(↑) Attend a Nina Hagen concert.

This former German opera singer turned punk rocker had an amazing voice.

(↑) Attend a Cyndi Lauper concert.

(↑) Attend an X concert.

My favorite song by X is Johnny Hit and Run Paulene. Billy Zoom plays a high-energy staccato guitar; John Doe sings disturbing lyrics; Exene harmonizes with her haunting voice; D. J. Bonebrake punishes the pig skins. During a live show, they all sweat like crazy from jumping around as though possessed.

(↓) Attend a concert by The Seekers.

My mother used to sing Georgy Girl and Waltzing Matilda. Judith Durham had a wonderful voice, so did my Mom.

(↑) Attend a concert by Foreigner.

❏ Attend a concert by The Cure.

(↑) Attend a Judy Collins concert.

(↑) Attend a Police concert.

While growing up, the Police were a favorite band. I attended many of their shows.

(↑) Attend a Foghat concert.

(↓) Attend a Michael Jackson concert.

RIP, Michael.

(↑) Attend a Beach Boys concert.

My favorite Beach Boys song is Good Vibrations.

(↑) Attend a Prince concert.

RIP, Prince.

(↓) Attend a David Bowie concert.

David Bowie (real name of David Robert Jones) was a musical genius. RIP, David.

(↑) Attend an English Beat concert.

My favorite English Beat song is Sole Salvation.

❏ Attend a concert by ELO.

Jeff Lynne is a musical genius.

(↑) Attend a J. Geils Band concert.

My favorite J. Geils Band song is Must of Got Lost.

(↑) Attend a Heart concert.

(↑) Attend a Stephen Stills concert.

(↑) Attend a Flock of Seagulls concert.

My favorite Flock of Seagulls song is Wishing.

(↑) Attend a concert by The Fixx.

My favorite The Fixx song is Red Skies at Night.

(↑) Attend an Elvis Costello concert.

My favorite Elvis Costello song is Watching the Detectives.

(↓) Attend a performance by the classical guitar maestro Andrés Segovia.

RIP, Andrés.

❏ Attend a U2 concert.

(↑) Attend a Pat Benatar concert.

(↑) Attend a Rolling Stones concert.

RIP, Charlie.

(↑) Attend a T-Rex concert.

(↑) Attend a concert by The Who.

RIP, Keith.

(↑) Attend a Bruce Springsteen concert.

(↓) Attend a concert by The Three Degrees.

RIP, Fayette.

(↑) Attend a Da Endorphine concert.

I met Thanida Thamwimon, also known as Da, at a small venue in Sakon Nakhon, Thailand.

Chapter 9
History

When I was young, history was my least favorite subject. I never enjoyed second- or third-hand accounts. I didn't enjoy memorizing names and dates, without understanding what actually happened. Looking back, my teachers hadn't traveled to the places they taught about. They didn't have a deep understanding of their subject. To be fair, few people had the means to travel the world at that time, especially high-school teachers. They were good people. They tried hard. They shared their book knowledge.

Once I started traveling the world, I acquired a strong interest in history. In school I learned about the places Alexander the Great had conquered. When I actually went to those places, I saw many of them were empty—almost no one had ever even been there. No one wanted to be there. Conquering meant being there and saying: "This is my territory" in ancient Macedonian. In most cases there was no resistance, as there was no population. I went where Alexander the Great had gone and understood more clearly what he'd done. I enjoyed retracing his steps much more than I did reading about his conquests.

Now that I have more context and have traveled extensively, history has become one of my favorite subjects. When I read an account, I often relate a personal experience to it. I know where places are and have a sense of the people living there. I went to many historical sites and also examined artifacts in museums. My perspective has grown. I appreciate and understand history better. I read historical accounts with a critical eye, filtering out biases and prejudices of historians. I connect far-flung events. The puzzle pieces fall into place.

When I want to learn about a historical event, I try to visit the site. My interests generate more bucket-list items. I try to check them off. Many fit nicely into the travel category as well.

(↑) Visit Norbulingka—the Dali Lama's Summer Palace—in Lhasa, Tibet.

(↑) See a footprint of the Prophet Muhammad.

(↑) Visit the Aral Sea area in Uzbekistan.

The disappearing Aral Sea is considered one of the greatest man-made disasters in history. The Soviet Union's mismanagement of water was done on an epic scale.

(↑) See the Code of Hammurabi at the Louvre Museum in Paris, France.

I'm fascinated by the legal text in the ancient Code of Hammurabi.

❑ Visit the Taj Mahal in Agra, India.

(↑) Visit the Forbidden City in Beijing, China.

(↑) Visit Bang Rachan in the Sing Buri province of Thailand.

According to Thai legend, when the Burmese invaded Thailand in 1765, the tiny village of Bang Rachan repelled the Burmese army for five months. Eventually, the army broke through and sacked Ayutthaya—the old capital city of Thailand—bringing down the 400-year-old Kingdom of Siam. There's a beautiful monument to the eleven village leaders at the site.

(↑) Visit the Killing Fields of Cheung Ek in Cambodia.

The Killing Fields are a terribly sad place. I cried.

(↑) Visit Samarkand, Uzbekistan.

The ancient Silk Road city of Samarkand has many well-preserved mosques and mausoleums. In 1220, 800 years ago, it was conquered by the Mongols under Genghis Khan.

(↑) Visit King Midas's tomb in Gordion, Turkey.

King Midas's tomb is thought to be the oldest wooden structure in the world. Because of the depth of his burial, the wood survived.

(↑) Visit the Duomo in Milan, Italy.

(↑) Visit Emmanuel Frémiet's Joan of Arc statue in the Place des Pyramides in Paris, France.

Where I grew up, teachers taught that Joan of Arc was a great heroine.

(↑) See the Rosetta Stone at the British Museum in London, United Kingdom.

(↑) Visit the New Bedford Whaling Museum in Massachusetts.

(↑) Visit the Manassas Battlefield in Virginia.

❑ See the Dead Sea Scrolls.

(↑) Visit the Corinth Canal in Greece.

(↑) See a replica of Lucy at the National Museum of Ethiopia in Addis Ababa. Note that due to its fragile nature, the real skeleton isn't available for public viewing and is stored in a special safe at the National Museum in Addis Ababa.

(↑) Visit Angkor Wat in Siem Reap, Cambodia.

The complex of temples is so large and beautiful that I went there three times.

(↑) Visit the Death Railway in Kanchanaburi, Thailand.

I hiked along the Death Railway far north of where most tourists visit. In places such as Hellfire Pass, it's stunning to see how much bedrock WWII captives chiseled out with primitive tools. The terrain along the abandoned railway is rugged.

(↑) Visit the Valley of the Kings in Luxor, Egypt.

I hiked through the area around the Valley of the Kings and visited many tombs.

(↑) Visit the Acropolis in Athens, Greece.

When I first saw the Parthenon, I was stunned by its beauty.

(↑) Visit Normandy, France.

I went to the Normandy American Cemetery and Memorial in Colleville-sur-Mer, Normandy on several occasions. On each succeeding visit, I saw fewer WWII veterans. There aren't many still alive. Each time that I visited, I was deeply moved, as I watched how much the cemetery and memorial meant to them. Based on their expressions and tears, I knew some were reliving D-Day. A visit without seeing any veterans is going to be terribly sad.

(↑) Visit the Ban Chiang archaeological site in Udon Thani, Thailand.

This prehistoric UNESCO world-heritage site is considered one of the most important in Southeast Asia.

(↑) Visit the ancient Coliseum in Rome, Italy.

(↑) Visit Petra in Jordan.

During my visit, I walked across the expansive Petra and back.

(↑) Visit the Statue of Liberty on Liberty Island in New York.

(↑) See the Great Sphinx on the Giza Plateau in Egypt.

(↑) Visit ancient cities throughout the old Roman Empire.

I visited many ancient Roman cities, including Ostia Antica on the west coast of Italy. It's considered the best preserved.

(↑) See the largest book in the world at Kuthodaw Pagoda in Mandalay, Myanmar.

(↑) Visit the Sagrada Família in Barcelona, Spain.

While living in Barcelona for a year, I became fascinated by the works of Antoni Gaudí. He was an amazing architect.

(↑) Visit the Florence Cathedral in Italy.

(↑) Retrace part of Marco Polo's route in Central Asia.

(↑) Visit the historic city of Segovia in central Spain.

(↑) Visit the bridge over the River Kwai in Kanchanaburi, Thailand.

(↑) Take a trip on the Perfume River near the city of Hue in Vietnam.

(↑) Visit Stratford-upon-Avon—the birthplace of William Shakespeare—in central England.

(↑) Visit the Terracotta Army in Xi'an, China.

When in Xi'an, I met the farmer who discovered the Terracotta Army.

(↑) Visit the Huntington Library in San Marino, California.

The library has an outstanding collection of rare books.

❏ Visit the Suez Canal in Egypt.

(↑) Visit the Eiffel Tower in Paris, France.

(↑) Visit the Saint Mark's Basilica in Venice, Italy.

(↑) Crawl through the Cu Chi Tunnels on the outskirts of Ho Chi Minh City in Vietnam.

(↑) Visit Wat Rong Khun (the White Temple) in Chiang Rai, Thailand.

(↑) Cruise the Rhine River through Germany.

(↑) Visit the opal-mining town of Coober Pedy in Australia.

(↑) See Big Ben in London, United Kingdom.

(↑) Visit the archaeological site of Gonur Depe in Yakeper, Turkmenistan.

(↑) Cruise the Yangtze River through the Three Gorges in China before the Chinese flood the area, creating a deep lake above the power plant at the Three Gorges Dam.

(↑) Visit the Hoover Dam in Nevada.

(↑) Visit the Saint Stephen's Cathedral in Vienna, Austria.

(↑) Visit the Oracle at Delphi in Greece.

(↑) Visit the Edinburgh Castle in Scotland.

(↑) Visit the Warsaw Ghetto in Poland.

I walked around the Warsaw Ghetto. I also went to Kraków, where I saw Oskar Schindler's Enamel Factory, which became well-known because of its depiction in the Steven Spielberg movie Schindler's List.

(↑) Visit the London Bridge in the United Kingdom.

(↑) Visit the Blue Mosque in Istanbul, Turkey.

(↑) See the Samarkand Kufic Quran in Tashkent, Uzbekistan.

(↑) Visit Red Square in Moscow, Russia.

(↑) Visit a gold mine in Johannesburg, South Africa.

(↑) Visit the Panama Canal.

(↑) Visit the Antietam Battlefield in Maryland.

(↑) Visit Olduvai Gorge in Tanzania.

I always had a fascination with paleoanthropology and been interested in the work of the Leakey family. I got goosebumps walking around Olduvai Gorge.

(↑) See the treasures of Tutankhamun.

(↑) Visit Ground Zero and go to the top of One World Trade Center in New York City.

(↑) Visit the Dachau Concentration Camp in Germany.

(↑) Visit the Saint Paul's Cathedral in London, United Kingdom.

(↑) Visit the Ukrainian National Chernobyl Museum in Kiev.

(↑) Visit the Great Wall of China.

(↑) Visit Plymouth Rock in Massachusetts.

(↑) Visit the St. Peter's Basilica and Vatican City in Rome, Italy.

(↑) Go to the top of the Empire State Building in New York City.

(↑) Visit the sacred Indigenous site Uluru (Ayer's Rock) in Central Australia.

Although the trails were closed due to temperatures exceeding 120°F, I walked around anyway. I carried several liters of water. The rock has many interesting formations. I see why it's sacred to the Indigenous people.

(↑) See Emperor Akihito and Empress Michiko of Japan at the Tokyo Imperial Palace.

(↑) Visit the Palace at Versailles in France.

The palace and gardens are simply amazing.

(↑) Visit the Saint Basil's Cathedral in Moscow, Russia.

(↑) Visit the Catacombs of Paris in France.

❑ Visit the State Hermitage Museum in Saint Petersburg, Russia.

(↑) Visit the Hearst Castle in San Simeon, California.

(↑) Visit the Gettysburg Battlefield in Pennsylvania.

(↑) Visit Stonehenge in Wiltshire, United Kingdom.

(↑) Visit the Cologne Cathedral in Germany.

(↑) Visit Williamsburg, Virginia.

(↑) Visit the Mosque of Córdoba in Spain.

(↑) Visit the monuments and The Mall in Washington, DC.

I went to many monuments in DC, but not all 200+ of them. I walked along The Mall on many occasions and ran the Marine Corps Marathon through DC. Some of the better-known monuments I visited are as follows: Lincoln Memorial, Franklin Delano Roosevelt Memorial, Vietnam Memorial, Korean War Veterans Memorial, Martin Luther King Jr. Memorial, Jefferson Memorial, National World War II Memorial, and Washington Monument.

(↑) Visit Mount Rushmore near Keystone, South Dakota.

(↑) Visit the Westminster Abbey in London, United Kingdom.

(↑) On the spring equinox, visit the ruins of Chichén Itzá in Mexico's Yucatan Peninsula.

(↑) Visit Leonardo da Vinci's house near Vinci, Italy.

(↑) Visit the Canterbury Cathedral in the United Kingdom.

(↑) Visit the Newport Mansions in Rhode Island.

(↑) Visit Machu Picchu in Peru.

(↑) Visit the Saint John's Co-Cathedral in Valletta, Malta.

(↑) See King Bhumibol, Rama IX, the ninth king of Thailand in person.

(↑) Visit the Saint Mary's Cathedral in Sydney, Australia.

(↑) Visit Dracula's House, Bran Castle in Transylvanian, Romania.

(↑) Visit the Notre Dame Cathedral in Paris, France.

Over the years I went into the cathedral on three different occasions. When I was in Europe in 2019, the cathedral burned. I went to see it three days after the fire. A huge crowd gathered. There was a collective sadness.

(↑) Visit the pyramids in San Juan Teotihuacán in Mexico.

(↑) Visit the Kigali Genocide Memorial in Rwanda.

(↑) Visit Bunker Hill in Boston, Massachusetts.

(↑) Visit the Saint Andrew's Cathedral in Sydney, Australia.

❏ Visit the Smithsonian Institution's 19 museums.

I made it to 11 of the Smithsonian museums.

(↑) Visit the Bastogne War Museum in Belgium.

(↑) Visit the Winchester Cathedral in the United Kingdom.

My Mom used to sing the 1966 song "Winchester Cathedral" by The New Vaudeville Band.

(↑) See a Gutenberg Bible.

(↑) Visit Giza to see the great pyramids of Egypt.

(↑) Visit the Darvaza Gas Crater in Turkmenistan.

Soviet engineers intentionally set fire to the gas deposit in 1971, thinking it would burn out in a few weeks. The "Gates of Hell" have been burning steadily for 50+ years. I can't imagine the environmental impact or the dollar value of the natural gas wasted. It's a hot and smelly place. In my yurt there was a giant camel spider.

❏ Visit the ancient ruins in Tulum, Mexico.

(↑) Visit Ancient Troy in Turkey.

(↑) Visit the Anne Frank House in Amsterdam, Netherlands.

As a child, I read the *Diary of Anne Frank*. I cried. As an adult, I read it again. I cried. On my second reading, I questioned whether Anne or her father wrote the bulk of the diary. In either case her story is incredible and one that I won't ever forget.

Chapter 10
Education

I list a number of general educational goals here. Related bucket-list items can be found in Part IV, describing professional activities.

(↑) Obtain a bachelor's degree.

I earned a Bachelor of Arts degree in mathematics from Pomona College at age 21.

(↑) Obtain a Masters degree.

I earned a Masters in computer science from the University of Washington (UW) at age 24.

(↑) Obtain a Doctor of Philosophy degree, PhD.

I earned a PhD in computer science from the UW at age 27.

(↑) Participate in simulated Moon and Mars walks at the Belgium Space Center in Transinne.

(↑) Obtain the highest score in my district on the National Mathematics Exam.

During the National Mathematics Exam, I sat in the rear of a large room next to my friend Peter. About halfway through the exam, bored students started chatting. Peter said: "Hey, quiet down. Greenlaw's back here." They stopped talking. I won.

(↑) Become one of the world-leading experts on parallel computation.

I'm considered by many computer scientists to be the world-leading expert on P-completeness theory—a branch of parallel computation that deals with problems which are hard to parallelize.

(↑) See a moon rock.

(↑) Serve as one of the commencement speakers at my high-school graduation.

(↑) Serve as a commencement speaker for a university's graduation ceremony.

In February 2006, as the keynote speaker, I addressed an audience of 4,000+ people at the University of Science and Management Malaysia (USM) in Shah Alam. My speech was titled: "International Collaborations in Education." During the impressive ceremony, there were two traditional bands that alternated playing music throughout, except during my speech.

(↑) Visit with different groups of Native Americans.

(↑) Visit the Space Center Houston and the Kennedy Space Center in Cape Canaveral, Florida.

(↑) Have Dr. R. Nelson Smith announce my name as the high scorer of a chemistry exam at Pomona College.

I traveled to the Los Angeles, California area on my own from Rhode Island to attend Pomona College—an institution that always sits near the top of US News & World Report's Rankings. Although my teachers wanted me to attend an Ivy League institution, my Dad encouraged me to head west. In my freshman year, I enrolled in the largest and most competitive class, namely freshman chemistry. A third of the freshmen class and some sophomores were enrolled, mostly cut-throat pre-med students. After the first exam, our bald professor R. Nelson Smith announced the high scorer on the exam.

After the second exam, Professor Smith announced: "The high score was a 93 by Raymond Greenlaw." I heard my new Californian friend and beer-drinking buddy Don Hume shout: "Greenlaw!?" Don was in disbelief. The rest of the class stared at Don and me. I refrained from smiling, but I beamed inside. I wasn't a chemistry major; I wasn't pre-med. I attended a public high school. My classmates were from all over the world and many had attended elite, private high schools. Everyone asked me why I was taking chemistry. I said: "For fun." They scratched their heads. It wasn't a required course. I enjoyed science. I was a mathematics major.

(↑) Visit with a Maasai tribe in Tanzania.

I learned a lot from these tall and fearless cattle herders.

(↑) Win the Most Outstanding Student Award in high school.

(↑) Publish one of the first books ever written about the Internet and World Wide Web.

❏ Become a medical doctor.

(↑) Become one of the world-leading experts on cybersecurity accreditation.

(↑) Learn to communicate in a foreign language.

I studied French for three years in high school. While in college, at my Dad's urging, I studied German. I became fluent. Because of my travels to Spanish-speaking countries, I picked up Spanish. I can communicate, but my grammar is atrocious. I learned some Italian. I studied Japanese. I learned Thai on my own. I have a vocabulary of 3,500+ words. I understand Thais better than they understand me. I can't hit all five tones perfectly. As part of my travels, to the extent possible, I learn 20 words in each new language that I encounter.

(↑) Visit the Boston Museum of Science as a teenager.

I grew up about 50 miles south of Boston, Massachusetts. As a young teenager, I feared the city. I was awed by its great institutions. At the Boston Museum of Science, I encountered brainy Harvard and MIT students walking around discussing exhibits. I was mesmerized by their level of intelligence. I was blown away by the sophistication of the displays.

(↑) Watch a space launch.

(↑) Visit with the Indigenous people of Australia.

(↑) Read many of the classic, great books.

Chapter 11
Personal Writing

My Mom was an English major in college. In high school I took a creative-writing course. She read drafts of my work. She made suggestions. I wrote better. Because of her influence, I selected English classes for electives. I wrote poetry. I wrote songs. I attended a liberal arts college. There I enrolled in a creative-writing course. I wrote short stories. I read classmates' stories.

When I attended graduate school, my writing focused on technical subjects. Those publications are discussed in later chapters in Part IV. Because I wrote so much for my job, personal writing suffered, but I continued to write poetry. As my academic career drew to a close, I focused on personal-writing projects—the books and stories added to my bucket list over the years. This chapter describes those projects.

❑ Write *A Bicycle Rider's Apology*.

A Bicycle Rider's Apology describes my rides at RAAM 2013 and 2014. I apologize to my crew members. While supporting me, they were pushed beyond their limits.

(↑) Write *PALMARÈS*.

PALMARÈS describes my athletic history. It details my achievements in sport.

❑ Write *Ladyboy*.

Ladyboy follows the story of a gay man. After a sexual encounter with a Thai ladyboy, he's finally able to confront his troubling inner feelings.

(↑) Outline the ten novels planned in *The Thai Wife Series of Novels*.

I finished the outlines for the ten novels in *The Thai Wife Series*. The narrator of the novels is a Nobel laureate in literature, awarded for his writings about Thailand. He discovers a set of unfinished novels in his apartment in Annapolis, Maryland. As he begins to edit *The Thai Wife Series of Novels*, bringing them to the Nobel level, the coronavirus pandemic strikes. It wreaks havoc on his family. While dealing with personal issues, including numerous affairs, the Nobel laureate relays the story of Doctor Adventure.

Doc is a decorated Navy SEAL and cybersecurity expert. His polyorchidism results in an unusually high testosterone level. His intensity leads to questionable behavior in the field, and Doc is fired from the NSA. He secretly continues covert cyber operations in Thailand, as a critical but underground asset. His cyberattacks target Chinese assets. Doc's cover involves exploring Thailand's massage parlors and bars, while searching for a Thai wife.

Doc falls in love with a series of gorgeous Thai ladies. Each time that he's about to pop the big question disaster strikes. He continues his quest for finding the perfect Thai wife through dozens of steamy sexual encounters. He meets several ladyboys, and his own sexuality is called into question.

(↑) Write *The Thai Wife Story JOY*, Book 1 of *The Thai Wife Series of Novels*.

After ten years off and on, I completed the first book in *The Thai Wife Series of Novels*. In *The Thai Wife Story JOY*, the narrator explains how he first discovered the novels. During the COVID-19 pandemic, he takes a leave of absence from his professorship at Naval Academy to complete them. He describes Doc's love affair with a beautiful underage masseuse named Joy. Doc meets another Navy SEAL operating out of Bangkok. They plot cyber-attacks against the Chinese. When Doc is forced to relocate to Chiang Mai, he decides to propose marriage to Joy. He misses his opportunity. Heartbroken, Joy remains behind in the salacious Thai capital. She continues her life as a sex worker. In parallel, the narrator describes how his father tragically succumbs to COVID-19. Through this difficult time, the narrator seeks comfort in a Vietnamese woman who works for his boss at the Academy.

❏ Write *Breaking Three*.

Breaking Three is a novel about a man who tries to run a marathon in under three hours.

(↑) Write *The Thai Wife Story STAR*, Book 2 of *The Thai Wife Series of Novels*.

In *The Thai Wife Story STAR*, the Navy SEAL Tom, who took on the moniker Doctor Adventure, continues his covert cybersecurity operations in Thailand. He moves his base from Bangkok to Chiang Mai. Tom continues his search for a Thai wife. He learns from Bpee, the gorgeous ladyboy working at Lucky Massage in Bangkok, that his first true Thai love, Joy, has committed suicide by hanging. He focuses on work and successfully carries out a cyber-attack against the Chinese. Tom explores the massage parlors in Chiang Mai to overcome his grief and work pressures. He meets a beautiful ladyboy named Wan. The American is troubled by his attraction to her.

Tom falls in love with a beautiful, bronze-skinned, Thai goddess named Star. When he decides to propose marriage, he learns that Star is already married. Along with her husband, the deceitful, materialistic beauty plots the Navy SEAL's murder. As Tom struggles with Joy's suicide, Star's deceit, and his own sexuality, his judgment falters. The suspense builds as Tom appears to have met his match.

The narrator continues his story paralleling the main plot. He loses his mother to COVID-19. He continues a love affair with his boss's Vietnamese assistance. A sexy Thai delivery girl catches his fancy. They engage in lustful relationship. While juggling two lovers and settling his parents' affairs, he feels it's impossible to remain on schedule for editing the remaining eight novels in *The Thai Wife Series*. He drinks heavily.

❏ Write *The Thai Wife Story SUGAR*, Book 3 of *The Thai Wife Series of Novels*.

In *The Thai Wife Story SUGAR*, the Navy SEAL Tom continues his search for a Thai wife. He learns that the ladyboy Bpee from Lucky Massage in Bangkok deceived him. His first love Joy is still alive. She didn't commit suicide. The stakes in the cyberwar with China intensify. Tom is asked to eliminate a key hacker in the PLA. The narrator withdraws himself from the novels. His drinking becomes a serious problem. Cam Tu, his Vietnamese lover, is the only stabilizing force in his life. She encourages him to continue writing.

(↑) Write *Raymond's Checklist for Traveling in the USA*, Book 1 of *Raymond's Checklist Series*.

Traveling in the USA is a book to quantify how much of America someone has seen. It presents a checklist of about 1,000 destinations. I visited 60% of them. A ranking system is provided. I rate as a Traveler+. To become an Excursionist–, I need to visit 11 additional places.

(↑) Write *Raymond's Checklist for Traveling in Thailand*, Book 2 of *Raymond's Checklist Series*.

Traveling in the Thailand is a book to quantify how much of Thailand someone has seen. It presents a checklist of 600+ destinations. I visited 65% of them. A ranking system similar to that used in *Traveling in the USA* is provided. I rate as a Traveler. To become a Traveler+, I need to visit 19 additional places.

I'm proportionally better traveled in Thailand than the US. My ranking systems bears this out. However, because the US is roughly 20 times the size of Thailand, I covered about 20 times as much ground in the US as in Thailand.

(↑) Write *The Hazards of Cycling in Thailand: Guidelines for Tourists*.

During 15 years of visiting and living in Thailand, I cycled its roads in nearly all provinces. I crossed the entire country dozens of times by bicycle in every possible direction. I saw many accidents. I had many close calls. I wanted to share my experience and knowledge with others. Although *The Hazards of Cycling in Thailand: Guidelines for Tourists* is written in a light style, many serious safety concerns are addressed.

(↑) Write *Raymond's Checklist for Traveling the World*, Book 3 of *Raymond's Checklist Series*.

Rather than merely counting countries, *Traveling the World* is a book to quantify how much of the Earth someone has seen. It presents a checklist of 3,600+ destinations. To my knowledge it's the most comprehensive list of destinations ever produced about world travel. The book categories all known landmasses. I visited 29% of them. A ranking system similar to that used in *Traveling in the USA* is provided. I rate as an Excursionist–. To become an Excursionist, I need to visit 161 additional places.

❏ Write *Peter*.

Peter is about my best friend's life.

(↑) Write *Raymond's Checklist for His Personal Bucket List*, Book 4 of *Raymond's Checklist Series*, second edition.

Personal Bucket List refers to this book. Working on it helped put my life in perspective. It helped me set more goals and form new dreams, and also reinforced the notion of using one's time wisely. I'm lucky that I never encountered a bad patch in life. Knock on wood. I've been healthy and energetic. COVID-19 put a damper on many things. I hope *Personal Bucket List* motivates readers to form new dreams and follow them.

❏ Write *A*.

A explains how to become a straight-A student.

(↑) Write *Raymond's Checklist for Gear for a Long Hike*, Book 5 of *Raymond's Checklist Series*, second edition.

I receive frequent requests to share my thoughts about hiking gear. So I decided to write *Gear for a Long Hike*. I'm a minimalist. My list gives hikers a great starting point for assembling their gear for a long-distance hike or for a thru-hike of a mega-trail.

(↑) Write *Raymond's Checklist Cycling Gear*, Book 6 of *Raymond's Checklist Series*, second edition.

I receive frequent requests to share my thoughts about cycling gear. So I decided to write *Cycling Gear*. My list gives cyclists a great starting point for assembling their gear for a long ride or for a complete traverse of a mega-trail or continent.

❑ Write *The Last Great Trip*, Book 7 of the *Raymond's Checklist Series*.

In 2019 I took an around-the-world backpacking trip and visited 65+ countries and territories. The epic adventure covered 120,000+ miles. Many people asked what I was carrying. *The Last Great Trip* provides them with the answer and thoughts about travel after the COVID-19 pandemic.

❑ Write *Triathlon Gear*, Book 8 of the *Raymond's Checklist Series*.

Having competed in triathlon for five decades, I receive many inquiries about my gear and preparations for a race. In *Triathlon Gear* I share my experience and knowledge with others.

(↑) Write *The Pacific Crest Trail: Its Fastest Hike*, second edition.

The Pacific Crest Trail: Its Fastest Hike describes my FKT hike of the PCT. It's a no-holds-barred account of my mental and physical states, as I pushed northward against the clock in dramatic high-mountain scenery. I overcame fear, danger, and adversity. Jim Leisy of

Franklin, Beedle & Associates, Inc. assisted me with the publication of *The Pacific Crest Trail: Its Fastest Hike*. RIP, Jim.

❑ Write *A Few More Magnets,* Book 9 of the *Raymond's Checklist Series*.

During my 2019 epic around-the-world trip, I learned some valuable lessons. *A Few More Magnets* assists other travelers who embark on an extended journey. It contains my trip itinerary.

❑ Finish *The Dancer*.

While attending graduate school, I produced a draft of *The Dancer*. It's about the life of a stripper.

(↑) Write *Bob: My Dad, the Fisherman: A Father and Son's Relationship*.

Bob: My Dad, the Fisherman is a tribute to my father. After he passed, I wrote it for my Mom and other family members. I read *Bob* when I'm missing my Dad.

❑ Write *Murder at the Embassy House*.

I lived at the Embassy House Condominium in Chiang Mai, Thailand for a year. *Murder at the Embassy House* is a novel about a heinous crime that took place on the grounds there.

(↑) (With Saowaluk Rattanaudomsawat) Write *Essential Conversational Thai: Learn to Speak Thai Quickly, while Traveling in Thailand*.

When I first moved to Thailand, I couldn't find a suitable book that taught foreigners how to speak Thai. Most books focused solely on grammar and the Thai alphabet—44 consonants and 32 vowels with many similar-looking characters—rather than teaching how to communicate. Over time, I understood that the Thai educational system focuses on rote learning. Most books teaching Thai are written by Thais. With my graduate student Saowaluk "Yui" Rattanaudomsawat, I wrote the book that I wished for when I began to learn Thai. In *Essential Conversational Thai*, we teach Thai for foreigners wanting to hold conversations. My approach goes against rote learning.

Essential Conversational Thai helped many foreigners communicate in Thai. In the dictionary included in the back of the book, I often look up forgotten words. The dictionary is presented in a phonetic format. Without knowing the Thai alphabet and the ordering of its 76 characters, it's impossible to make use of a standard Thai dictionary.

Note that I learned the Thai alphabet and how to read and write Thai, but most foreigners don't want to invest the amount of time required for those tasks. Thai people prefer to speak English with foreigners. In many villages Thais are afraid to speak with foreigners. Even if a foreigner is speaking Thai, the local is only listening for English. In remote locations, communication is difficult.

❑ Write *On Communication*.

On Communication is intended to teach people who are in a relationship how to communicate. Although serious, it's humorous.

(↑) Write *You'll Never Walk Alone: Love Poems for My Sweetheart*.

I wrote *You'll Never Walk Alone*, a collection of 50+ heart-felt poems, for my sweetheart.

❏ Write *The Zero-Hour Workweek*.

The Zero-Hour Workweek describes how to use time wisely once retired.

(↑) Write *Poems of Raymond Greenlaw, 1986-2005*.

I gathered my poems from a 20-year period. I updated them slightly, formatted them, and organized them into *Poems of Raymond Greenlaw*.

❏ Write *The Bar Girl Next Door*.

(↑) Write *Trapped in Thailand's Cave*.

The *Trapped in Thailand's Cave* novel blends Thai legends, ghost stories, and spiritual beliefs with the real-life story of the soccer boys who were rescued after being trapped for nine days in a flooded cave in northern Thailand.

❏ Write *Lucy and Molly*.

Lucy and Molly is the heartbreaking story about the love shared between a cat and a dog who spend their lives together. It's based on my cat Killface and dog Dottie who lived happily together for 15+ years.

Chapter 12
Self

I collect a number of miscellaneous bucket-list items here. They're of a general personal nature.

(↑) While my Mom was alive, establish a scholarship in perpetuity in her name at her alma mater—the University of Rhode Island (URI).

I setup the *Rox-Ellene Greenlaw English Scholarship* in perpetuity at URI. Before passing, Mom attended the presentation of her scholarship on seven occasions. The named scholarship was a great honor for her. It's awarded annually in perpetuity. The recipient sends me and my sister a thank-you letter. The letters move me and bring my Mom to the forefront of my thoughts. RIP, Mom.

❑ When I'm 100 years old, see Halley's Comet for a second time.

When I was 25, Halley's Comet passed by in 1986. It returns in the vicinity of Earth approximately every 75 years.

(↑) Visit Arlington National Cemetery in Virginia.

When visiting Arlington National Cemetery, I get teary eyed.

❑ Meet Dr. Jane Goodall.

I admire her genius, spirit of adventure, brilliant research, conservation efforts, and work with chimpanzees.

(↑) Win a fishing derby.

(↑) Form my own company.

I formed two businesses: ABET Consulting Services and Roxy Publishing. I consult with universities and assist them with their accreditation needs, particularly in the areas of computing, engineering, technology, and applied sciences. In computing I help institutions with cybersecurity, computer science, information technology, information systems, software engineering, and computer engineering. My publishing company publishes books on a wide range of topics. It's named after my mother.

(↑) Catch a steelhead in one of Washington State's rivers.

Catching a steelhead isn't as easy as it sounds. The average steelhead fisherman catches one fish every seven years. I only lived in Washington State for six. I caught and released three fish. The big one got away.

❑ Father a daughter and a son.

(↑) Stay in a hotel with 25+ kings and heads of state.

At the time of Thailand's King Rama IX's 60th year anniversary of being on the throne, I stayed at the

Mandarin Oriental Hotel in Bangkok for a week. I checked in at the same time as several kings and VIPs. Many other heads of state checked in before me.

(↑) Visit the Jack Daniel's Distillery in Lynchburg, Tennessee.

(↑) Go to the top of Building 101 in Taipei, Taiwan.

❏ Stay at the Ice Hotel in Jukkasjärvi, Sweden.

(↑) Visit Wall Drugstore in Wall, South Dakota.

My hiking trail-name is Wall.

(↑) Drink margaritas at Hussong's Cantina in Tijuana, Mexico.

❏ Have dinner with Naomi Campbell.

(↑) Enter my guacamole recipe in a celebrity-chef, benefit cooking contest and win a prize.

(↑) Visit the cities where my parents were born: Northampton, Massachusetts (mother) and Worcester, Massachusetts (father).

❏ Volunteer for the Peace Corps.

(↑) Experience an eight-hand manicure and pedicure.

(↑) Learn how to make Scrimshaw.

Prior to the ban on ivory, my father was a Scrimshaw artist in the old whaling tradition.

❏ Become a boat captain.

(↑) Stay for a week at the Mandarin Oriental Hotel in Kuala Lumpur, Malaysia.

(↑) Drink a bottle of Dom Pérignon vintage champagne.

❑ Become a sushi chef.

Growing up in the Greenlaw household meant eating fresh fish daily—fish that we caught ourselves. My Mom cooked it. When I traveled to Japan, I became fond of raw fish.

(↑) Attend the Nutcracker Ballet performance with my friend Paul and our mothers at the Wang Theatre in Boston, Massachusetts.

Not too long before my Mom passed away, my friend Paul and I took his mother Lynne and my mother Roxy to this wonderful show in Boston. We had a marvelous time.

(↑) Read the Brother Grimm's Fairy Tales in German.

(↑) Be a philanthropist.

❑ Teach a course in the technical aspects of cryptocurrencies and the history of money.

(↑) Get a four-hands massage.

(↑) Provide moral and financial support for a friend to complete graduate school.

(↑) Visit the Petronas Towers in Kuala Lumpur, Malaysia.

❑ Become an expert bicycle mechanic.

(↑) Watch a meteorite shower.

(↑) Learn to speak the Thai language.

(↑) Drink margaritas at Señor Frog's in Playa del Carmen, Mexico.

❑ Kayak around the Americas.

(↑) Eat sashimi in Tokyo, Japan.

(↑) Purchase a condo in Thailand.

(↑) Consume ten Maine lobsters in one sitting.

❑ Take a ride on a nuclear submarine.

(↑) Become a multi-millionaire.

(↑) Eat a scorpion.

When being hosted, I'm polite and eat what's served. I ate scorpion, snake, bamboo rats, ants, puffin, kangaroo, various animal organs, camel, blood sausage, cockroaches, durian, grasshoppers, putrefied shark, ant eggs, dog, horse, fried baby birds, bear, century eggs, puffer fish, ram's testicles, seagull, emu, alligator, fish eyes, chicken feet, tripe, surströmming, whale, shark-fin soup, escargot, pickled eggs, octopus, mescal worms, reindeer, frog legs, crocodile, and a few things I won't list because they might upset readers.

Perhaps I was too polite. However, in many cultures turning down an expensive delicacy is considered rude and/or insulting. Norms change. Items that were acceptable to eat 50 years ago are now forbidden. When I queried about a dish's taste, the server invariably responded with: "Chicken." I tend to disagree.

(↑) Sample the cuisine of 150+ countries and territories.

(↑) Race at Andretti's Indoor Karting and Games in Atlanta, Georgia.

At Andretti's I turned in the second fastest lap of the entire day. My colleagues were impressed with my driving skills and lack of fear.

(↑) Have dinner with a Malaysian king and queen.

❑ Learn to ride a unicycle.

(↑) Visit the vineyards of Spain, Germany, Australia, Chile, Italy, France, Argentina, and Georgia (the country).

(↑) Take my mother on a sightseeing trip to Nova Scotia, Canada.

❑ Learn to draw.

I took a drawing class in college. My professor told us to draw. I drew. He didn't teach us to draw. I didn't learn how to draw.

(↑) Consume jello shots at Carlos 'N Charlie's in Cancun, Mexico.

(↑) Be in the first group of people to use email.

Email was invented in 1972. I started using it in the late 1970s. At the time few people whom I knew had ever heard of email. There was no one to whom I could send a message. In the 1990s when family and friends discovered email, they asked me excitedly about it:

"Have you heard of email?" I always responded with a polite: "Yes."

❏ Visit 80% of the destinations on the Traveler's Century Club list.

I visited 55% of the 329 destinations on the Traveler's Century Club list. I don't have the ambition to travel to all places on the list.

(↑) Take a week-long fishing trip to Alaska with my Dad.

My father loved fishing. He held two fishing world records. The trip to Alaska culminated our father-and-son relationship. I wrote down some of our shared times in *Bob: My Dad, the Fisherman*. RIP, Dad.

❏ Act in a professional play.

I did some acting in my Shakespeare class in high school.

(↑) Meet Sebastian Junger and discuss his book *The Perfect Storm: A True Story of Men against the Sea*.

(↑) Spend a week at Club Med.

I spent individual weeks at Club Meds in the Dominican Republic, the Maldives, and Turks and Caicos.

❏ Help to reduce the number of cybercrimes originating from Africa.

(↑) Have dinner with the director of the National Security Agency.

(↑) Tour wineries in Napa Valley, California.

Part II
Specific Travel

This part of the book includes bucket-list items for specific sets of travel destinations. There are chapters on UN countries; capitals of UN countries; world territories; world islands; USA's states; USA's state capitals; USA's second cities; USA's national parks, seashores, and lakeshores; USA's national forests and grasslands; USA's national monuments; USA's territories; USA's extreme points; Thailand's provinces; Thailand's national and marine parks; Thailand's extreme points; Thailand's mountains; and Thailand's scuba-diving sites.

Chapter 13
UN Countries

After my trip to Europe as a teenager, I added visiting all UN-recognized countries[2] to my bucket list. I have quite a few to go. For the most part, I haven't made specific trips to check off certain countries, but rather my interests led me to various destinations around the world. Since I turned 18, I'm averaging three new countries per year. At this rate it'll take me another 20 years to visit the remaining ones. I'll need to accelerate my rate of travel to hit them all. It's possible I'll deem a few places too dangerous to visit.

I added brief remarks to a handful of countries. For countries without notes, this omission shouldn't be interpreted negatively. I enjoyed almost everywhere I went. As of this writing, the COVID-19 pandemic has put a damper on travel. I won't be able to check off any new boxes until 2022. I list the countries in alphabetical order, so they can be searched easily.

❑ Visit all UN countries.

❑ Visit Afghanistan.

---

[2] This list is from the website un.org and is current as of this writing.

While in Tajikistan, I drove along the Afghan border for several hundred miles. I threw a rock across the Panj River into Afghanistan. Unfortunately, I wasn't able to cross the border. At a shared weekend market, I tried. I failed. The mountains and villages looked beautiful.

(↑) Visit Albania.

I enjoyed meeting the locals, hiking in the rugged Accursed Mountains, visiting the capital city of Tirana, and traveling around to smaller villages.

❑ Visit Algeria.

(↑) Visit Andorra.

❑ Visit Angola.

I plan to visit in 2022.

(↑) Visit Antigua and Barbuda.

I thoroughly enjoyed hiking and diving in Antigua.

(↑) Visit Argentina.

(↑) Visit Armenia.

(↑) Visit Australia.

I visited five of six states in Australia and all three internal territories.

(↑) Visit Austria.

I visited seven of nine states in Austria.

(↑) Visit Azerbaijan.

(↑) Visit the Bahamas.

(↑) Visit Bahrain.

❏ Visit Bangladesh.

When I was in Kolkata, India, I was extremely close to the border of Bangladesh.

(↑) Visit Barbados.

(↑) Visit Belarus.

(↑) Visit Belgium.

I visited all 11 of Belgium's provinces. In my humble opinion, Belgium has the best beer in the world.

(↑) Visit Belize.

❏ Visit Benin.

❏ Visit Bhutan.

(↑) Visit Bolivia.

(↑) Visit Bosnia and Herzegovina.

When I walked into Bosnia and Herzegovina from Croatia, a black car with darkened windows pulled beside me. I got ready to run. After rolling down the window, a nice guy handed me a giant chocolate bar and said: "Welcome to Bosnia!" I thanked him. I enjoyed that chocolate. I met many other hospitable and friendly people in the country. I even got invited and stayed in people's homes.

❑ Visit Botswana.

I plan to visit in 2022.

(↑) Visit Brazil.

(↑) Visit Brunei.

(↑) Visit Bulgaria.

❑ Visit Burkina Faso.

❑ Visit Burundi.

❑ Visit Cabo Verde.

(↑) Visit Cambodia.

❑ Visit Cameroon.

(↑) Visit Canada.

I visited seven of ten provinces.

❑ Visit the Central African Republic.

❑ Visit Chad.

(↑) Visit Chile.

(↑) Visit China.

I visited 26 of 32 regions in China.

(↑) Visit Colombia.

❑ Visit Comoros.

❑ Visit Congo.

(↑) Visit Costa Rica.

❑ Visit Côte D'Ivoire.

(↑) Visit Croatia.

I visited 18 of 21 counties in Croatia.

(↑) Visit Cuba.

I want to return and see more of this beautiful country. I want to interact more with the locals.

(↑) Visit Cyprus.

(↑) Visit Czechia, also known as the Czech Republic.

❑ Visit the Democratic Republic of the Congo.

While traveling with my friend Paul to Rwanda, I came within three miles of the Democratic Republic of the Congo. At the time we felt it was too dangerous to cross the border.

(↑) Visit Denmark.

❑ Visit Djibouti.

(↑) Visit Dominica.

(↑) Visit the Dominican Republic.

(↑) Visit Ecuador.

(↑) Visit Egypt.

Egypt has some of the most aggressive street hawkers in the world. I met friendly people, too.

(↑) Visit El Salvador.

❏ Visit Equatorial Guinea.

❏ Visit Eritrea.

(↑) Visit Estonia.

After meeting an Estonian hiker on the Via Dinarica Trail, I decided to go to Estonia.

(↑) Eswatini.

When I traveled there, the Kingdom of Eswatini was called Swaziland. The absolute monarchy changed its name in 2018.

(↑) Visit Ethiopia.

(↑) Visit Fiji.

(↑) Visit Finland.

(↑) Visit France.

❏ Visit Gabon.

❏ Visit Gambia.

(↑) Visit Georgia.

The people are big and strong. Everyone makes their own wine and bread. The mountains are spectacular. The locals are friendly.

(↑) Visit Germany.

I want to visit the old East Germany.

❑ Visit Ghana.

(↑) Visit Greece.

(↑) Visit Grenada.

(↑) Visit Guatemala.

❑ Visit Guinea.

❑ Visit Guinea Bissau.

(↑) Visit Guyana.

❑ Visit Haiti.

❑ Visit Honduras.

(↑) Visit Hungary.

(↑) Visit Iceland.

I lived in Iceland for several months. It's a beautiful country with well-educated and friendly people. I visited all eight regions of Iceland.

(↑) Visit India.

(↑) Visit Indonesia.

❑ Visit Iran.

When traveling in Turkmenistan, I came close to entering Iran.

❏ Visit Iraq.

(↑) Visit Ireland.

(↑) Visit Israel.

(↑) Visit Italy.

I made about 40 trips to Italy. I worked at the University of Roma La Sapienza. I love the people, food, sights, history, culture, and scenery. I followed the three-week Giro d'Italia bicycle race in 2019. It took me into a few new parts of Italy. Overall, I visited 17 of 20 regions.

(↑) Visit Jamaica.

(↑) Visit Japan.

I visited seven of eight regions in Japan.

(↑) Visit Jordan.

(↑) Visit Kazakhstan.

A student from Kazakhstan studied with me. After learning more about the country from him, I traveled there. It's a massive country. The people whom I met were friendly.

(↑) Visit Kenya.

❏ Visit Kiribati.

❏ Visit Kuwait.

(↑) Visit Kyrgyzstan.

I took a grand tour of the country. I visited six of eight districts. The people whom I met were incredibly kind.

(↑) Visit Laos.

I love riding my bicycle in Laos. The terrain is challenging. The people are extremely friendly. There are many remote areas, having little vehicular traffic.

(↑) Visit Latvia.

❑ Visit Lebanon.

(↑) Visit Lesotho.

❑ Visit Liberia.

❑ Visit Libya.

(↑) Visit Liechtenstein.

(↑) Visit Lithuania.

(↑) Visit Luxembourg.

(↑) Visit Madagascar.

❑ Visit Malawi.

(↑) Visit Malaysia.

I had a visiting professorship at a university near Kuala Lumpur. I made 10+ trips to Malaysia.

(↑) Visit the Maldives.

❑ Visit Mali.

(↑) Visit Malta.

❑ Visit the Marshall Islands.

❑ Visit Mauritania.

(↑) Visit Mexico.

I went to Mexico dozens of times. I love the people, food, scenery, culture, and weather. I traveled thousands of miles throughout the country. It's diverse. I did a lot of scuba diving and climbing in Mexico.

(↑) Visit the Federated States of Micronesia.

I visited the islands of Truk and Yap. The best sashimi I ever ate was on Yap.

(↑) Visit Moldova.

(↑) Visit Monaco.

❑ Visit Mongolia.

When in Inner Mongolia, I traveled to the Mongolian border with the intention of crossing. If I entered Mongolia, I wouldn't be allowed back in China, from where my return flights were booked. I wasn't able to rearrange my schedule. Arghhh!

(↑) Visit Montenegro.

I walked across Montenegro.

(↑) Visit Morocco.

❏ Visit Mozambique.

While driving in northeast South Africa, I was only a couple miles from the border of Mozambique.

(↑) Visit Myanmar.

I made six trips to Myanmar. It's a beautiful place. As of this writing, the country is in turmoil.

❏ Visit Namibia.

I plan to move to Namibia for a year in 2022.

❏ Visit Nauru.

(↑) Visit Nepal.

(↑) Visit the Netherlands.

When 18, I walked down a street alone in Amsterdam one night. Out of my peripheral vision, I thought I saw a nude, sexy woman signaling to me. While shaking my head in denial, I proceeded. Then I saw another and another. I went back to the first window. She smiled. I smiled. I wasn't mistaken. I missed the memo about the Red Light District. I love Amsterdam. The people are open minded.

(↑) Visit New Zealand.

I traveled in the north island of New Zealand.

❏ Visit Nicaragua.

❏ Visit Niger.

❏ Visit Nigeria.

❑ Visit North Korea.

When in South Korea, I planned to take a tour across the border into North Korea. The tour got canceled. Arghhh!

(↑) Visit North Macedonia.

(↑) Visit Norway.

(↑) Visit Oman.

❑ Visit Pakistan.

(↑) Visit Palau.

(↑) Visit Panama.

❑ Visit Papua New Guinea.

(↑) Visit Paraguay.

I drove around the perimeter of Paraguay. I visited 15 of 18 departments. Paraguay is a little bigger than California. The country doesn't attract many tourists. The people are friendly. It gets hot in their summer months, 100°+F.

(↑) Visit Peru.

(↑) Visit the Philippines.

I went to 12 islands in the Philippines. The people are positive, loud, energetic, friendly, and religious. The scenery is excellent. Manila is sprawling and chaotic.

(↑) Visit Poland.

(↑) Visit Portugal.

(↑) Visit Qatar.

(↑) Visit Romania.

(↑) Visit Russia.

The people whom I met in Russia were very friendly and helpful. Outside of Moscow, things were reasonably priced.

(↑) Visit Rwanda.

The people of Rwanda are beautiful and friendly.

(↑) Visit Saint Kitts and Nevis.

(↑) Visit Saint Lucia.

(↑) Visit Saint Vincent and the Grenadines.

❑ Visit Samoa.

(↑) Visit San Marino.

❑ Visit São Tomé and Príncipe.

(↑) Visit Saudi Arabia.

❑ Visit Senegal.

(↑) Visit Serbia.

❑ Visit the Seychelles.

❑ Visit Sierra Leone.

(↑) Visit Singapore.

While traveling between North America and Asia, I made dozens of 2-3 day stopovers in Singapore. It has great restaurants and shopping.

(↑) Visit Slovakia.

(↑) Visit Slovenia.

The scenery is fantastic, and the people are friendly.

❏ Visit the Solomon Islands.

❏ Visit Somalia.

(↑) Visit South Africa.

The food in South Africa is excellent. The wildlife and scenery are spectacular.

(↑) Visit South Korea.

❏ Visit South Sudan.

(↑) Visit Spain.

I lived in Barcelona for one year. I visited 36 of 54 provinces in Spain. I like the weather, mountains, beaches, and museums.

(↑) Visit Sri Lanka.

(↑) Visit Suriname.

(↑) Visit Sweden.

I visited 17 of 21 lands in Sweden.

(↑) Visit Switzerland.

I made 10+ trips to Switzerland. I visited 20 of 26 cantons. Due to its natural beauty, it's one of my favorite countries.

❑ Visit Syria.

I hope things calm down in Syria at some point.

(↑) Visit Tajikistan.

With an average elevation of 10,455 feet, Tajikistan is one of the highest countries in the world. I took a grand tour of the country. I visited all five regions and 35 of 58 districts. If you enjoy plov and bread, you'll enjoy their food.

(↑) Visit Tanzania.

I love Tanzania. The people are welcoming and friendly. There are many scenic areas.

(↑) Visit Thailand.

Thailand has been my base for a number of years. I have bicycled and walked across the entire country. I have traveled to all 77 of its provinces. Outside the main tourist cities, Thais enjoy a peaceful and relaxing life style. Most people are farmers. The food is excellent.

❑ Visit Timor-Leste.

❑ Visit Togo.

❑ Visit Tonga.

(↑) Visit Trinidad and Tobago.

I traveled to Trinidad and Tobago twice: for scuba diving and as a stop-over between other Caribbean countries.

❑ Visit Tunisia.

(↑) Visit Turkey.

I took a grand tour of Turkey and visited many archaeological sites. The history is amazing. The weather is good. The food is hearty. The whirling dervishes and belly dancers are impressive.

(↑) Visit Turkmenistan.

I took a grand tour of Turkmenistan. Tourists are monitored carefully. I visited five of six regions. The desert scenery is spectacular. Ashgabat is perhaps the cleanest city in the world. The white-marble buildings designed by French architects and built with Italian marble are something to behold. The 1,000,000+ trees planted in and around Ashgabat in the desert are impressive.

❑ Visit Tuvalu.

(↑) Visit Uganda.

I found the people of Uganda to be welcoming, happy, smiling, and friendly. The mountains are beautiful. The roads are primitive.

(↑) Visit Ukraine.

(↑) Visit the United Arab Emirates.

(↑) Visit the United Kingdom of Great Britain and Northern Ireland.

(↑) Visit the United States of America.

I was born in the US.

(↑) Visit Uruguay.

(↑) Visit Uzbekistan.

I visited 12 of 14 regions in Uzbekistan.

(↑) Visit Vanuatu.

(↑) Visit Venezuela.

(↑) Visit Vietnam.

Everything I ever heard about Vietnam was the exact opposite of what I encountered. The people are friendly, even toward Americans. The countryside is beautiful, as are the beaches. Due to the French influence, the roads are well built and the bakeries are wonderful. The food is delicious. The people are hard working.

❑ Visit Yemen.

Before planning a visit, I need to wait until things settle down in Yemen.

(↑) Visit Zambia.

(↑) Visit Zimbabwe.

The farms in the countryside look beautiful.

Chapter 14
Capitals of UN Countries

I added to my bucket list visiting all capital cities of the world. Most of these places are extremely interesting from historical, political, architectural, and cultural points of view. Usually, the best museums, monuments, restaurants, architecture, and entertainment are found in a country's capital city. The people are interesting.

While visiting some countries, I missed their capital cities. I regret that. When visiting new countries, I hope I'll have the chance to visit their capitals as well. The capitals are listed in alphabetical order by country.

❑ Visit the capital cities of all UN countries.

❑ Visit Afghanistan: Kābul.

(↑) Visit Albania: Tirana.

❑ Visit Algeria: Algiers.

(↑) Visit Andorra: Andorra La Vella.

❑ Visit Angola: Luanda.

(↑) Visit Antigua and Barbuda: Saint John's.

(↑) Visit Argentina: Buenos Aires.

(↑) Visit Armenia: Yerevan.

(↑) Visit Australia: Canberra.

(↑) Visit Austria: Vienna.

(↑) Visit Azerbaijan: Baku.

(↑) Visit the Bahamas: Nassau.

(↑) Visit Bahrain: Manama.

❑ Visit Bangladesh: Dhaka.

(↑) Visit Barbados: Bridgetown.

(↑) Visit Belarus: Minsk.

(↑) Visit Belgium: Brussels.

(↑) Visit Belize: Belmopan.

❑ Visit Benin: Porto-Novo.

❑ Visit Bhutan: Thimphu.

(↑) Visit Bolivia: La Paz.

(↑) Visit Bosnia and Herzegovina: Sarajevo.

❑ Visit Botswana: Gaborone.

❑ Visit Brazil: Brasília.

(↑) Visit Brunei: Bandar Seri Begawan.

(↑) Visit Bulgaria: Sofia.

❑ Visit Burkina Faso: Ouagadougou.

❑ Visit Burundi: Bujumbura.

❑ Visit Cabo Verde: Praia.

(↑) Visit Cambodia: Phnom Penh.

❑ Visit Cameroon: Yaoundé.

(↑) Visit Canada: Ottawa.

❑ Visit the Central African Republic: Bangui.

❑ Visit Chad: N'Djamena.

(↑) Visit Chile: Santiago.

(↑) Visit China: Beijing.

(↑) Visit Colombia: Bogota.

❑ Visit Comoros: Moroni.

❑ Visit Congo: Brazzaville.

(↑) Visit Costa Rica: San Jose.

❑ Visit Côte D'Ivoire: Yamoussoukro.

(↑) Visit Croatia: Zagreb.

(↑) Visit Cuba: Havana.

(↑) Visit Cyprus: Nicosia.

(↑) Visit Czechia: Prague.

❏ Visit the Democratic Republic of the Congo: Kinshasa.

(↑) Visit Denmark: Copenhagen.

❏ Visit Djibouti: Djibouti.

(↑) Visit Dominica: Roseau.

(↑) Visit the Dominican Republic: Santo Domingo.

(↑) Visit Ecuador: Quito.

(↑) Visit Egypt: Cairo.

(↑) Visit El Salvador: San Salvador.

❏ Visit Equatorial Guinea: Malabo.

❏ Visit Eritrea: Asmara.

(↑) Visit Estonia: Tallinn.

(↑) Eswatini: Mbabane.

(↑) Visit Ethiopia: Addis Ababa.

(↑) Visit Fiji: Suva.

(↑) Visit Finland: Helsinki.

(↑) Visit France: Paris.

❏ Visit Gabon: Libreville.

❏ Visit Gambia: Banjul.

(↑) Visit Georgia: Tbilisi.

❑ Visit Germany: Berlin.

❑ Visit Ghana: Accra.

(↑) Visit Greece: Athens.

(↑) Visit Grenada: Saint George's.

(↑) Visit Guatemala: Guatemala City.

❑ Visit Guinea: Conakry.

❑ Visit Guinea Bissau: Bissau.

(↑) Visit Guyana: Georgetown.

❑ Visit Haiti: Port-au-Prince.

❑ Visit Honduras: Tegucigalpa.

(↑) Visit Hungary: Budapest.

(↑) Visit Iceland: Reykjavik.

❑ Visit India: New Delhi.

(↑) Visit Indonesia: Jakarta.

❑ Visit Iran: Tehrān.

❑ Visit Iraq: Baghdād.

(↑) Visit Ireland: Dublin.

(↑) Visit Israel: Jerusalem.

(↑) Visit Italy: Rome.

(↑) Visit Jamaica: Kingstown.

(↑) Visit Japan: Tokyo.

(↑) Visit Jordan: Amman.

❑ Visit Kazakhstan: Nur-Sultan.

(↑) Visit Kenya: Nairobi.

❑ Visit Kiribati: Tarawa.

❑ Visit Kuwait: Kuwait.

(↑) Visit Kyrgyzstan: Bishkek.

(↑) Visit Laos: Vientiane.

(↑) Visit Latvia: Riga.

❑ Visit Lebanon: Beirut.

(↑) Visit Lesotho: Maseru.

❑ Visit Liberia: Monrovia.

❑ Visit Libya: Tripoli.

(↑) Visit Liechtenstein: Vaduz.

(↑) Visit Lithuania: Vilnius.

(↑) Visit Luxembourg: Luxembourg.

❑ Visit Madagascar: Antananarivo.

- ❏ Visit Malawi: Lilongwe.

- (↑) Visit Malaysia: Kuala Lumpur.

- ❏ Visit the Maldives: Male.

- ❏ Visit Mali: Bamako.

- (↑) Visit Malta: Valletta.

- ❏ Visit the Marshall Islands: Majuro.

- ❏ Visit Mauritania: Nouakchott.

- (↑) Visit Mexico: Mexico City.

- ❏ Visit Micronesia, Federated States of: Palikir.

- (↑) Visit Moldova: Chisinau.

- (↑) Visit Monaco: Monaco.

- ❏ Visit Mongolia: Ulaanbaatar.

- ❏ Visit Montenegro: Podgorica.

When I was hiking the Via Dinarica Trail in the Balkans, I walked across Montenegro. I was close to Podgorica. I met some people who were heading into the city, but I didn't have the time or the energy to go with them. I regret that now.

- ❏ Visit Morocco: Rabat.

- ❏ Visit Mozambique: Maputo.

- ❏ Visit Myanmar: Yangon.

❑ Visit Namibia: Windhoek.

I plan to work in Windhoek in 2022.

❑ Visit Nauru: Yaren District.

(↑) Visit Nepal: Kathmandu.

(↑) Visit the Netherlands: Amsterdam.

(↑) Visit New Zealand: Wellington.

❑ Visit Nicaragua: Managua.

❑ Visit Niger: Niamey.

❑ Visit Nigeria: Abuja.

(↑) Visit North Macedonia: Skopje.

(↑) Visit Norway: Oslo.

(↑) Visit Oman: Muscat.

❑ Visit Pakistan: Islāmābād.

(↑) Visit Palau: Ngerulmud, Koror.

(↑) Visit Panama: Panama City.

❑ Visit Papua New Guinea: Port Moresby.

(↑) Visit Paraguay: Asuncion.

(↑) Visit Peru: Lima.

(↑) Visit the Philippines: Manila.

(↑) Visit Poland: Warsaw.

(↑) Visit Portugal: Lisbon.

(↑) Visit Qatar: Doha.

(↑) Visit Romania: Bucharest.

(↑) Visit Russia: Moscow.

(↑) Visit Rwanda: Kigali.

(↑) Visit Saint Kitts and Nevis: Basseterre.

(↑) Visit Saint Lucia: Castries.

(↑) Visit Saint Vincent and the Grenadines: Kingstown.

❏ Visit Samoa: Apia.

(↑) Visit San Marino: San Marino.

❏ Visit São Tomé and Príncipe: São Tomé.

❏ Visit Saudi Arabia: Riyadh.

❏ Visit Senegal: Dakar.

(↑) Visit Serbia: Belgrade.

❏ Visit the Seychelles: Victoria.

❏ Visit Sierra Leone: Freetown.

(↑) Visit Singapore: Singapore.

(↑) Visit Slovakia: Bratislava.

(↑) Visit Slovenia: Ljubljana.

❏ Visit the Solomon Islands: Honiara.

❏ Visit Somalia: Mogadishu.

(↑) Visit South Africa: Pretoria.

(↑) Visit South Korea: Seoul.

❏ Visit South Sudan: Juba.

(↑) Visit Spain: Madrid.

(↑) Visit Sri Lanka: Colombo.

(↑) Visit Suriname: Paramaribo.

(↑) Visit Sweden: Stockholm.

(↑) Visit Switzerland: Bern.

❏ Visit Syria: Damascus.

(↑) Visit Tajikistan: Dushanbe.

❏ Visit Tanzania: Dodoma.

(↑) Visit Thailand: Bangkok.

❏ Visit Timor-Leste: Dili.

❏ Visit Togo: Lomé.

❏ Visit Tonga: Nukuʻalofa.

(↑) Visit Trinidad and Tobago: Port of Spain.

- ❏ Visit Tunisia: Tunis.

- (↑) Visit Turkey: Ankara.

- (↑) Visit Turkmenistan: Ashgabat.

- ❏ Visit Tuvalu: Funafuti.

- (↑) Visit Uganda: Kampala.

- (↑) Visit Ukraine: Kiev.

- (↑) Visit the United Arab Emirates: Abu Dhabi.

- (↑) Visit the United Kingdom of Great Britain and Northern Ireland: London.

- (↑) Visit the United States of America: Washington, DC.

- (↑) Visit Uruguay: Montevideo.

- (↑) Visit Uzbekistan: Tashkent.

- (↑) Visit Vanuatu: Port Vila.

- (↑) Visit Venezuela: Caracas.

- (↑) Visit Vietnam: Hanoi.

- ❏ Visit Yemen: Ṣanʻāʼ.

- ❏ Visit Zambia: Lusaka.

- (↑) Visit Zimbabwe: Harare.

Chapter 15
World Territories

There are many interesting regions in the world that aren't countries. In this chapter I focus on non-US territories and independent regions. I added them to my bucket list. The USA's territories are handled in a separate chapter. Territories are land areas that belong to certain countries but aren't considered countries themselves. There are other landmasses that are independent republics or autonomous regions. Many of these places are more remote and challenging to reach than regular countries. Territories may become countries. Some territories listed here fit easily into the islands chapter as well.

The territories aren't ordered in any particular manner. I provide an indication of where they're located.

❏ Visit all world territories.

(↑) Visit New Caledonia (Noumea,[3] French Territory).

---

[3] I list the capital of a territory if I went there. This doesn't mean that I only went to the capital. Usually, I visited many locations within the territory.

❑ Visit the Andaman and Nicobar Islands Union Territory of India (west of the Andaman Sea and east of the Bay of Bengal).

(↑) Visit Antarctica (Argentine Territory, Chilean Territory, and United Kingdom Territory).

I was only in a few places in Antarctica. These territorial claims overlap in some areas.

(↑) Visit the Gorno Badakhshan Autonomous Oblast (Khorog, shared between Tajikistan and Afghanistan).

(↑) Visit Reunion Island (Saint-Denis, French Territory).

❑ Visit the Chagos Archipelago and Diego Garcia Island (British Indian Ocean Territory with the claim disputed by Mauritius).

(↑) Visit Antarctica (Patriot Hills).

This trip entailed an expensive flight with near week-long delays on both ends. The landing on the glacier at Patriot Hills was spectacular. I thought that my teeth would turn into powder from the vibrations caused by landing on a natural glacier. Before reaching a stop on the rough ice, the plane slid for 10+ miles.

On the return flight to Ushuaia, Argentina, a helicopter was transported back inside the cabin, right where we were sitting. The rotor blade always seemed to be at throat level. I often thought: "I hope that bungee cord doesn't break." The helicopter had made the first North to South Pole flight.

❑ Visit the Wallis and Futuna Territory (France, South Pacific).

(↑) Visit Saint Maarten (Philipsburg, Netherlands).

(↑) Visit Aruba (Oranjestad, Netherlands).

❑ Visit the Northwest Territories (Canada).

(↑) Visit Bermuda (Hamilton, British Overseas Territory).

❑ Visit the Nunavut Territory (Canada).

(↑) Visit Bonaire (Kralendijk, Netherlands).

❑ Visit the Yukon Territory (Canada).

(↑) Visit the Capital Territory in Canberra, Australia.

❑ Visit the Ashmore and Cartier Islands External Territory (Australia, Indian Ocean).

(↑) Visit the Cayman Islands (Georgetown, British Overseas Territory).

❑ Visit the Christmas Island External Territory (Australia, Indian Ocean).

(↑) Visit Taiwan (Taipei, Region of China).

(↑) Visit the Cook Islands (Avarua District).

❑ Visit the Cocos (Keeling) Islands External Territory (Australia, Indian Ocean).

(↑) Visit the US Virgin Islands (Charlotte Amalie).

(↑) Visit Curaçao (Willemstad, Netherlands).

❏ Visit the Coral Sea Islands External Territory (Australia, South Pacific).

(↑) Visit the Northern Territory (Australia).

(↑) Visit Dubai (an emirate in the United Arab Emirates).

❏ Visit Heard Island and the McDonald Islands External Territory (Australia, Indian Ocean).

(↑) Visit the Ellsworth Mountains (Chilean territory in Antarctica).

❏ Visit the Norfolk Island External Territory (Australia, South Pacific).

(↑) Visit French Guiana (Cayenne, French Territory).

(↑) Visit the Republika Srpska (located in the Bosnia and Herzegovina area of the Balkan Peninsula).

❏ Visit the Chatham Islands Territory (New Zealand).

(↑) Visit French Polynesia (French Territory).

(↑) Visit Gibraltar (Gibraltar, British Overseas Territory).

❏ Visit the Tokelau Territory (New Zealand, South Pacific Ocean).

(↑) Visit Hong Kong (City of Victoria, Region of China).

(↑) Visit the Jervis Bay Territory (Australia).

❏ Visit Sharjah in the United Arab Emirates.

Sharjah is the third largest and third most populous emirate in the UAE.

(↑) Visit Tibet (Lhasa, Region of China).

(↑) Visit the Turks and Caicos Islands (British Overseas Territory).

Chapter 16
World Islands

I'm fascinated by islands. Maybe it's because I grew up in an area with many beautiful beaches. Early on in life I went to places such as Block Island, Martha's Vineyard, and Nantucket. Check times three. I love such places. In this chapter I present my bucket list for islands. I present the islands in alphabetical order, so it's easy to search the list for a particular island.

In a few cases, an island might be listed twice using separate names or by specifying the name of the group of islands, where a particular island is located. I adopted this convention because some readers might be familiar with one name, but not the other. Some islands are remote and difficult to check off, whereas others are near the mainland and easy to check off, if you're in the area.

For the most part, I haven't specified where an island is located. It didn't seem to make sense to me to say things such as: "Pacific Ocean," as it covers 30% of the planet. A pointer to an unfamiliar body of water, such as the Beaufort or Ligurian Sea, won't help most readers. Geographic coordinates probably wouldn't be too beneficial either. For unfamiliar islands it's easy enough to check online for a location.

To reach all the islands that I traveled to required an enormous amount of time, energy, planning, and money. I probably covered 1,000,000+ miles getting to these destinations. To complete my bucket list, I have many more miles to go.

❑ Visit the Admiralty Islands (Papua New Guinea).

(↑) Visit the Aegean Islands.

(↑) Visit Aitutaki Island.

Long ago, when I googled for the most beautiful place on Earth, Aitutaki came up as the first hit. It's an extremely beautiful place and definitely one of the most beautiful islands in the world. To reach Aitutaki required six flights over a few days on multiple airlines. Other remote islands on my bucket list require similar amounts of travel from the US.

❑ Visit the Åland Islands (Baltic Sea).

(↑) Visit Ambergris Caye.

(↑) Visit Amelia Island.

(↑) Visit Antigua Island.

(↑) Visit Aquidneck Island.

❑ Visit the Austral Islands (French Polynesia).

(↑) Visit Babeldoab Island.

(↑) Visit Bainbridge Island.

(↑) Visit Baisha Island.

❑ Visit the Balearic Islands (Mediterranean Sea).

(↑) Visit the private Balesin Island.

(↑) Visit Bali.

(↑) Visit Baranof Island.

❑ Visit Barbuda Island (Caribbean Sea).

(↑) Visit Block Island.

(↑) Visit Bohol Island.

(↑) Visit Boracay Island.

(↑) Visit Borneo.

❑ Visit Bouvet Island (South Atlantic Island).

(↑) Visit Brewster Island.

(↑) Visit Brunswick Island.

❑ Visit the Canary Islands (Atlantic Ocean).

(↑) Visit Cape Breton Island.

(↑) Visit Castaway Island.

(↑) Visit Cebu Island.

(↑) Visit Chichagof Island.

(↑) Visit Chuuk (Truk).

❑ Visit Clipperton Island (Eastern Pacific Ocean).

(↑) Visit Cockspur Island.

(↑) Visit Conanicut Island.

(↑) Visit the Cooks Islands (Southern Group).

(↑) Visit Corfu.

❏ Visit Corsica Island (Mediterranean Sea).

(↑) Visit Cozumel.

(↑) Visit Crete.

(↑) Visit Cumberland Island.

(↑) Visit the Cyclades Islands.

(↑) Visit Daufuskie Island.

(↑) Visit Delos Island.

(↑) Visit Dukit Island.

(↑) Visit Dutch Island.

❏ Visit Easter Island (Chile).

(↑) Visit Edisto Island.

(↑) Visit Efaté Island.

(↑) Visit Eil Malk Island.

❏ Visit the Falkland Islands (South Atlantic Ocean).

❏ Visit the Faroe Islands (between the Norwegian Sea and the North Atlantic Ocean).

(↑) Visit Fenwick Island.

(↑) Visit Fidalgo Island.

(↑) Visit the Florida Keys.

(↑) Visit French Polynesia.

I listed separately numerous islands in French Polynesia that I specifically want to visit.

❑ Visit the French Southern Lands (Kerguelen Islands, St. Paul and Amsterdam Islands, Crozet Islands, and the Scattered Islands).

(↑) Visit Fripp Island.

(↑) Visit Gagil-Tamil Island.

(↑) Visit the Galapagos (numerous islands).

(↑) Visit Galveston Island.

(↑) Visit Gato Island.

(↑) Visit Grand Bahama.

(↑) Visit Grande Terre.

(↑) Visit the Great Barrier Reef.

❑ Visit Greenland.

(↑) Visit Gyoo Island.

(↑) Visit Half-Moon Bay Cay.

(↑) Visit Heimaey.

(↑) Visit Herisson Island.

(↑) Visit Hilton Head Island.

(↑) Visit Hispaniola.

(↑) Visit Hoko Island.

(↑) Visit Honshu Island.

(↑) Visit Huxi Island.

(↑) Visit Ifari Island.

(↑) Visit Ile aux Carnards.

(↑) Visit the Ionian Islands (Ionian Sea off the west coast of Greece).

(↑) Visit Iririki Island.

(↑) Visit Isla del Sol.

(↑) Visit Isla Grande de Tierra del Fuego.

(↑) Visit the Isle of Hope.

(↑) Visit the Isle of Shoals.

(↑) Visit Jamestown Island.

❑ Visit Jan Mayen Island (Arctic Ocean between the Greenland and Norwegian Seas).

(↑) Visit Java.

(↑) Visit Jekyll Island.

(↑) Visit John's Island.

❏ Visit the Juan Fernández Islands, including Robinson Crusoe, Alejandro Selkirk, and Santa Clara (Chile).

(↑) Visit Kani.

(↑) Visit Kanifinholu Island.

(↑) Visit Kauai.

(↑) Visit Kent Island.

(↑) Visit Key West.

(↑) Visit Kiawah Island.

(↑) Visit Koh Bayu.

(↑) Visit Koh Bon.

(↑) Visit Koh Chang.

(↑) Visit Koh Ha.

(↑) Visit Koh Hin Pousar.

(↑) Visit Koh Kai.

(↑) Visit Koh Klang.

(↑) Visit Koh Lanta.

(↑) Visit Koh Miang.

(↑) Visit Koh Nang Yuan.

(↑) Visit Koh Payu.

(↑) Visit Koh Ri.

(↑) Visit Koh Samui.

(↑) Visit Koh Similan.

(↑) Visit Koh Surin Nuea.

(↑) Visit Koh Surin Tai.

(↑) Visit Koh Tachai.

(↑) Visit Koh Tao.

(↑) Visit Koror Island.

(↑) Visit Krabi.

(↑) Visit Kyushu.

❏ Visit the Leeward Islands (French Polynesia).

(↑) Visit the Lesser Antilles.

(↑) Visit the Lesser Sunda Islands.

(↑) Visit Leyte Island.

(↑) Visit Little St. Simons Island.

(↑) Visit Little Tybee Island.

(↑) Visit Livingstone Island.

(↑) Visit Longboat Key.

(↑) Visit Long Island.

(↑) Visit Looe Key.

❏ Visit the Loyalty Islands (New Caledonia).

When I was in New Caledonia for ten days, due to strong winds causing very rough seas, I was unable to make a trip out to the Loyalty Islands.

(↑) Visit Luzon Island.

(↑) Visit Mactan Island.

(↑) Visit Magdalena Island.

(↑) Visit Magong Island.

(↑) Visit Malakal Island.

(↑) Visit Malapascua Island.

(↑) Visit the Mamanuca Islands.

(↑) Visit Manhattan Island.

❏ Visit Margarita Island (Venezuela).

(↑) Visit the Marianas Islands.

❏ Visit the Marquesas Islands (French Polynesia).

(↑) Visit Martha's Vineyard.

❏ Visit Martinique Island (Caribbean Sea).

(↑) Visit Mecherchar (Jelly Fish Lake).

(↑) Visit Mercer Island.

(↑) Visit Mount Desert Island.

(↑) Visit Muharraq Island.

(↑) Visit Mykonos Island.

(↑) Visit Nantucket Island.

(↑) Visit Nassau.

(↑) Visit Negros Island.

(↑) Visit the New Hebrides Islands.

❑ Visit the Northern Gilberts (Kiribati).

❑ Visit the Northern Group of the Cook Islands: Manihiki, Nassau, Penryhn, Pukapuka, Rakahanga, and Suwarrow.

(↑) Visit North Island.

(↑) Visit Oahu.

(↑) Visit Observatory Island.

(↑) Visit Orcas Island.

(↑) Visit Ossabaw Island.

(↑) Visit Palawan.

(↑) Visit Panglao Island.

(↑) Visit Pelelui Island.

(↑) Visit the Penghu Islands.

- ❏ Visit Peter I Island (Bellingshausen Sea).

- (↑) Visit Phi Phi Island.

- ❏ Visit the Phoenix Islands (Kiribati).

- (↑) Visit Phuket Island.

- (↑) Visit Pine Island.

- ❏ Visit the Pitcairn Islands (South Pacific Ocean).

- (↑) Visit Prince Edward Island.

- (↑) Visit Providenciales.

- (↑) Visit Prudence Island.

- (↑) Visit Rarotonga.

- (↑) Visit the Rock Islands.

- (↑) Visit the Rosario Islands.

- (↑) Visit Saint Simons Island.

- (↑) Visit Saint Thomas Island.

- (↑) Visit Sanibel Island.

- (↑) Visit the San Juan Islands.

- ❏ Visit Santa Catalina Island.

- (↑) Visit Santorini.

- (↑) Visit Sapello Island.

❑ Visit Sardinia.

I planned a trip to Sardinia. I was in Italy on the mainland ready to depart. My friend became ill, and she couldn't travel. We canceled the trip. The good news is she recovered.

(↑) Visit Sea Island.

(↑) Visit Sentosa Island.

(↑) Visit the Shepherd Islands.

(↑) Visit Siargao Island.

❑ Visit Sicily.

(↑) Visit the Similian Islands.

❑ Visit Sint Eustatius Island (Caribbean Sea).

(↑) Visit Siquidor Island.

(↑) Visit Skidaway Island.

(↑) Visit the Society Islands.

❑ Visit South Georgia and the South Sandwich Islands (South Atlantic Ocean).

❑ Visit the Southern Gilberts (Kiribati).

❑ Visit the South Orkney Islands (Southern Sea).

❑ Visit the South Shetland Islands (Scotia Sea).

❑ Visit the Spratly Islands (South China Sea).

(↑) Visit Staten Island.

❑ Visit the Subantarctic Islands of New Zealand, including the Antipodes Islands, Auckland Islands, Bounty Islands, Campbell Islands, and Snares Islands.

(↑) Visit the Surin Islands.

(↑) Visit Suva Island.

(↑) Visit Table Island.

(↑) Visit Tahiti.

(↑) Visit Talahi Island.

(↑) Visit the Tierra del Fuego Archipelago.

(↑) Visit Tobago.

❑ Visit the Tuamotu-Gambier Islands (French Polynesia).

(↑) Visit Tubbatha Reef.

(↑) Visit Tybee Island.

(↑) Visit Vancouver Island.

(↑) Visit Vanua Levu.

(↑) Visit Vashon Island.

(↑) Visit Victoria Island.

(↑) Visit the Visayas Islands.

(↑) Visit Viti Levu.

(↑) Visit Weno Island.

(↑) Visit the West Carolines.

(↑) Visit Whidbey Island.

(↑) Visit Whitemarsh Island.

(↑) Visit Wilmington Island.

(↑) Visit the Windward Islands (French Polynesia).

(↑) Visit Xiyu.

(↑) Visit Yap.

Chapter 17
USA's States

Although I didn't travel much outside of New England as a child, I attended college in Southern California. Twice I traveled from Rhode Island to California by Greyhound bus. After a while I noticed that I'd been to quite a few states. I added the goal of visiting all 50 states and the District of Columbia to my bucket list. I reached 49 states and DC prior to 2005, but it wasn't until I made a special trip to visit North Dakota in November 2015 that I completed the circuit. It's a beautiful state. I recommend going there in the summer, if possible. I list the states in alphabetical order.

(↑) Visit all 50 US states and the District of Columbia.

(↑) Visit Alabama.

(↑) Visit Alaska.

(↑) Visit Arizona.

(↑) Visit Arkansas.

(↑) Visit California.

I lived in California for four years.

(↑) Visit Colorado.

(↑) Visit Connecticut.

(↑) Visit Delaware.

(↑) Visit the District of Columbia.

(↑) Visit Florida.

(↑) Visit Georgia.

I lived in Georgia for 12 years.

(↑) Visit Hawaii.

(↑) Visit Idaho.

(↑) Visit Illinois.

(↑) Visit Indiana.

(↑) Visit Iowa.

(↑) Visit Kansas.

(↑) Visit Kentucky.

(↑) Visit Louisiana.

(↑) Visit Maine.

(↑) Visit Maryland.

I lived part-time in Maryland over the span of six years.

(↑) Visit Massachusetts.

(↑) Visit Michigan.

(↑) Visit Minnesota.

(↑) Visit Mississippi.

(↑) Visit Missouri.

(↑) Visit Montana.

(↑) Visit Nebraska.

(↑) Visit Nevada.

(↑) Visit New Hampshire.

I lived in New Hampshire for ten years.

(↑) Visit New Jersey.

(↑) Visit New Mexico.

(↑) Visit New York.

(↑) Visit North Carolina.

(↑) Visit North Dakota.

As noted, North Dakota is the last state that I checked off my bucket list. It isn't really on the way to anywhere, apologies to Saskatchewan and Manitoba.

(↑) Visit Ohio.

(↑) Visit Oklahoma.

(↑) Visit Oregon.

(↑) Visit Pennsylvania.

(↑) Visit Rhode Island.

I was born in the smallest state in the US and lived there for 18 years.

(↑) Visit South Carolina.

(↑) Visit South Dakota.

(↑) Visit Tennessee.

(↑) Visit Texas.

(↑) Visit Utah.

(↑) Visit Vermont.

(↑) Visit Virginia.

(↑) Visit Washington.

I lived in Washington State for six years.

(↑) Visit West Virginia.

(↑) Visit Wisconsin.

(↑) Visit Wyoming.

Chapter 18
USA's State Capitals

I'm missing a couple state capitals: Lansing and Madison. It's clear that I'll need to make special trips to check them off my list. I plan to make them a priority in the near future. I list the capitals in alphabetical order by state.

❑ Visit the capital city of every US state.

(↑) Visit Alabama: Montgomery.

(↑) Visit Alaska: Juneau.

(↑) Visit Arizona: Phoenix.

(↑) Visit Arkansas: Little Rock.

(↑) Visit California: Sacramento.

(↑) Visit Colorado: Denver.

(↑) Visit Connecticut: Hartford.

(↑) Visit Delaware: Dover.

(↑) Visit Florida: Tallahassee.

(↑) Visit Georgia: Atlanta.

(↑) Visit Hawaii: Honolulu.

(↑) Visit Idaho: Boise.

(↑) Visit Illinois: Springfield.

(↑) Visit Indiana: Indianapolis.

(↑) Visit Iowa: Des Moines.

(↑) Visit Kansas: Topeka.

(↑) Visit Kentucky: Frankfort.

(↑) Visit Louisiana: Baton Rouge.

(↑) Visit Maine: Augusta.

(↑) Visit Maryland: Annapolis.

(↑) Visit Massachusetts: Boston.

❏ Visit Michigan: Lansing.

I hope to get there soon.

(↑) Visit Minnesota: St. Paul.

(↑) Visit Mississippi: Jackson.

(↑) Visit Missouri: Jefferson City.

(↑) Visit Montana: Helena.

(↑) Visit Nebraska: Lincoln.

(↑) Visit Nevada: Carson City.

(↑) Visit New Hampshire: Concord.

(↑) Visit New Jersey: Trenton.

(↑) Visit New Mexico: Santa Fe.

(↑) Visit New York: Albany.

(↑) Visit North Carolina: Raleigh.

(↑) Visit North Dakota: Bismarck.

(↑) Visit Ohio: Columbus.

(↑) Visit Oklahoma: Oklahoma City.

(↑) Visit Oregon: Salem.

(↑) Visit Pennsylvania: Harrisburg.

(↑) Visit Rhode Island: Providence.

(↑) Visit South Carolina: Columbia.

(↑) Visit South Dakota: Pierre.

(↑) Visit Tennessee: Nashville.

(↑) Visit Texas: Austin.

(↑) Visit Utah: Salt Lake City.

(↑) Visit Vermont: Montpelier.

(↑) Visit Virginia: Richmond.

(↑) Visit Washington: Olympia.

(↑) Visit West Virginia: Charleston.

❑ Visit Wisconsin: Madison.

I hope to get there soon.

(↑) Visit Wyoming: Cheyenne.

Chapter 19
USA's Second Cities

Many states have an important "second city." It's often mistaken for the capital of the state. For example, in Florida there's Miami, in Alaska there's Anchorage, in California there's Los Angeles, and in Washington State there's Seattle. Such second cities are important due to their historical value, population, culture, industry, or general location. I added all these important cities to my bucket list. I checked off many of them. In some cases a state may have more than one "second city." I list them in alphabetical order by state.

❑ Visit the second cities of every US state.

(↑) Visit Alabama: Birmingham.

(↑) Visit Alabama: Mobile.

(↑) Visit Alaska: Anchorage.

❑ Visit Alaska: Fairbanks.

(↑) Visit Arizona: Flagstaff.

(↑) Visit Arizona: Tucson.

(↑) Visit Arkansas: Fort Smith.

(↑) Visit California: Los Angeles.

(↑) Visit California: San Diego.

(↑) Visit California: San Francisco.

(↑) Visit Colorado: Colorado Springs.

(↑) Visit Colorado: Leadville.

(↑) Visit Connecticut: New Haven.

(↑) Visit Delaware: Wilmington.

(↑) Visit Florida: Jacksonville.

(↑) Visit Florida: Miami.

(↑) Visit Georgia: Augusta.

(↑) Visit Georgia: Savannah.

(↑) Visit Idaho: Coeur d'Alene.

(↑) Visit Idaho: Pocatello.

(↑) Visit Illinois: Chicago.

(↑) Visit Indiana: Fort Wayne.

❑ Visit Iowa: Cedar Rapids.

(↑) Visit Kansas: Wichita.

(↑) Visit Kentucky: Louisville.

(↑) Visit Kentucky: Lexington.

(↑) Visit Louisiana: New Orleans.

(↑) Visit Louisiana: Shreveport.

(↑) Visit Maine: Bangor.

(↑) Visit Maine: Portland.

(↑) Visit Maryland: Baltimore.

(↑) Visit Maryland: Cumberland.

(↑) Visit Massachusetts: Provincetown.

(↑) Visit Massachusetts: Springfield.

(↑) Visit Michigan: Detroit.

❑ Visit Michigan: Grand Rapids.

(↑) Visit Minnesota: Duluth.

(↑) Visit Minnesota: Minneapolis.

(↑) Visit Mississippi: Gulfport.

❑ Visit Mississippi: Tupelo.

(↑) Visit Missouri: Kansas City.

(↑) Visit Missouri: St. Louis.

(↑) Visit Montana: Billings.

(↑) Visit Montana: Missoula.

(↑) Visit Nebraska: Omaha.

(↑) Visit Nevada: Las Vegas.

(↑) Visit Nevada: Reno.

(↑) Visit New Hampshire: Manchester.

(↑) Visit New Hampshire: Portsmouth.

(↑) Visit New Jersey: Atlantic City.

(↑) Visit New Jersey: Newark.

(↑) Visit New Mexico: Albuquerque.

(↑) Visit New Mexico: Las Cruces.

(↑) Visit New York: Lake Placid.

(↑) Visit New York: New York City.

(↑) Visit New York: Rochester.

(↑) Visit North Carolina: Ashville.

(↑) Visit North Carolina: Charlotte.

(↑) Visit North Dakota: Fargo.

❑ Visit North Dakota: Minot.

(↑) Visit Ohio: Cincinnati.

(↑) Visit Ohio: Cleveland.

❑ Visit Oklahoma: Tulsa.

(↑) Visit Oregon: Ashland.

(↑) Visit Oregon: Eugene.

(↑) Visit Oregon: Portland.

(↑) Visit Pennsylvania: Philadelphia.

(↑) Visit Pennsylvania: Pittsburgh.

(↑) Visit Rhode Island: Newport.

(↑) Visit South Carolina: Charleston.

(↑) Visit South Carolina: Greenville.

(↑) Visit South Dakota: Rapid City.

(↑) Visit South Dakota: Sioux Falls.

(↑) Visit Tennessee: Chattanooga.

(↑) Visit Tennessee: Memphis.

(↑) Visit Texas: Dallas.

(↑) Visit Texas: El Paso.

(↑) Visit Texas: Houston.

(↑) Visit Utah: Moab.

(↑) Visit Vermont: Brattleboro.

(↑) Visit Vermont: Burlington.

(↑) Visit Virginia: Arlington.

(↑) Visit Virginia: Virginia Beach.

(↑) Visit Washington: Seattle.

(↑) Visit Washington: Spokane.

(↑) Visit West Virginia: Morgantown.

❑ Visit Wisconsin: Green Bay.

❑ Visit Wisconsin: Milwaukee.

(↑) Visit Wyoming: Rock Springs.

Chapter 20
USA's National Parks, Seashores, and Lakeshores

I met a Dutch fellow not too long ago on a trip to Australia. He was a nice guy. We talked for a while. He spent quite a bit of time in the USA. After commiserating about the absurd heat in Alice Springs, we began discussing the USA's national parks. He emphatically stated that the US has the most beautiful national parks in the world. I smiled and nodded wholeheartedly. We laughed.

I added all national parks, seashores, and lakeshores in the US to my bucket list. These places are a great source of pride for American people. The parks are special for their natural beauty, wildlife, and geology, and as such have been designated as places that should be preserved for all future generations. I included all national parks, seashores, and lakeshores sorted by the state(s) in which they occur.

The first national park in the US was Yellowstone National Park and was designated as such in 1872 by Ulysses S. Grant, the 18th President of the US. The first national seashore was established in 1953. These steps were incredibly important ones in preserving areas of great natural beauty, the flora, and the fauna in the US.

❏ Visit all the USA's national parks, seashores, and lakeshores.

(↑) Visit Alaska's Denali National Park and Preserve (formerly Mount McKinley National Park).

❏ Visit Alaska's Gates of the Arctic National Park.

(↑) Visit Alaska's Glacier Bay National Park.

❏ Visit Alaska's Katmai National Park and Preserve.

(↑) Visit Alaska's Kenai Fjords National Park.

❏ Visit Alaska's Kobuk Valley National Park.

❏ Visit Alaska's Lake Clark National Park.

❏ Visit Alaska's Wrangell-St. Elias National Park.

❏ Visit American Samoa's National Park of American Samoa.

(↑) Visit Arizona's Grand Canyon National Park.

(↑) Visit Arizona's Petrified Forest National Park.

(↑) Visit Arizona's Saguaro National Park.

❏ Visit Arkansas's Hot Springs National Park.

❏ Visit California's Channel Islands National Park.

(↑) Visit California's Death Valley National Park.

(↑) Visit California's Joshua Tree National Park.

(↑) Visit California's Kings Canyon National Park.

(↑) Visit California's Lassen Volcanic National Park.

(↑) Visit California's Point Reyes National Seashore.

(↑) Visit California's Redwood National Park.

(↑) Visit California's Sequoia National Park.

(↑) Visit California's Yosemite National Park.

❏ Visit Colorado's Black Canyon of the Gunnison National Park.

❏ Visit Colorado's Great Sand Dunes National Park and Preserve.

❏ Visit Colorado's Mesa Verde National Park.

(↑) Visit Colorado's Rocky Mountain National Park.

❏ Visit Florida's Biscayne National Park.

(↑) Visit Florida's Canaveral National Seashore.

❏ Visit Florida's Dry Tortugas National Park.

(↑) Visit Florida's Everglades National Park.

(↑) Visit Florida and Mississippi's Gulf Islands National Seashore.

(↑) Visit Georgia's Cumberland Island National Seashore.

❏ Visit Hawaii's Volcanoes National Park.

❏ Visit Hawaii's Haleakalā National Park.

❑ Visit Indiana's Indiana Dunes National Park.

(↑) Visit Kentucky's Mammoth Cave National Park.

(↑) Visit Maine's Acadia National Park.

❑ Visit Maryland and Virginia's Assateague Island National Seashore.

(↑) Visit Massachusetts's Cape Cod National Seashore.

❑ Visit Michigan's Isle Royale National Park.

❑ Visit Michigan's Pictured Rocks National Lakeshore.

❑ Visit Michigan's Sleeping Bear Dunes National Lakeshore.

❑ Visit Minnesota's Voyageurs National Park.

(↑) Visit Missouri's Gateway Arch National Park.

(↑) Visit Montana's Glacier National Park.

❑ Visit Nevada's Great Basin National Park.

❑ Visit New Mexico's Carlsbad Caverns National Park.

❑ Visit New York's Fire Island National Seashore.

(↑) Visit North Carolina's Cape Hatteras National Seashore.

(↑) Visit North Carolina and Tennessee's Great Smoky Mountains National Park.

❑ Visit North Carolina's Cape Lookout National Seashore.

❑ Visit North Dakota's **Theodore Roosevelt National Park.**

❑ Visit Ohio's **Cuyahoga Valley National Park.**

(↑) Visit Oregon's Crater Lake National Park.

❑ Visit South Carolina's Congaree National Park.

(↑) Visit South Dakota's Badlands National Park.

❑ Visit South Dakota's Wind Cave National Park.

❑ Visit Texas's Big Bend National Park.

In 55 hours, I drove alone from Lee, New Hampshire to Squaw Valley, California to run the Western States 100 ultra-marathon unsupported. After running the race, I drove to San Diego. When I began heading back to Lee, I thought that I would drive to Big Bend. However, upon reaching the Fort Stockton area, I saw I still had 100 miles to go to the park.

No problem, I thought: "You just ran 100 miles." But then, it entailed another 150+ miles driving around the park and an additional 100 miles back to I-10. Because I planned to drive the southern route through Baton Rouge, I still had another 2,500 miles to drive home. I opted out of visiting Big Bend. Now I regret that decision. I never made it back to that area. When opportunity knocks, you need to open the door.

❑ Visit Texas's **Guadalupe Mountains National Park.**

❑ Visit Texas's Padre Island National Seashore.

❏ Visit the United States Virgin Islands' Virgin Islands National Park.

(↑) Visit Utah's Arches National Park.

❏ Visit Utah's Bryce Canyon National Park.

(↑) Visit Utah's Canyonlands National Park.

❏ Visit Utah's Capitol Reef National Park.

❏ Visit Utah's Zion National Park.

(↑) Visit Virginia's Shenandoah National Park.

(↑) Visit Washington's Mount Rainier National Park.

(↑) Visit Washington's North Cascades National Park.

(↑) Visit Washington's Olympic National Park.

❏ Visit Wisconsin's Apostle Islands National Lakeshore.

(↑) Visit Wyoming's Grand Teton National Park.

(↑) Visit Wyoming's Yellowstone National Park.

Chapter 21
USA's National Forests and Grasslands

The USA's national forests and grasslands are special protected areas. They possess great natural beauty and support a wide range of flora and fauna. These places provide many recreational opportunities and should be preserved for future generations to enjoy. I love these places and added them to my bucket list. I included all national forests and grasslands sorted by the state(s) in which they occur.

The first national forest in the US was Shoshone National Forest established in 1891 by Benjamin Harrison, the 23rd President of the US. The first national grasslands were established in the 1930s.

❑ Visit all the USA's national forests and grasslands.

(↑) Visit Alabama's **Conecuh National Forest**.

(↑) Visit Alabama's **Talladega National Forest**.

❑ Visit Alabama's **Tuskegee National Forest**.

❑ Visit Alabama's **William B. Bankhead National Forest**.

(↑) Visit Alaska's Chugach National Forest.

(↑) Visit Alaska's Tongass National Forest.

(↑) Visit Arizona and New Mexico's Apache National Forest.

(↑) Visit Arizona's Coconino National Forest.

(↑) Visit Arizona and New Mexico's Coronado National Forest.

(↑) Visit Arizona's Kaibab National Forest.

(↑) Visit Arizona's Prescott National Forest.

(↑) Visit Arizona's Sitgreaves National Forest.

(↑) Visit Arizona's Tonto National Forest.

(↑) Visit Arkansas and Oklahoma's Ouachita National Forest.

(↑) Visit Arkansas's Ozark National Forest.

❑ Visit Arkansas's St. Francis National Forest.

(↑) Visit California's Angeles National Forest.

❑ Visit California's Butte Valley National Grassland.

(↑) Visit California's Cleveland National Forest.

(↑) Visit California and Nevada's Inyo National Forest.

(↑) Visit California and Oregon's Klamath National Forest.

(↑) Visit California and Nevada's Lake Tahoe Basin National Forest.

(↑) Visit California's Lassen National Forest.

(↑) Visit California's Los Padres National Forest.

(↑) Visit California's Mendocino National Forest.

❑ Visit California's Modoc National Forest.

(↑) Visit California's Plumas National Forest.

(↑) Visit California and Oregon's Rogue River National Forest.

(↑) Visit California's San Bernardino National Forest.

(↑) Visit California's Sequoia National Forest.

(↑) Visit California's Shasta National Forest.

(↑) Visit California's Sierra National Forest.

(↑) Visit California's Six Rivers National Forest.

(↑) Visit California's Stanislaus National Forest.

(↑) Visit California's Tahoe National Forest.

(↑) Visit California and Nevada's Toiyabe National Forest.

(↑) Visit California's Trinity National Forest.

(↑) Visit Colorado's Arapahoe National Forest.

(↑) Visit Colorado's Comanche National Grassland.

(↑) Visit Colorado's Eldorado National Forest.

(↑) Visit Colorado's Grand Mesa National Forest.

(↑) Visit Colorado's Gunnison National Forest.

(↑) Visit Colorado and Utah's Manti-La Sal National Forest.

❑ Visit Colorado's Pawnee National Grassland.

(↑) Visit Colorado's Pike National Forest.

(↑) Visit Colorado's Rio Grande National Forest.

(↑) Visit Colorado's Roosevelt National Forest.

(↑) Visit Colorado's Routt National Forest.

(↑) Visit Colorado's San Isabel National Forest.

(↑) Visit Colorado's San Juan National Forest.

❑ Visit Colorado's Uncompahgre National Forest.

(↑) Visit Colorado's White River National Forest.

(↑) Visit Florida's Apalachicola National Forest.

(↑) Visit Florida's Ocala National Forest.

(↑) Visit Florida's Osceola National Forest.

(↑) Visit Georgia's Chattahoochee National Forest.

(↑) Visit Georgia's Oconee National Forest.

(↑) Visit Idaho's **Boise National Forest**.

(↑) Visit Idaho and Montana's **Bitterroot National Forest**.

(↑) Visit Idaho and Utah's **Cache National Forest**.

(↑) Visit Idaho's **Caribou National Forest**.

❏ Visit Idaho's **Challis National Forest**.

❏ Visit Idaho's **Clearwater National Forest**.

(↑) Visit Idaho's **Coeur d'Alene National Forest**.

❏ Visit Idaho's **Curlew National Grassland**.

(↑) Visit Idaho, Montana, and Washington's **Kaniksu National Forest**.

(↑) Visit Idaho and Montana's **Kootenai National Forest**.

(↑) Visit Idaho's **Nez Perce National Forest**.

(↑) Visit Idaho's **Payette National Forest**.

(↑) Visit Idaho's **Salmon National Forest**.

(↑) Visit Idaho and Utah's **Sawtooth National Forest**.

❏ Visit Idaho's **St. Joe National Forest**.

(↑) Visit Idaho and Wyoming's **Targhee National Forest**.

(↑) Visit Idaho and Oregon's **Wallowa National Forest**.

- ❑ Visit Illinois's Midewin National Tallgrass Prairie.

- (↑) Visit Illinois's **Shawnee National Forest**.

- ❑ Visit Indiana's **Hoosier National Forest**.

- ❑ Visit Kansas's Cimarron National Grassland.

- (↑) Visit Kentucky's **Daniel Boone National Forest**.

- (↑) Visit Kentucky, **Virginia**, and West Virginia's **Jefferson National Forest**.

- ❑ Visit Louisiana's **Kisatchie National Forest**.

- (↑) Visit Maine and New Hampshire's **White Mountain National Forest**.

- ❑ Visit Michigan's **Hiawatha National Forest**.

- ❑ Visit Michigan's Huron National Forest.

- ❑ Visit Michigan's **Manistee National Forest**.

- ❑ Visit Michigan's **Ottawa National Forest**.

- ❑ Visit Minnesota's **Chippewa National Forest**.

- (↑) Visit Minnesota's **Superior National Forest**.

- ❑ Visit Mississippi's **Bienville National Forest**.

- ❑ Visit Mississippi's Delta National Forest.

- ❑ Visit Mississippi's De Soto National Forest.

- (↑) Visit Mississippi's Holly Springs National Forest.

❑ Visit Mississippi's Homochitto National Forest.

❑ Visit Mississippi's Tombigbee National Forest.

(↑) Visit Missouri's Mark Twain National Forest.

(↑) Visit Montana's Beaverhead National Forest.

❑ Visit Montana and South Dakota's Custer National Forest.

(↑) Visit Montana's Deerlodge National Forest.

(↑) Visit Montana's Flathead National Forest.

(↑) Visit Montana's Gallatin National Forest.

(↑) Visit Montana's Helena National Forest.

(↑) Visit Montana's Lewis and Clark National Forest.

(↑) Visit Montana's Lolo National Forest.

❑ Visit Nebraska's Nebraska National Forest.

❑ Visit Nebraska's Oglala National Grassland.

❑ Visit Nebraska's Samuel R. McKelvie National Forest.

❑ Visit Nevada's Humboldt National Forest.

(↑) Visit New Mexico's Carson National Forest.

(↑) Visit New Mexico's Cibola National Forest.

(↑) Visit New Mexico's Gila National Forest.

❏ Visit New Mexico's **Kiowa National Grassland**.

❏ Visit New Mexico's Lincoln National Forest.

(↑) Visit New Mexico's **Santa Fe National Forest**.

(↑) Visit New York's Finger Lakes National Forest.

(↑) Visit North Carolina and Tennessee's **Cherokee National Forest**.

(↑) Visit North Carolina's **Croatan National Forest**.

(↑) Visit North Carolina's **Nantahala National Forest**.

(↑) Visit North Carolina's **Pisgah National Forest**.

(↑) Visit North Carolina's **Uwharrie National Forest**.

❏ Visit North Dakota's **Cedar River National Grassland**.

❏ Visit North Dakota's Little Missouri National Grassland.

❏ Visit North Dakota's **Sheyenne National Grassland**.

(↑) Visit Ohio's **Wayne National Forest**.

❏ Visit Oklahoma and Texas's **Black Kettle National Grassland**.

❏ Visit Oklahoma and Texas's **Rita Blanca National Grassland**.

(↑) Visit Oregon's Crooked River National Grassland.

(↑) Visit Oregon's Deschutes National Forest.

(↑) Visit Oregon's Fremont National Forest.

(↑) Visit Oregon's Malheur National Forest.

(↑) Visit Oregon's Mount Hood National Forest.

(↑) Visit Oregon's Ochoco National Forest.

(↑) Visit Oregon's Siskiyou National Forest.

(↑) Visit Oregon's Siuslaw National Forest.

❑ Visit Oregon and Washington's Umatilla National Forest.

(↑) Visit Oregon's Umpqua National Forest.

❑ Visit Oregon's Whitman National Forest.

(↑) Visit Oregon's Willamette National Forest.

(↑) Visit Oregon's Winema National Forest.

(↑) Visit Pennsylvania's Allegheny National Forest.

❑ Visit Puerto Rico's El Yunque National Forest.

(↑) Visit South Carolina's Francis Marion National Forest.

(↑) Visit South Carolina's Sumter National Forest.

(↑) Visit South Dakota's Buffalo Gap National Grassland.

(↑) Visit South Dakota and Wyoming's Black Hills National Forest.

❑ Visit South Dakota's Fort Pierre National Grassland.

❑ Visit South Dakota's Grand River National Grassland.

❑ Visit Texas's Angelina National Forest.

❑ Visit Texas's Caddo National Grassland.

❑ Visit Texas's Davy Crockett National Forest.

❑ Visit Texas's Lyndon B. Johnson National Grassland.

❑ Visit Texas's McClellan Creek National Grassland.

❑ Visit Texas's Sabine National Forest.

(↑) Visit Texas's Sam Houston National Forest.

❑ Visit Utah and Wyoming's Ashley National Forest.

❑ Visit Utah's Dixie National Forest.

(↑) Visit Utah's Fishlake National Forest.

(↑) Visit Utah's Uinta National Forest.

(↑) Visit Utah and Wyoming's Wasatch National Forest.

(↑) Visit Vermont's Green Mountain National Forest.

(↑) Visit Virginia and West Virginia's George Washington National Forest.

❑ Visit Washington's Colville National Forest.

(↑) Visit Washington's Gifford Pinchot National Forest.

(↑) Washington's Mount Baker National Forest.

(↑) Washington's Okanogan National Forest.

(↑) Washington's Olympic National Forest.

(↑) Washington's Snoqualmie National Forest.

(↑) Washington's Wenatchee National Forest.

(↑) West Virginia's Monongahela National Forest.

❑ Wisconsin's Chequamegon National Forest.

❑ Wisconsin's Nicolet National Forest.

(↑) Wyoming's Bighorn National Forest.

(↑) Wyoming's Bridger National Forest.

(↑) Wyoming's Medicine Bow National Forest.

(↑) Wyoming's Shoshone National Forest.

(↑) Wyoming's Teton National Forest.

❑ Wyoming's Thunder Basin National Grassland.

Chapter 22
USA's National Monuments

As of this writing, there are 131 places in the US with formal designations as national monuments. These are places of great historical significance. The list of national monuments changes over time. Sometimes places are added while at other times places are removed. In some cases national monuments have become national parks. I added visiting all national monuments to my bucket list. I list them here in alphabetical order by state.

❏ Visit all the USA's national monuments.

(↑) Visit Alabama's Birmingham Civil Rights National Monument.

❏ Visit Alabama's Freedom Riders National Monument.

❏ Visit Alabama's Russell Cave National Monument.

(↑) Visit Alaska's Admiralty Island National Monument.

❏ Visit Alaska's Aleutian Islands World War II National Monument.

❑ Visit Alaska's Aniakchak National Monument.

❑ Visit Alaska's Cape Krusenstern National Monument.

❑ Visit Alaska's Misty Fjords National Monument.

❑ Visit American Samoa's Rose Atoll Marine National Monument.

❑ Visit Arizona's Agua Fria National Monument.

❑ Visit Arizona's Canyon de Chelly National Monument.

❑ Visit Arizona's Casa Grande Ruins National Monument.

❑ Visit Arizona's Chiricahua National Monument.

❑ Visit Arizona's Grand Canyon-Parashant National Monument.

❑ Visit Arizona's Hohokam Pima National Monument.
Note that this monument is not open to the public.

(↑) Visit Arizona's Ironwood Forest National Monument.

❑ Visit Arizona's Montezuma Castle National Monument.

❑ Visit Arizona's Navajo National Monument.

(↑) Visit Arizona's Organ Pipe Cactus National Monument.

❑ Visit Arizona's Pipe Spring National Monument.

(↑) Visit Arizona's Sonoran Desert National Monument.

❑ Visit Arizona's Sunset Crater Volcano National Monument.

❑ Visit Arizona's Tonto National Monument.

❑ Visit Arizona's Tuzigoot National Monument.

❑ Visit Arizona's Vermilion Cliffs National Monument.

❑ Visit Arizona's Walnut Canyon National Monument.

❑ Visit Arizona's Wupatki National Monument.

❑ Visit the Atlantic Ocean's Northeast Canyons and Seamounts Marine National Monument.

❑ Visit California's Berryessa Snow Mountain National Monument.

(↑) Visit California's Cabrillo National Monument.

(↑) Visit California's California Coastal National Monument.

(↑) Visit California's Carrizo Plain National Monument.

(↑) Visit California's Castle Mountains National Monument.

❑ Visit California's César E. Chávez National Monument.

(↑) Visit California's Devils Postpile National Monument.

❑ Visit California's Fort Ord National Monument.

(↑) Visit California's Giant Sequoia National Monument.

❑ Visit California's Lava Beds National Monument.

(↑) Visit California's Mojave Trails National Monument.

(↑) Visit California's Muir Woods National Monument.

❑ Visit California's Saint Francis Dam Disaster National Monument.

(↑) Visit California's Sand to Snow National Monument.

(↑) Visit California's San Gabriel Mountains National Monument.

(↑) Visit California's Santa Rosa and San Jacinto Mountains National Monument.

❑ Visit California's Tule Lake National Monument.

❑ Visit Colorado's Browns Canyon National Monument.

❑ Visit Colorado's Canyon of the Ancients National Monument.

❑ Visit Colorado's Chimney Rock National Monument.

❏ Visit Colorado's Colorado National Monument.

❏ Visit Colorado and Utah's Dinosaur National Monument.

❏ Visit Colorado's Florissant Fossil Beds National Monument.

❏ Visit Colorado and Utah's Hovenweep National Monument.

❏ Visit Colorado's Yucca House National Monument.

❏ Visit the District of Columbia's Belmont-Paul Women's Equality National Monument.

❏ Visit the District of Columbia's President Lincoln and Soldiers' Home National Monument.

❏ Visit Florida's Castillo de San Marcos National Monument.

❏ Visit Florida's Fort Matanzas National Monument.

(↑) Visit Georgia's Fort Frederica National Monument.

(↑) Visit Georgia's Fort Pulaski National Monument.

❏ Visit the Hawaii and US Minor Outlying Islands's Papahānaumokuākea Marine **National Monument.**

❏ Visit Idaho's Craters of the Moon National Monument.

❏ Visit Idaho's Hagerman Fossil Beds National Monument.

❑ Visit Illinois's Pullman National Monument.

❑ Visit Iowa's Effigy Mounds National Monument.

❑ Visit Kentucky's Camp Nelson Heritage National Monument.

❑ Visit Kentucky's Mill Springs Battlefield National Monument.

❑ Visit Louisiana's Poverty Point National Monument.

(↑) Visit Maine's Katahdin Woods and Waters National Monument.

(↑) Visit Maryland's Fort McHenry National Monument.

(↑) Visit Maryland's Harriet Tubman Underground Railroad National Monument.

❑ Visit Minnesota's Grand Portage National Monument.

❑ Visit Minnesota's Pipestone National Monument.

❑ Visit Mississippi's Medgar and Myrlie Evers Home National Monument.

❑ Visit Missouri's George Washington Carver National Monument.

(↑) Visit Montana's Little Bighorn Battlefield National Monument.

❑ Visit Montana's Pompeys Pillar National Monument.

❏ Visit Montana's Upper Missouri River Breaks National Monument.

❏ Visit Nebraska's Agate Fossil Beds National Monument.

❏ Visit Nebraska's Homestead National Monument.

❏ Visit Nebraska's Scotts Bluff National Monument.

❏ Visit Nevada's Basin and Range National Monument.

❏ Visit Nevada's Gold Butte National Monument.

❏ Visit Nevada's Tule Springs Fossil Beds National Monument.

❏ Visit New Mexico's Aztec Ruins National Monument.

❏ Visit New Mexico's Bandelier National Monument.

❏ Visit New Mexico's Capulin Volcano National Monument.

(↑) Visit New Mexico's El Malpais National Monument.

❏ Visit New Mexico's El Morro National Monument.

❏ Visit New Mexico's Fort Union National Monument.

(↑) Visit New Mexico's Gila Cliff Dwellings National Monument.

❏ Visit New Mexico's Kasha-Katuwe Tent Rocks National Monument.

❏ Visit New Mexico's Organ Mountains-Desert Peaks National Monument.

❏ Visit New Mexico's Petroglyph National Monument.

❏ Visit New Mexico's Prehistoric Trackways National Monument.

❏ Visit New Mexico's Rio Grande del Norte National Monument.

❏ Visit New Mexico's Salinas Pueblo Missions National Monument.

❏ Visit New Mexico's White Sands National Monument.

❏ Visit New York's African Burial Ground National Monument.

❏ Visit New York's Castle Clinton National Monument.

❏ Visit New York's Fort Stanwix National Monument.

❏ Visit New York's Governors Island National Monument.

(↑) Visit New York and New Jersey's Statue of Liberty National Monument.

❏ Visit New York's Stonewall National Monument.

❏ Visit the Northern Marianas Islands and Guam's Marianas Trench Marine National Monument.

❏ Visit Ohio's Charles Young Buffalo Soldiers National Monument.

(↑) Visit Oregon's Cascade-Siskiyou National Monument.

(↑) Visit Oregon's John Day Fossil Beds National Monument.

❏ Visit Oregon's Newberry Volcanic National Monument.

❏ Visit Oregon's Oregon Caves National Monument.

❏ Visit South Dakota's Jewel Cave National Monument.

❏ Visit Texas's Alibates Flint Quarries National Monument.

❏ Visit Texas's Military Working Dog Teams National Monument.

❏ Visit Texas's Waco Mammoth National Monument.

❏ Visit the US Minor Outlying Islands's Pacific Remote Islands Marine National Monument.

❏ Visit the US Virgin Islands's Buck Island Reef National Monument.

❏ Visit the US Virgin Islands's Virgin Islands Coral Reef National Monument.

❏ Visit Utah's Bears Ears National Monument.

❏ Visit Utah's Cedar Breaks National Monument.

❏ Visit Utah's Grand Staircase-Escalante National Monument.

❏ Visit Utah's Jurassic National Monument.

❏ Visit Utah's Natural Bridges National Monument.

❏ Visit Utah's Rainbow Bridge National Monument.

❏ Visit Utah's Timpanagos Cave National Monument.

❏ Visit Virginia's Booker T. Washington National Monument.

❏ Visit Virginia's Fort Monroe National Monument.

(↑) Visit Virginia's George Washington Birthplace National Monument.

❏ Visit Washington's Hanford Reach National Monument.

(↑) Visit Washington's Mount St. Helens Volcanic National Monument.

(↑) Visit Washington's San Juan Islands National Monument.

(↑) Visit Wyoming's Devils Tower National Monument.

❏ Visit Wyoming's Fort Butte National Monument.

Chapter 23
USA's Territories

The USA's territories are spread far and wide around the world. Only recently have they come onto my radar. Not all these places are inhabited. Some require special permission to visit. From my research and from what little I've seen, these places are beautiful and worth visiting. I added them to my bucket list. Some territories are extremely remote. For this reason I added a couple age-related bucket-list items. I present the territories in alphabetical order by their name. I provide a general indication of where they're located.

❏ Visit all the USA's territories.

❏ By age 65 visit at least eight US territories.

❏ By age 70 visit at least 12 US territories.

❏ Visit American Samoa (South Pacific Ocean).

❏ Visit the Bajo Nuevo Bank (Caribbean Sea), disputed claim with Columbia.

❏ Visit Baker Island (Central Pacific Ocean).

(↑) Visit Guam (North Pacific Ocean).

I visited the beautiful island of Guam several times.

❏ Visit Howland Island (Central Pacific Ocean).

❏ Visit Jarvis Island (Line Island, South Pacific Ocean).

❏ Visit the Johnston Atoll (North Pacific Ocean).

❏ Visit Kingman Reef (Line Island, North Pacific Ocean).

❏ Visit the Midway Atoll, formerly Brooks Island (North/Central Pacific Ocean).

❏ Visit Navassa Island (Caribbean Sea), also claimed by Haiti.

Visit the Northern Mariana Islands (North Pacific Ocean).
   ❏ Northern Islands
   ❏ Rota
   ❏ Saipan
   ❏ Tinian

❏ Visit the Palmyra Atoll (Line Island, North/Central Pacific Ocean).

❏ Visit Puerto Rico (between the Caribbean and North Atlantic Seas).

❏ Visit the Serranilla Bank (Caribbean Sea), disputed claim with Columbia and Honduras.

(↑) Visit the US Virgin Islands (Caribbean Sea).

❑ Visit Wake Island (North Pacific Ocean).

Some people consider Wake Island to be the most remote destination in the world.

Chapter 24
USA's Extreme Points

From time-to-time, I read about the extreme points of the USA in the news. Spurred on by these stories, I added them to my bucket list. Some are easily accessible, but only if you happen to be in the area. To reach others may be incredibly demanding and even life threatening. Anyone who has climbed to the summit of Denali (Mount McKinley) in Alaska—the highest point in North America—can attest to this fact. These items aren't listed in any particular order.

❏ Visit all the extreme points in the USA (the ones on this list).

(↑) Climb to the highest point in the USA: 20,310 feet Denali, Alaska.

(↑) Visit the lowest point in the USA: 279 feet below sea level Badwater, California.

Badwater is a desolate yet very beautiful place. It's extremely hot.

❏ Visit the highest dam in the USA: 770 feet, Oroville Dam, Oroville, California.

Construction of the Oroville Dam on the Feather River began in the year I was born. We're the same age. In 2017 the dam's spillways suffered damage. They've been under repair for a number of years.

(↑) Visit the deepest lake in the USA: 1,960 feet, Crater Lake, Oregon.

I visited Crater Lake on several occasions. It always impresses with its beauty and crystal-clear water.

(↑) Visit the longest river in the USA: 2,348 miles, the Mississippi River flows through Minnesota, Wisconsin, Iowa, Illinois, Missouri, Kentucky, Tennessee, Arkansas, Mississippi, and Louisiana.

I saw the mighty Mississippi flood. From a safe distance, it's a spectacular sight to behold.

❏ Visit the place in the USA where the lowest temperature was recorded: −80°F, Prospect Creek, Alaska.

I want to visit Prospect Creek in the summer.

(↑) Go to the top of the tallest building in the USA: 1,776 feet with antenna, One World Trade Center, New York City, New York.

I went to One World Trade Center with my friends Paul and Helen Göransson, and Wongduean "Kig" Bohthong. The trip was a pilgrimage and a time to reflect. It brought tears to my eyes.

(↑) Hike into the largest crater in the USA: 3,907 feet in diameter, Barringer Meteor Crater, near Winslow, Arizona.

It's truly amazing how big a hole a small meteor can make.

(↑) Visit the largest lake in the USA: 31,700 square miles, Lake Superior in Wisconsin, Michigan, Minnesota, and Canada.

❑ Visit the highest volcano in the USA: 16,550 feet, Mount Bona, Alaska.

There are guided 12-day trips to the top of Mount Bona via non-technical routes.

(↑) Visit the place in the USA where the highest temperature was recorded: 134.1°F, Furnace Creek, California.

When I went to Furnace Creek, the temperature was only around 115°F.

(↑) Visit the place with the fastest ground-wind speed ever recorded in the USA: 231 mph, Mount Washington Summit, New Hampshire.

I was on the summit of Mount Washington in 65 mph winds. On a cold, windy day, it's dangerous. Many people have perished on the mountain. The highest ground-wind speed ever recorded in the world is 253 mph in Barrow, Australia. This record broke the 62-year old record set on Mount Washington.

(↑) Visit the largest desert in the USA: 190,000 square miles, Great Basin Desert in Arizona, Idaho, Oregon, Nevada, and Utah.

(↑) See the biggest tree in the USA by volume: 52,500 cubic feet, General Sherman, Tulare County, California.

I first visited the General Sherman tree many years ago. I returned numerous times to marvel at it. The tree moves me. General Sherman was under threat from raging wildfires in 2021. Precautions taken to protect the 2,500-year-old tree succeeded. I followed the news about General Sherman closely. When he was declared safe, I felt relieved.

(↑) Visit the deepest canyon in the USA: 7,993 feet, Hells Canyon in Oregon, Washington, and Idaho.

Chapter 25
Thailand's Provinces

Thailand is known throughout the world as the "Land of Smiles." It's a lovely destination with beautiful people. Most tourists visit well-known places such as Bangkok, Chiang Mai, Pattaya, and Phuket. These fun destinations provide interesting activities. More adventurous people visit additional places such as Bpai, Chiang Rai, Sukhothai, and some islands.

Given the wide range of cultures and customs in Thailand, I felt that to understand its people more fully, I should explore all its provinces. I added them to my bucket list. Most Thais claim the south of Thailand isn't safe. When I wrote the first edition of this book, I still had five southern provinces to check off. Since then, I visited the deep south. I found it to be one of the most beautiful and cleanest places in the country. (Recall my commentary from Chapter 3.) From the first edition, I left my original notes about these five provinces in place.

Through my travels around Thailand, I gained a good understanding of its people, history, cultures, customs, geography, politics, food, economy, weather, educational system, and royal family. Without personally visiting all provinces, I couldn't have achieved this understanding. I list the provinces in alphabetical order.

(↑) Visit all 77 of Thailand's provinces.

This item is repeated from Chapter 3. There I provided commentary.

(↑) Visit Amnat Charoen province.

(↑) Visit Ang Thong province.

(↑) Visit Bangkok City province.

(↑) Visit Bueng Kan province.

(↑) Visit Buriram province.

(↑) Visit Chachoengsao province.

(↑) Visit Chai Nat province.

(↑) Visit Chaiyaphum province.

(↑) Visit Chanthaburi province.

(↑) Visit Chiang Mai province.

(↑) Visit Chiang Rai province.

(↑) Visit Chonburi province.

(↑) Visit Chumphon province.

(↑) Visit Kalasin province.

(↑) Visit Kamphaeng Phet province.

(↑) Visit Kanchanaburi province.

(↑) Visit Khon Kaen province.

(↑) Visit Krabi province.

(↑) Visit Lampang province.

(↑) Visit Lamphun province.

(↑) Visit Loei province.

(↑) Visit Lopburi province.

(↑) Visit Mae Hong Son province.

(↑) Visit Maha Sarakham province.

(↑) Visit Mukdahan province.

(↑) Visit Nakhon Nayok province.

(↑) Visit Nakhon Pathom province.

(↑) Visit Nakhon Phanom province.

(↑) Visit Nakhon Ratchasima province.

(↑) Visit Nakhon Sawan province.

(↑) Visit Nakhon Si Thammarat province.

(↑) Visit Nan province.

(↑) Visit Narathiwat province.

This province borders Malaysia and is on the east coast on the Gulf of Thailand.

(↑) Visit Nong Bua Lamphu province.

(↑) Visit Nong Khai province.

(↑) Visit Nonthaburi province.

(↑) Visit Pathum Thani province.

(↑) Visit Pattani province.

This province is in the far south on the east coast on the Gulf of Thailand.

(↑) Visit Phang Nga province.

(↑) Visit Phatthalung province.

(↑) Visit Phayao province.

(↑) Visit Phetchabun province.

(↑) Visit Phetchaburi province.

(↑) Visit Phichit province.

(↑) Visit Phitsanulok province.

(↑) Visit Phra Nakhon Si Ayutthaya province.

(↑) Visit Phrae province.

(↑) Visit Phuket province.

(↑) Visit Prachinburi province.

(↑) Visit Prachuap Khiri Khan province.

(↑) Visit Ranong province.

(↑) Visit Ratchaburi province.

(↑) Visit Rayong province.

(↑) Visit Roi Et province.

(↑) Visit Sa Kaeo province.

(↑) Visit Sakon Nakhon province.

(↑) Visit Samut Prakan province.

(↑) Visit Samut Sakhon province.

(↑) Visit Samut Songkhram province.

(↑) Visit Saraburi province.

(↑) Visit Satun province.

This province borders Malaysia and is on the west coast on the Andaman Sea.

(↑) Visit Sing Buri province.

(↑) Visit Sisaket province.

(↑) Visit Songkhla province.

(↑) Visit Sukhothai province.

(↑) Visit Suphan Buri province.

(↑) Visit Surat Thani province.

(↑) Visit Surin province.

(↑) Visit Tak province.

(↑) Visit Trang province.

This province is on the west coast on the Andaman Sea.

(↑) Visit Trat province.

(↑) Visit Ubon Ratchathani province.

(↑) Visit Udon Thani province.

(↑) Visit Uthai Thani province.

(↑) Visit Uttaradit province.

(↑) Visit Yala province.

This province is in the far south and borders Malaysia.

(↑) Visit Yasothon province.

Chapter 26
Thailand's National and Marine Parks

Thailand's national and marine parks are a great source of pride for Thai people. These locations are special for their natural beauty, flora, wildlife, and geology, as such they've been preserved. I include all confirmed national and marine parks. I added these places to my bucket list. Numerous additional parks are being proposed.

The first national park to be established in Thailand was Khao Yai in 1961. It's the same age as me. The first national marine park was Khao Sam Roi Yot in 1966. The parks have difficulty in preventing illegal farming, poaching, logging, burning, fishing, and general encroachment. The park system is often criticized for excessive development of park lands.

Thailand falls in the middle in the worldwide rankings for corruption. The country is poor, and through corruption, the wealthy get private concessions on land. Those without means have little to lose if they violate park regulations. I hope parks receive better protection and are preserved as intended. The parks are listed in alphabetical order by province.

❑ Visit all national and marine parks in Thailand.

❑ Visit Buriram and Sa Kaeo's Ta Phraya National Park.

❑ Visit Chaiyaphum's Pa Hin Ngam National Park.

❑ Visit Chaiyaphum's Phu Laenkha National Park.

(↑) Visit Chaiyaphum's Sai Thong National Park.

❑ Visit Chaiyaphum's Tat Ton National Park.

❑ Visit Chanthaburi's Khao Khitchakut National Park.

❑ Visit Chanthaburi's Khao Sip Ha Chan National Park.

(↑) Visit Chanthaburi's Namtok Phlio National Park.

(↑) Visit Chiang Mai's Doi Inthanon National Park.

❑ Visit Chiang Mai's Doi Pha Hom Pok National Park.

(↑) Visit Chiang Mai's Doi Suthep-Pui National Park.

(↑) Visit Chiang Mai's Huai Nam Dang National Park.

(↑) Visit Chiang Mai's Khun Khan National Park.

(↑) Visit Chiang Mai's Mae Wang National Park.

(↑) Visit Chiang Mai's Op Luang National Park.

(↑) Visit Chiang Mai's Pha Daeng National Park.

(↑) Visit Chiang Mai's Si Lanna National Park.

(↑) Visit Chiang Rai, Lampang, and Phayao's Doi Luang National Park.

(↑) Visit Chiang Rai's Khun Chae National Park.

❏ Visit Chumphon's Mu Koh Chumphon National Marine Park.

❏ Visit Kamphaeng Phet's Khlong Lan National Park.

❏ Visit Kamphaeng Phet and Tak's Khlong Wang Chao National Park.

❏ Visit Kamphaeng Phet and Nakhon Sawan's Mae Wong National Park.

(↑) Visit Kanchanaburi's Chaloem Rattanakosin National Park.

(↑) Visit Kanchanaburi's Erawan National Park.

(↑) Visit Kanchanaburi's Khao Laem National Park.

❏ Visit Kanchanaburi's Khuean Srinagarindra National Park.

❏ Visit Kanchanaburi's Lam Khlong Ngu National Park.

(↑) Visit Kanchanaburi's Sai Yok National Park.

❏ Visit Kanchanaburi's Thong Pha Phum National Park.

(↑) Visit Khon Kaen and Chaiyaphum's Nam Phong National Park.

❏ Visit Khon Kaen's Phu Kao-Phu Phan Kham National Park.

(↑) Visit Khon Kaen and Loei's Phu Pha Man National Park.

❏ Visit Khon Kaen's Phu Wiang National Park.

(↑) Visit Krabi's Hat Noppharat Thara-Mu Koh Phi Phi National Marine Park.

❏ Visit Krabi's Khao Phanom Bencha National Marine Park.

(↑) Visit Krabi's Mu Koh Lanta National Marine Park.

(↑) Visit Krabi's Than Bok Khorani National Park.

❏ Visit Lampang's Chae Son National Park.

(↑) Visit Lampang and Tak's Mae Wa National Park.

(↑) Visit Lamphun's Doi Khun Tan National Park.

(↑) Visit Lamphun, Chiang Mai, and Tak's Mae Ping National Park.

(↑) Visit Loei's Phu Kradueng National Park.

(↑) Visit Loei's Phu Ruea National Park.

(↑) Visit Loei's Phu Suan Sai National Park.

(↑) Visit Mae Hong Son's Namtok Mae Surin National Park.

(↑) Visit Mae Hong Son's Salawin National Park.

❑ Visit Mae Hong Son's Tham Pla-Namtok Pha Suea National Park.

❑ Visit Mukdahan's Phu Pha Thoep National Park.

❑ Visit Mukdahan, Ubon Ratchathani, and Yasothon's Phu Sa Dok Bua National Park.

❑ Visit Nakhon Phanom and Nong Khai's Phu Langka National Park.

(↑) Visit Nakhon Ratchasima, Nakhon Nayok, Prachinburi, and Saraburi's Khao Yai National Park.

❑ Visit Nakhon Si Thammarat's Khao Luang National Park.

❑ Visit Nakhon Si Thammarat's Khao Nan National Park.

❑ Visit Nakhon Si Thammarat and Surat Thani's Namtok Si Khit National Park.

❑ Visit Nakhon Si Thammarat's Namtok Yong National Park.

(↑) Visit Nan's Doi Phu Kha National Park.

(↑) Visit Nan's Khun Nan National Park.

(↑) Visit Nan's Mae Charim National Park.

(↑) Visit Nan's Si Nan National Park.

❑ Visit Narathiwat, Pattani, and Yala's Budo-Su-Ngai Padi National Park.

❑ Visit Pattani, Songkhla, and Yala's Namtok Sai Khao National Park.

(↑) Visit Phang Nga's Ao Phang-Nga National Marine Park.

(↑) Visit Phang Nga's Khao Lak-Lam Ru National Marine Park.

(↑) Visit Phang Nga's Khao Lampi-Hat Thai Mueang National Marine Park.

(↑) Visit Phang Nga's Mu Koh Similan National Marine Park.

(↑) Visit Phang Nga's Mu Koh Surin National Marine Park.

❑ Visit Phang Nga's Si Phang-Nga National Park.

❑ Visit Phatthalung's Khao Pu-Khao Ya National Park.

❑ Visit Phayao's Doi Phu Nang National Park.

❑ Visit Phayao and Chiang Rai's Mae Puem National Park.

❑ Visit Phayao and Chiang Rai's Phu Sang National Park.

❑ Visit Phetchabun's Khao Kho National Park.

(↑) Visit Phetchabun's Nam Nao National Park.

❑ Visit Phetchabun's Tat Mok National Park.

❑ Visit Phetchaburi and Prachuap Khiri Khan's Kaeng Krachan National Park.

(↑) Visit Phitsanulok's Kaeng Chet Khwae National Park.

(↑) Visit Phitsanulok's Namtok Chat Trakan National Park.

❑ Visit Phitsanulok and Loei's Phu Hin Rong Kla National Park.

❑ Visit Phitsanulok and Phetchabun's Thung Salaeng Luang National Park.

(↑) Visit Phrae's Doi Pha Klong National Park.

❑ Visit Phrae's Mae Yom National Park.

(↑) Visit Phrae and Lampang's Wiang Kosai National Park.

(↑) Visit Phuket's Sirinat National Marine Park.

(↑) Visit Prachinburi and Nakhon Ratchasima's Thap Lan National Park.

(↑) Visit Prachuap Khiri Khan's Hat Wanakon National Marine Park.

❑ Visit Prachuap Khiri Khan's Khao Sam Roi Yot National Marine Park.

(↑) Visit Prachuap Khiri Khan's Kui Buri National Park.

❑ Visit Prachuap Khiri Khan's Namtok Huai Yang National Park.

(↑) Visit Ranong's Laem Son National Marine Park.

(↑) Visit Ranong's Lam Nam Kra Buri National Marine Park.

(↑) Visit Ranong's Mu Koh Ranong National Marine Park.

❑ Visit Ranong and Chumphon's Namtok Ngao National Park.

❑ Visit Ratchaburi's Chaloem Phrakiat Thai Prachan National Park.

❑ Visit Rayong and Chanthaburi's Khao Chamao-Khao Wong National Park.

❑ Visit Rayong's Khao Laem Ya-Mu Koh Samet National Marine Park.

❑ Visit Sa Kaeo and Prachinburi's Pang Sida National Park.

❑ Visit Sakon Nakhon and Ubon Ratchathani's Phu Pha Lek National Park.

❑ Visit Sakon Nakhon and Kalasin's Phu Phan National Park.

❑ Visit Sakon Nakhon, Mukdahan, and Nakhon Phanom's Phu Pha Yon National Park.

❑ Visit Saraburi's Namtok Sam Lan National Park.

❑ Visit Satun and Trang's Mu Koh Phetra National Marine Park.

❏ Visit Satun's Tarutao National Marine Park.

❏ Visit Satun's Thale Ban National Marine Park.

❏ Visit Sisaket and Ubon Ratchathani's Khao Phra Wihan National Park.

❏ Visit Songkhla's Khao Nam Khang National Park.

(↑) Visit Sukhothai's Ramkhamhaeng National Park.

(↑) Visit Sukhothai's Si Satchanalai National Park.

❏ Visit Suphan Buri's Phu Toei National Park.

❏ Visit Surat Thani's Kaeng Krung National Park.

(↑) Visit Surat Thani's Khao Sok National Park.

❏ Visit Surat Thani's Khlong Phanom National Park.

❏ Visit Surat Thani's Mu Koh Ang Thong National Marine Park.

❏ Visit Surat Thani's Tai Rom Yen National Park.

❏ Visit Surat Thani's Than Sadet-Koh Pha-Ngan National Park.

(↑) Visit Tak's Khun Phawo National Park.

(↑) Visit Tak's Lan Sang National Park.

(↑) Visit Tak's Mae Moei National Park.

❏ Visit Tak's Namtok Pha Charoen National Park.

(↑) Visit Tak's Taksin Maharat National Park.

❑ Visit Trang's Hat Chao Mai National Marine Park.

❑ Visit Trat's Mu Koh Chang National Marine Park.

❑ Visit Trat's Namtok Khlong Kaeo National Park.

(↑) Visit Ubon Ratchathani's Kaeng Tana National Park.

(↑) Visit Ubon Ratchathani's Pha Taem National Park.

❑ Visit Ubon Ratchathani's Phu Chong-Na Yoi National Park.

❑ Visit Udon Thani's Na Yung-Nam Som National Park.

(↑) Visit Uttaradit and Phrae's Lam Nam Nan National Park.

(↑) Visit Uttaradit's Phu Soi Dao National Park.

(↑) Visit Uttaradit's Ton Sak Yai National Park.

❑ Visit Yala's Bang Lang National Park.

Chapter 27
Thailand's Extreme Points

I added visiting Thailand's extreme points to my bucket list. The directional points here (farthest north and so on) are for the mainland. They don't include islands. Many places are easily accessible, but only if you're in the area. These items aren't listed in any particular order.

❑ Visit all the extreme points in Thailand (the ones on this list).

(↑) Stand on the highest mountain summit: 8,415 feet, Doi Inthanon in Chiang Mai.

(↑) Travel along and swim in the longest river flowing through Thailand: 2,614 miles, the Mekong River in the provinces of Amnat Charoen, Bueng Kan, Chiang Rai, Loei, Mukdahan, Nakhon Phahom, Nong Khai, and Ubon Ratchathani.

(↑) Travel along the longest river flowing entirely within Thailand: some sources say the Chi River is 475 miles long and others say that it's 651 miles; the Mun River is listed as 559 miles long.

I went to both the Chi and Mun Rivers.

❏ Visit the highest dam: 505 feet, the Bhumibol Dam in Tak.

The Bhumibol Dam is named after Thailand's ninth king.

(↑) Visit the place where the highest temperature was recorded: 112.3°F, Mae Hong Son City in the Mae Hong Son province.[4]

(↑) Visit the place where the lowest temperature was recorded: 29.5°F, Sakhon Nakhon City in the Sakhon Nakhon province in 1974, but this record may have been lowered in 2019 to 23°F at Doi Inthanon Summit in Chiang Mai.

❏ Visit the biggest tree in circumference: 79.4 feet in girth, Koh Yao Noi in Phang Nga.

(↑) Go to the eastern-most point: Pha Taem in Ubon Ratchathani province on the Laotian border.

(↑) Go to the western-most point: Mae Nam Salawin in Mae Sam Laep in the Mae Hong Son province on the Myanmar border.

❏ Visit the tallest building: 1,030 feet, the King Power Mahanakhon in Bangkok.

(↑) Go to the northern-most point: Mae Sai in the Chiang Rai province on the Myanmar border.

(↑) Go to the southern-most point: Betong in the Yala province on the Malaysian border.

---

[4] I cycled the 360-mile Mae Hong Son loop on that day in 2016.

Chapter 28
Thailand's Mountains

There are ten peaks in Thailand over 2,000 meters (6,562 feet) high. For reference Mount Washington in New Hampshire is 6,288 feet and Mount Mitchell in North Carolina is 6,684 feet. Although there are many other beautiful mountains in Thailand, I added just these ten to my bucket list. Many of these mountains are in national parks. Some summits are difficult to attain, not because of their great heights, but because of their location and the land laws—a guide may be required.

When climbing these peaks, sound judgment and caution must be exercised. It's easy to underestimate the difficulty of the climbs, and the dangers of Thailand's weather, wildlife, insects, and man-lit fires. For inexperienced hikers, it's best to hire a guide even if one isn't required. Some areas are closed at certain times of the year due to fire danger or other issues. It's important not to stray into areas where people are cultivating illegal drugs, hunting, or harvesting illegally in the forest.

The Thai words 'doi,' 'phu,' and 'khao' all mean mountain. Various sources provide different heights for these mountains, so they could be plus or minus a handful of meters either way. I specify heights in meters, as is done in Thailand. The mountains range in height from 6,575 to 8,415 feet. I sorted them from highest to lowest.

❑ Stand on the summit of the ten highest peaks in Thailand.

(↑) Go to the summit of Doi Inthanon: 2,565 meters in Chiang Mai.

❑ Go to the summit of Doi Pha Hom Pok: 2,296 meters in Chiang Mai.

(↑) Go to the summit of Doi Chiang Dao: 2,175 meters in Chiang Mai.

❑ Go to the summit of Khao Kacheu Lau: 2,152 meters in Tak.

❑ Go to the summit of Phu Soi Dao: 2,120 meters in Uttaradit.

❑ Go to the summit of Phu Khe: 2,079 meters in Nan.

❑ Go to the summit of Phu Lo: 2,077 meters in Nan.

❑ Go to the summit of Doi Mae Tho: 2,031 meters in Chiang Rai.

❑ Go to the summit of Doi Mae Ya: 2,005 meters in Mae Hong Son.

❑ Go to the summit of Doi Phong Sa Yan: 2,004 meters in Mae Hong Son.

Chapter 29
Thailand's Scuba-Diving Sites

Thailand's waters are a paradise. I added to my bucket list its top-50 dive sites. These are debatable. However, most top-50 lists will overlap significantly with my list. A "site" may consist of multiple named dive sites in a general location. For me to check a box, I only need to dive any of the sites in that location. For shallow sites, they can be snorkeled.

When diving, it's best not to exceed your certification level and abilities. Accidents happen, and a recompression chamber in Thailand may be far away. If you choose to dive with a scuba company in Thailand make sure it's reputable. I saw dive boats sinking with passengers on board ... In Thailand many tourists have died in speed-boating accidents.

To obtain more information about the dive sites here, to determine if a marine park fee is required, to obtain directions, to understand depths and currents, to determine best times to dive, and so on, you can conduct research online or visit a local scuba shop. I list the dive sites alphabetically by name. In Thai the word 'hin' means rock or stone.

❏ Dive the top-50 sites in Thailand (the ones on this list).

(↑) Dive Anemone Reef.

(↑) Dive Anita's Reef (Tsunami Memorial).

❏ Dive Aow Leuk.

(↑) Dive the Boonsung Wreck.

(↑) Dive Boulder City.

❏ Dive the Bremen Wreck.

(↑) Dive Christmas Point.

❏ Dive Chumphon Pinnacle.

(↑) Dive East of Eden.

(↑) Dive Elephant Head Rock (Hin Pusar).

❏ Dive the Hardeep Wreck.

(↑) Dive Hin Bida.

(↑) Dive Hin Daeng.

❏ Dive Hin Ga Daeng.

❏ Dive Hin Kuak Ma.

❏ Dive Hin Luk Bat.

(↑) Dive Hin Muang.

❏ Dive Hin Pae.

- ❏ Dive Hin Rap.
- ❏ Dive the HTMS Chang.
- (↑) Dive the HTMS Khram.
- ❏ Dive the HTMS Kut.
- ❏ Dive the HTMS Mataphon.
- ❏ Dive the HTMS Sattakut.
- (↑) Dive the Japanese Garden.
- (↑) Dive the King Cruiser Wreck.
- ❏ Dive Koh Bangu.
- (↑) Dive Koh Bida Nai.
- (↑) Dive Koh Bida Nok.
- (↑) Dive Koh Bon.
- ❏ Dive Koh Chi.
- ❏ Dive Koh Dok Mai.
- (↑) Dive Koh Haa.
- ❏ Dive Koh Khai.
- ❏ Dive Koh Khrok.
- ❏ Dive Koh Larn.
- (↑) Dive Koh Nang Yuan.

(↑) Dive Koh Phi Phi.

❑ Dive Koh Sak.

(↑) Dive Koh Tachai.

(↑) Dive Racha Noi.

(↑) Dive Racha Yai.

(↑) Dive Richelieu Rock.

(↑) Dive Sail Rock.

(↑) Dive Shark Fin Reef.

(↑) Dive Shark Point (Hin Musang).

❑ Dive Southern Rock.

(↑) Dive Stonehenge (Similan).

❑ Dive Twin Peaks.

(↑) Dive West of Eden.

Part III
Sporting Competitions and Activities

This part of the book includes bucket-list items for sporting competitions and activities. There are chapters on marathon running, ultra-marathon running, road and trail races, multi-sport and triathlon, cycling, scuba diving, mountaineering, and hiking. Additional details about many of the events described here are provided in my book *PALMARÈS*.

Chapter 30
Marathon Running

A standard marathon is 26.2 miles in length. This chapter presents my bucket-list for marathoning. Before describing it, I provide background and a few marathon-running stats.

Dave Wottle (1972 Olympic-gold medalist at 800 meters) inspired my brother to take up competitive running, and they inspired me. At age 11, I started training. Over the past 50 years, I ran more than 100,000 miles. Check. There was a time when I ran morning, noon, and night. I got called Forrest Gump. I usually took one day off per week. My biggest weeks exceeded 125 miles. Check. I gradually increased the length of long runs. My longest training run is 75 miles. Check. I stretched and did yoga to combat tightening and sore muscles.

My fastest marathon was at the Tucson Marathon in 2005, where at age 44, I ran a 2:51:45. When age-graded, it equates to a 2:41:15. I went the marathon distance or farther 584 times. Check. I ran 15 sub-three hour marathons. Check. When age-graded, I ran 25 sub-three hour marathons. Check. The average time of my ten best marathons is 2:53:31. Check. The average time of my ten best age-graded marathons is 2:49:19, which suggests that I got better with age. I had five age-graded performances under 2:50.

The average time of my 33 best marathons is 2:59:53. Check. The average time of my 45 best age-graded marathons is 2:59:45. Check. When considering my trail marathons and the hot marathons in Thailand, my average performance on a "reasonable" course, when age-graded, was sub-three hours. The average time of my best seven Boston Marathons is 2:57:53. The average age-graded time of my ten Boston Marathons is 2:58:53, and one of them took place the day after the London Marathon. Check. If I remove it, my average age-graded time drops to 2:57:17.

It was only in the process of writing this book that I noticed I had a 24-year streak in which I ran a marathon race every year. If I'd known that, I would have kept the streak alive. I ran the marathon distance or farther in training for 32 of the past 33 years. When I took my around-the-world trip in 2019, I missed one year. My 30-year streak ended. I never thought about it until now. Many runners use streaks to stay motivated. Some run every day for a minimum distance, say three miles, year after year. I knew a guy who snuck out his hospital bed to keep a 25-year streak alive.

I won one marathon overall—the Low Country Distance Classic Marathon in 2004 in South Carolina. Check. I won several races in the Masters category. Checks. My Masters wins are as follows:

- Low Country Distance Classic Marathon 2003
- Atlanta Marathon 2003
- Bay State Marathon 2004 (1st 40-49)
- Low Country Distance Classic Marathon 2004
- Rutledge Marathon 2009 (1st 45-49)

I finished in the top-ten overall at the following marathons:

- 10th Cape Cod Marathon 1993

- 5th Nipmuck Trail Marathon 1994
- 10th Nipmuck Trail Marathon 1997
- 3rd Tybee Marathon 1999
- 5th Myvatn Marathon 1999
- 7th Leadville Trail Marathon 2001
- 6th Tybee Marathon 2003
- 2nd Low Country Distance Classic Marathon 2003
- 5th Atlanta Marathon 2003
- 9th Bay State Marathon 2004
- 1st Low Country Distance Classic Marathon 2004
- 10th Phuket Marathon 2006
- 6th Chiang Mai Marathon 2008
- 4th Rutledge Marathon 2009

In many other marathons, I finished in the top ten in the Masters division. My most frequently run marathons are the Boston Marathon (ten times, check), the Tybee Marathon (six times), the Nipmuck Trail Marathon (five times, check), and the Phuket Marathon (four times). I tried to find good races nearby where I was living and support them. With this background let's get to my marathoning bucket list. I present marathons in chronological order.

(↑) Run 100,000+ miles.

(↑) Run training weeks of 125+ miles.

(↑) Run a training session of 75+ miles.

(↑) Run 15 sub-three hour marathons.

(↑) Average under 2:55 for my 10 fastest marathons.

I averaged 2:53:31 for my ten fastest marathons.

(↑) Run 25 age-graded sub-three hour marathons.

(↑) Average under three hours for my top-45 best age-graded marathons.

(↑) Average under an age-graded three hours for ten Boston Marathons.

I averaged an age-graded time of 2:58:53 in my ten Boston Marathons.

(↑) Run the Rhode Island Marathon in Newport, Rhode Island.

At age 28, my first marathon was run on home soil in beautiful Newport, Rhode Island. I ran a 3:23:06 on October 22, 1989. My Mom and Dad were there. My Mom cried because I was hurting so badly. After that, she didn't want to see me run. It was too painful. Although I hadn't trained too much, I pushed the pace hard. I ran the entire race. In the later stages, I passed many competitors who were walking.

(↑) Run the Nipmuck Trail Marathon in Ashford, Connecticut.

I ran my first Nipmuck Trail Marathon on June 10, 1990. I finished 15th. I fell in love with this low-key race. The aid stations were spotty clusters of self-service water jugs, sitting near the trail. We needed to jump over several fences. The trail is challenging and beautiful. The best trail runners in New England show up at this race. I went back in 1992 and finished 13th. In 1993 I ran a 3:37:15 and finished 12th. In 1994 I ran my best Nipmuck in a time of 3:24:11 and finished 5th. This was an excellent time on the tough course.

(↑) Run the Cape Cod Marathon in Falmouth, Massachusetts.

At the Cape Cod Marathon, my second road marathon, I ran a 3:03:36 on October 28, 1990. I took 20 minutes off the time from my first marathon. I ran a seven-minute pace, and I came close to breaking three hours. In 1991 I improved my time to 3:00:52 and finished 45th. I tried to break three hours, but failed.

(↑) Run the Maine Marathon in Portland, Maine.

I ran the Maine Marathon in a time of 2:54:22 on October 4, 1992. I finished in about 20th out of 400. It was the first time that I broke three hours.

(↑) Break three hours in the marathon.

(↑) Run the Cape Cod Marathon in Hyannis, Massachusetts.

At the Cape Cod Marathon in Hyannis on March 7, 1993 at age 31, I set my new PR of 2:53:31.

(↑) Finish in the top 10 at a marathon.

At the Cape Cod Marathon in Hyannis, I finished 10th out of 500 finishers. I listed my other top-10 finishes in the introduction to this chapter.

(↓) Run a sub-2:40 marathon.

With the progression of my times in the marathon, I added to my bucket list breaking 2:40. In 2005 at the Tucson Marathon, I pushed through the half marathon in a PR of 1:18:00 on pace to break 2:40. Even through 18 miles, I was on a sub-2:40. But, shortly thereafter, abdominal cramping made it hard for me to breathe. I slowed down considerably over the final miles, but I managed to run my best time of 2:51 by a handful of seconds.

My fast split convinced me that I was capable of a sub-2:40 on the right course and day. But, it never happened. As of this writing, my age-graded time at the Tucson Marathon of 2:41:15 is the best of my career.

(↑) Run the Rhode Island Marathon in Providence, Rhode Island.

I don't think the residents of Newport wanted the Rhode Island Marathon run through neighborhood, so it was moved to Providence. I ran a 3:01:49 on November 7, 1993. This marathon was the first road marathon where I didn't improve my time. The reason was because I'd run in a 100-mile ultra-marathon race three weeks earlier, and my legs hadn't recovered.

(↑) Run the Boston Marathon in Hopkinton, Massachusetts.

I grew up just south of Boston, and this race is important to me. All serious marathoners from the East Coast have the Boston Marathon on their bucket list, as do many runners from around the world. My first Boston Marathon took place when it was still a relatively small and exclusive marathon. The qualifying times are rigorous, so it's considered an elite marathon. On April 18, 1994, I ran a new best time of 2:52:25. I finished 684th out of 8,105 finishers. It was the biggest field I had ever run in to that point.

The following year I ran the race again on April 17, 1995 and improved my time by 24 seconds to a new PR of 2:52:01. In 1997 I finished my third Boston Marathon in 2:59:22. In 1998 I ran a 3:01:12. In 1999 I ran a 2:58:04. In 2000 I ran a 3:00:52. In 2004 I ran a

3:01:12 in one of the hottest Boston's on record. It's an age-graded time of 2:53:56. I finished high up in the Masters division. In 2005 I ran a 3:23:31 the day after running the London Marathon in England. In 2006 I ran a 3:14:38. In 2010 in my tenth Boston, I ran a 3:15:36.

The Boston Marathon holds many great memories for me. Let me relay one interesting story. One year, the Boston Athletics Association called me pre-race. They explained that my assigned number was coincidentally the number worn by a former Japanese champion. He was returning to celebrate his victory and run Boston again, 50 years later. It was quite something for a Japanese person to travel to America right after World War II. Never mind to come and win the Boston Marathon.

The champion requested to wear his lucky number. I immediately gave it up for him. I was happy to become part of his bucket list. He was a tremendous inspiration! The numbers at Boston are seedings by time. The race start is cordoned off into corrals, and you can enter a corral only if you possess a number in the appropriate range. As a return favor, the organizers gave me an elite number. It meant I could start directly behind the pros.

My starting position was the best I'd ever had at the race. I was usually in the second or third corral. My chip time would be the same as my actual time. I didn't have as good a run as I usually do at Boston. And, throughout the day, I heard the knowledgeable roadside fans saying things like: "Boy, that guy really blew up," "Look at that guy's number, how'd he end up way back here?," "How did that guy ever get such a low number?," and "He doesn't look like he could run a 2:18." Hearing such comments for three hours did little to improve my mental state. I thought of the old Japanese champion. I shook my head and smiled.

(↑) Finish 10 Boston Marathons.

(↑) Run the Burlington Marathon in Burlington, Vermont.

I ran the Burlington Marathon on May 29, 1994 in a time of 2:54:04. The course is beautiful.

(↑) Run the Marathon Popular de Valencia (Compensada) in Valencia, Spain.

On February 4, 1996 at age 34, I ran the Valencia Marathon in a time of 2:58:21. The format featured delayed starting times, based on your age and gender. Since I was a young male, I started in the final group. I enjoyed this format because there were runners whom you could key off throughout.

There were only three aid stations in the race, and it was a hot day. At one aid station, I grabbed a big bottle that the volunteers were using to fill small cups. Someone shouted at me in Spanish (the equivalent of): "Don't take that!" The guy chased me. He caught me as I finished the last sip. I said: "Gracias," while passing him back the empty. He shook his finger. I smiled. I ran.

At the finish line, a volunteer handed me a bag of Valencia oranges. I was too cramped and exhausted to take advantage of the free massage. I didn't have sufficient energy to carry the oranges around either. I'd walked a few miles to reach the starting line, and I needed to walk back to reach my hotel.

(↑) Run an international marathon.

In Valencia, Spain I ran my first international marathon. I ran other international marathons in Spain, the United Kingdom, Iceland, and Thailand.

(↑) Run the Catalunya Marathon in Barcelona, Spain.

I ran the Catalunya Marathon on March 17, 1996. It was fun to run the 1992 course from the Barcelona Olympics. While cheering roadside, it seemed all spectators were smoking. I remember "An-e-mal!" being shouted. Completing the final 400 meters in the Olympic stadium to a huge, enthusiastic crowd thrilled me, even though the packed stadium existed only in my mind. In reality there were about 2,500 fans.

(↑) Run the Bay State Marathon in Lowell, Massachusetts.

I ran the Bay State Marathon on October 13, 1996. I ran a 2:53:46 and finished 18th. My Mom came to this race, and I wanted to perform well. I ran a good race finishing in the top 2.5%. On October 17, 2004 at age 43, I returned. I ran 14 seconds slower in a time of 2:54:00, which is an age-graded time of 2:45:38. I finished 9th overall and 2nd in the Masters division.

(↑) Run the Tybee Marathon in Tybee Island, Georgia.

I ran a 2:54:26 at the Tybee Marathon in 1999. In 2000 I ran a 3:03:40. At age 40 in 2002, I ran a 3:09:50. In 2003 I ran a 2:56:37. In 2005 I ran a 3:09:16. In 2008 I ran a 3:24:53. This race was one minute slower than my first marathon, 20 years earlier.

(↑) Finish on the podium at a marathon.

I finished 3rd at the Tybee Marathon in 1999. I ran an excellent race in hot and humid conditions. At one point I thought I might win. I pushed all the way to the finish, but the winner maintained his pace. I listed my other top-marathon finishes at the beginning of this chapter.

(↑) Finish on the Masters podium at a marathon.

At age 41 in 2003, I ran a 2:56:37 to finish 2nd master at the Tybee Marathon in Georgia. I won the Masters division at the Bluffton Marathon in 2003. I won the Masters division at the Atlanta Marathon that year, too. There are a number of other races where I finished in the top three in the Masters division.

(↑) Run the Myvatn Marathon in Myvatn, Iceland.

On June 25, 1999 at age 37, I finished the Myvatn Marathon in 2:55:26 in 5th.

(↑) Run a midnight marathon.

The Myvatn Marathon in Iceland is a midnight marathon. It starts at 12 AM. Iceland sits far north, so it isn't completely dark at midnight around the time of the summer solstice. Myvatn means mosquito in Icelandic. This race is the mosquito-lake marathon. I carried mosquito netting, as we ran around the lake. I was exhausted while finishing at 3:00 AM.

(↑) Run the Leadville Trail Marathon in Leadville, Colorado.

While out drinking margaritas in Leadville, I met a group of runners. They informed me that the next day they were running the Leadville Trail Marathon. They weren't drinking. I asked if I could sign up, and they said: "Yes." At that moment I added this race to my bucket list. I ran a 4:30:29. The group reunited at the finish and laughed. I blame the slow time on the time on the elevation—the lowest point of the mountainous race is 9,300 feet—not the margaritas.

(↑) Run a high-altitude marathon.

The Leadville Trail Marathon with a low point of 9,300 feet checks this box.

(↑) Run the Bluffton Low Country Distance Classic in Bluffton, South Carolina.

On October 26, 2003 at age 42, I ran the Bluffton Marathon in a time of 3:12:56, which is an age-graded time of 3:05:12. I finished 2nd overall and won the Masters division. On October 31, 2004 at age 43, I won this race overall in 3:02:49.

(↑) Win the Masters division at a marathon.

I finished first in the Masters division at the Bluffton Marathon in South Carolina in 2003 and 2004. I finished first at the Atlanta Marathon in 2003.

(↑) Win a marathon.

In 2004 at age 43, I won the Bluffton Marathon in South Carolina. On a day with temperatures touching 100°F and the heat index well over 120°F, I ran a 3:02:49, including a bathroom break.

(↑) Run the Atlanta Marathon in Atlanta, Georgia.

On November 27, 2003 at age 42, I ran a time of 2:54:55 at the Atlanta Marathon. This is an age-graded time of 2:47:54. This race marked one of my best performances. I negative split the course. It has lots of rolling hills. It was hot and humid. At the halfway point, I was in 18th. Then in rapid succession, I heard: "You're in 15th," "You're in 12th," "You're in 10th," and "You're in 8th," ... I thought: "I can win this." I won the Masters division and finished 6th overall. I received a nice award—a blanket with lettering—on the podium.

(↑) Run the London Marathon in London, England.

On April 17, 2005 at age 43, I ran this iconic marathon in a time of 3:02:38 and finished 1,294th out of 35,261. The start line in London was chaos with one of the largest fields ever assembled for a marathon. There were probably 40,000+ starters. Three separate starting venues helped spread out the field of runners. When the different groups of runners merged, it was beautiful, like the confluence of three colorful rivers mixing with the bobbing runners providing turbulent water. I enjoyed the sights and smells, as the course traversed London's neighborhoods. I saved something for the next day's Boston Marathon.

(↑) Run a marathon in which a world record is broken.

In the 2005 London Marathon, Paula Radcliffe set a world record for a women's only marathon, as the elite women ran separately. At one point she flew by me on the opposite side of the road, as did the world-class men's field.

(↑) Complete the London-Boston Marathon double on consecutive days.

The London Marathon is always run on a Sunday and the Boston Marathon always on the third Monday in April, but there are few times when the days are consecutive. In 2005 they were. On April 18, 2005 at age 43, I ran a 3:02:38 at the London Marathon in England and the next day ran the Boston Marathon in 3:23:31 in Massachusetts. My friend Paul and I completed this bucket-list item together.

(↑) Run the Tucson Marathon in Tucson, Arizona.

On December 5, 2005 at age 44, I ran the Tucson Marathon in a time of 2:51:45, which is an age-graded time of 2:41:15. This is my PR. In 2010 at age 49, I ran a 3:10:03, which is an age-graded time of 2:51:46.

(↑) Run the ING Temple Marathon in Bangkok, Thailand.

On March 19, 2006 at age 44, I finished the Temple Marathon in 3:15:27. Like most marathons in Thailand, this one was super-hot and humid. The early start meant many barking and chasing dogs, especially for the leaders. The race was billed as a cultural event and passed by dozens of temples. It turned into a survival test.

(↑) Run the Phuket Marathon in Phuket, Thailand.

On June 18, 2006, I ran the Phuket Marathon in 3:35:36. I was the first Westerner to finish on the hot, humid, and hilly course. Like many marathons in Thailand, the race started in the dark. The early morning starts mean many aggressive dogs, the inability to enjoy the scenery, and the higher likelihood of getting lost. The advantage is less traffic. In 2008 I ran a 3:22:04, which placed me 2nd in my age group. In 2009 I ran a 3:52:00 in hot and humid conditions. In 2010 I ran a 3:54:11 in tough conditions.

(↑) Run the Pattaya Marathon in Pattaya, Thailand.

On July 15, 2007 at age 45, I ran the Pattaya Marathon in 3:30:09. While walking to the starting line at 3:30 AM, a couple bargirls propositioned me: "Hey mister, you wanna go?" I replied: "No thanks, I'm on my way to run a marathon." One girl asked: "Short time? Up to you. He-he-he." I smiled and laughed. They were disappointed.

(↑) Run the Marine Corps Marathon in Washington, DC.

On October 28, 2007 at age 46, I ran the Marine Corps Marathon in 3:02:52, which is an age-graded time of 2:49:40. I finished 218th out of 20,667. I wanted to run this race to honor the US military and to see the beautiful sights of Washington, DC. In 2008 I arrived at the starting line late. I ran a 4:17:51 from the back of the pack.

(↑) Run the Chiang Mai Marathon in Chiang Mai, Thailand.

On December 28, 2008 at age 47, I ran the Chiang Mai Marathon in 3:03:10, which is an age-graded time of 2:47:42. I placed 6th overall.

(↑) Run the Kentucky Derby Marathon in Louisville, Kentucky.

On April 25, 2009 at age 47, I ran the Kentucky Derby Marathon in 3:14:02. The temperature and humidity were high.

(↑) Run the Rutledge Marathon in Rutledge, Tennessee.

On November 14, 2009 at age 48, I ran the Rutledge Marathon in 3:18:28 and finished 4th overall.

(↑) Run the Baltimore Marathon in Baltimore, Maryland.

On October 15, 2011 at age 50, I ran the Baltimore Marathon in 3:26:07. Although not training for a marathon, I was living in Annapolis, so decided to add this nearby race to my bucket list.

(↑) Run the Khon Kaen Marathon in Khon Kaen, Thailand.

On January 29, 2012 at age 50, I ran the Khon Kaen Marathon in 3:21:14. This race inspired my friend Kae to add marathoning to her bucket list. She now has completed several marathons.

(↑) Run the Sukhothai Marathon in Sukhothai, Thailand.

On June 26, 2016 at age 54, I ran the Sukhothai Marathon in 3:41:00. With my intense focus on cycling, I hadn't run a marathon for almost four and a half years. This was the longest gap in my marathon-running career since I ran my first marathon on home soil in Rhode Island in 1989. My 24-year streak of running at least one marathon every year from 1989-2012 ended four years earlier. As I mentioned in the introductory remarks of this chapter, I achieved the streak without being aware of it.

I often said to myself that from the age of 28 onward, I could have run a marathon on any day. I believe that statement to be true. Thus if I'd been paying closer attention to my streak, I easily could have kept it alive. In fact, during the intervening years, when I didn't run a marathon race, I did run farther than the marathon distance in training.

When I ran my 54th marathon at the Khon Kaen race, I was 54 years old. One month after this race, my average number of marathons dropped below one per year. I hope to bring it back up to one marathon per year for the remainder of my life.

(↑) Run the Lampang Marathon in Lampang, Thailand.

On October 25, 2020 at age 59, I ran the Lampang Marathon in 4:21:08. I jumped into this marathon with my friend Sanpawat "Bobby" Kantabutra, but I'd done *no* run training. I got Bobby into marathon running about ten years earlier. He wanted to add this item to his bucket list, so I added it to mine. In hindsight, I'm glad we ran, as the COVID-19 pandemic has made it difficult to enter any athletic events in 2021.

(↑) Visit the city of Marathon in Greece.

I drove there and visited the museum. It wasn't easy to find.

❏ Run the New York City Marathon.

(↓) Run under 3:30 in the marathon during an Ironman race.

The best I could manage was a 3:52 on a hot, hilly course at Ironman Canada in Penticton, British Columbia.

❏ Average one marathon per year for my lifetime.

At age 54 I ran my 54th marathon. Since then, I fell behind. The lack of races in 2020 and 2021, due to the COVID-19 pandemic, has me falling further behind.

(↑) Run the Nipmuck Trail Marathon in Ashford, Connecticut five or more times.

(↓) Run the 100th Boston Marathon.

Although I ran in 1995 and 1997, I regret missing the 100th running in 1996. I lived in Spain at the time and wasn't able to return for the race.

❏ Run the Berlin Marathon.

❏ Run a marathon on each continent, besides Antarctica.

I never had the desire to run a marathon in the cold of Antarctica. I ran marathons in Asia, Europe, and North America. I hope to run a marathon in Africa in 2022.

(↑) Cover the marathon distance in a day 500+ times.

There are 584 days when I covered the marathon distance or farther.

Chapter 31
Ultra-Marathon Running

An ultra-marathon is a run of 50 km (31.1 miles) or farther. This chapter presents my bucket-list items for ultra-marathoning. Before describing my bucket list, I present background and a few ultra-running stats.

My childhood friend Claire became a world-class marathoner. We reconnected on the opposite coast, while attending graduate school at the UW. Claire's friend Kim Moody was an outstanding ultra-marathoner. Kim ran a 6:01 for 50 miles in 1986. Her time still ranks high on the all-time list. During our long runs, Claire's stories about Kim inspired me.

Claire told me about the Western States 100. I added it to my bucket list. In order to gain entry into that race—the Grand Daddy of all ultra-marathons—I needed to qualify by running a 50-mile race. I chose the Sunmart Texas Trail 50 for my first ultra. I finished third. Check. That thrust me into a period where I would run ultra-marathons during three decades. More checks. Although I don't race ultras anymore, I do sometimes go out for 35-mile training runs. When I'm hiking, I often exceed the ultra-distance. I enjoy covering a long distance on foot. Maybe there's something etched in my DNA from the great human migrations.

I set my best time for 50 miles of 6:27:05 at the Texas Trail 50, which is run on trails. Although not nearly as fast as Kim, a 7:45 pace per mile on trails is a solid effort. At the Western States 100, I set my best for 100 miles in a time of 22:13:20. When training days are included, I went the ultra-distance or farther 254 times. Check. Those runs alone exceeded 10,000 miles. I had many other efforts between 26.2 and 31 miles.

I won my age group at the competitive Texas Trail 50. Check. I finished in the top-ten overall at the following races: Laugavegurinn 55K, the Mountain Masochist 50 (two times), the Nifty Fifty, the Nugget 50, the Strolling Jim (two times), the Texas Trail 50 (four times), and the US Nationals 100K Championships. Checks.

I completed six 100-mile runs and thirteen 50-mile runs. The hardest race I ever completed was the Wasatch Front 100, which has 47,300 feet of elevation change, or almost exactly nine vertical miles of up and down. Check. I lost eight toenails in that race. All the 100-mile runs I completed were at high altitude, and living at sea-level made these tough bucket-list accomplishments.

Next I present a few facts about my personal records (PRs) and a summary of my wins and top-ten placings.

Personal records:
- PR 50 miles: 6:27:05 at the Texas Trail 50, 1997
- PR 100K: 8:20:43 at the US Nationals 100K, 1998
- PR 100 miles: 22:13:20 at the Western States 100, 1994

Wins:
- Age group at Texas Trail 50

Top ten:
- Laugavegurinn 55K
- Mountain Masochist (2 times)
- Nifty Fifty
- Nugget 50
- Strolling Jim (2 times)
- Texas Trail 50 (4 times)
- US Nationals 100K Championships

Basic stats:
- Number of 100-mile runs completed: 6
- Number of 50-mile runs completed: 13
- Number of times going the ultra-distance (50K or farther): 254
- Hardest race: Wasatch Front 100

With this background I present my ultra-marathoning bucket list.

(↑) Run the Sunmart Texas Trail 50 in Huntsville, Texas.

On December 15, 1990 at age 29, I ran the Texas Trail 50. I finished my first ultra (50.2 miles) in 7:17:15 in 3rd. I started out conservatively, not knowing what to expect. I passed runners throughout. I came close to second place. Strangely, this would be my only podium finish in an ultra-marathon.[5] At the time I figured that in the near future I would win an ultra. I was wrong.

In 1991 I ran a 7:48:49 on the course. In 1992 I ran a 6:47:25, which was a new PR for 50 miles. In 1997 I improved my PR to 6:27:05 and finished 7th in a strong

---

[5] See the Nugget 50.

field. I averaged 7:42 pace per mile on the trails. In 1998 I ran a 7:37:59.

(↑) Run the Western States 100 Mile Endurance Run starting at Squaw Valley and finishing in Auburn, California.

With a single ultra-marathon under my belt, I took on one of the hardest runs in the world, having 41,060 feet of elevation change. On June 29, 1991 at age 29, I ran the Western States 100 in 26:33:02. The temperature *fluctuates* 100°F on race day—from 18°F to 118°F. On June 25, 1994, I returned and improved to a 22:13:20, which is my PR for 100 miles.

(↑) Run the Leadville Trail 100 in Leadville, Colorado.

On August 15, 1992 at age 31, I ran the Leadville Trail 100, but dropped out at Twin Lakes, completing 61 miles in 15:19:10. The Leadville Trail 100 has 31,200 feet of elevation change, a minimum altitude of 9,200 feet, and a max of 12,600. I went out hard and was in the top ten at 50 miles. My split time was 9:40:57. The altitude bothered me. I sat down and tried to recover. I failed. I progressed slowly. I stopped. I continued. I put my hands on my knees. I vomited. Night approached. Temperatures dropped. I had no pacer. I continued vomiting from altitude sickness. I smelled horrendous. I evaluated my predicament. The prognosis wasn't good. I felt weak and broken. I dropped out.

On August 21, 1993 at age 32, I returned and finished the Leadville Trail 100 in 23:53:48. I avenged my earlier DNF.

(↑) Pace my friend Paul to a finish at the Leadville Trail 100.

I paced Paul in his first attempt at the Leadville Trail 100. After a courageous effort, he dropped out around mile 70. We returned the following year. Over the last 40 miles, I paced him to a successful finish. I helped Paul check this item off his bucket list, as he had me, when he paced me to my finish in 1993.

(↑) Run the Mountain Masochist Trail Run near the Blue Ridge Parkway, Virginia.

On October 24, 1992 at age 31, I ran the Mountain Masochist Trail Run in 7:58:00 and finished 7th. This race has 16,200 feet of elevation change. I returned in 1994 and improved my time and place to 7:51:00 and 6th, respectively.

(↑↓) Run the Nugget 50 in North San Juan, California.

On May 22, 1993 at age 32, I entered the Nugget 50. This race had a crazy ending. There was deep snow on the course. The five lead runners were stopped by race officials. I was one of them. Although the original plan called for an aid station ahead, it wouldn't be there. No vehicles could pass. Officials weren't sure what to do: allow runners to proceed or direct them to turn around. Runners would be on their own. Safety became a serious concern.

The organizers finally made the decision to change the race to a 36-mile, out-and-back run. We accepted that decision. I pressed on hard with Brian Purcell—a former winner of the Western States 100, the Westfield (a 544-mile ultra in Australia), and many other ultras. We chatted. Brian was one of the top ultra-runners in the world, tough as nails. I hung on for grim death.

When we reached 31 miles, Brian and I were stopped again. This time a different official told us the race had changed to a 50 miler over a different route. With the wishy-washy officiating, Brian and I decided to run the 36 miler, as did many others. We finished tied for first, shaking our heads in disbelief about what had transpired.

(↑) Run the Angeles Crest 100 Mile Endurance Run starting in Wrightwood and finishing at the Rose Bowl in California.

On October 9, 1993 at age 32, I ran the Angeles Crest 100, but dropped out at Chantry Flats, completing 76 miles in 17:11:00. I made an attempt to win this race and started out fast with the leader, Fred Shufflebarger. It was a big mistake, but while it was dark, I had to stay with Fred or I would have been totally lost. When I went to the bathroom, Fred dropped me. I made wrong turns that cost me time.

I became sick. I vomited. I became dehydrated. I lost toenails. I sat down for an hour. Almost no one passed me. I debated what to do. When I reached Chantry Flats at mile 76, I was still in the top ten. However, facing nighttime without support, suffering from bad feet, and feeling weak from hours of vomiting, I decided to quit. Due to redlining my effort in an attempt to win, I went too deep. I cracked. My will broke. I could have slept for eight hours and walked to the finish. Fred ended up winning. I pushed him for 30 miles. His time still stands as one of the fastest ever run on the course.

On September 30, 2000 at age 39, I returned and ran a 27:18:40 at the Angeles Crest 100. I avenged my earlier DNF. I didn't go for the win. I ran sensibly.

(↑) Run the Comrades Marathon from Durban to Pietermaritzburg (up), South Africa.

When apartheid ended in South Africa in 1994, the great Comrades Marathon opened to foreign runners. I immediately added it to my bucket list. On June 17,

1996 at age 34, I ran the Comrades Marathon in 7:38:51. It's the largest ultra-marathon in the world and steeped in tradition. It was inspiring to see Nelson Mandela at the finish line.

On June 16, 2000 at age 38, I returned for another Comrades up run. Despite suffering from horrendous diarrhea, I improved my time from four years earlier and ran a 7:23:47.

(↑) Earn a silver medal at the Comrades Marathon in South Africa for running under 7 hours and 30 minutes.

(↑) Run the JFK 50 in Boonsboro, Maryland.

On November 23, 1996 at age 35, I ran the JFK 50 in 6:46:20. This was a new PR for 50 miles. On a more challenging course, I improved my time from the Texas Trail 50 by one minute and five seconds.

(↑) Run the Wasatch Front 100 in East Layton, Utah.

On September 6, 1997 at 36, I ran the Wasatch Front 100, but dropped out at Upper Big Water, completing 59.2 miles in 13:15:00. I was in the best climbing shape of my life. Unfortunately, a few days before the race, I caught a terrible cold. I shouldn't have raced at all, but with my crew coming in from all around the world, I decided to give it my best shot. At high altitude I had trouble breathing due to my nasal congestion, coughing, and sore lungs. I was unable to finish.

I returned to the race on September 11, 1999. I completed the course in 29:25:00. I redeemed myself at the race referred to as "One Hundred Miles of Heaven and Hell." In addition to nine miles of elevation change, a portion of the race is run on animal-track trails. My legs got scratched to hell. Route finding was difficult. The footing was rough. The rugged scenery was heavenly. The air was fresh and clean. The course lived up to its billing.

(↑) Run the US National 100K Championships in Pittsburgh, Pennsylvania.

On March 30, 1998 at age 36, I ran the US 100K Championships in 8:20:43. My split time for 50 miles was 6:31:00. I averaged 8:02 pace per mile.

(↑) Run the Laugavegurinn 55K in Landmannalaugar, Iceland.

While living in Iceland, I learned about this race. The cross-country run traverses obsidian fields, glaciers, sandy stretches, rocky areas, valleys, and mountains. It skirts nasty smelling sulfur vents that disrupt one's breathing and block vision completely. The race includes river fords in deep, fast-moving, ice-cold water. I added it to my bucket list. On July 24, 1999 at age 37, I ran the Laugavegurinn 55K in 5:20:15 and finished 4th.

(↑) Run the Strolling Jim 40 in Wartrace, Tennessee.

On May 4, 2002 at age 40, I ran the Strolling Jim (41.2 miles) in 5:22:26 and finished 6th. I returned on May 1, 2004 two years later. I ran a 5:28:25 and finished 5th.

(↑) Run the Nifty 50, New England Championships in Coventry, Rhode Island.

On November 17, 2002 at age 41, I ran the Nifty 50 in 6:55:55 and finished 4th. My Mom and family members came to see me race on home soil. I went out fast with the goal of setting a new personal best for 50 miles. The rolling hills took a toll, as did the chilly weather, and I struggled at the end. With my Mom and family cheering me on, I hung on for 4th place. This was the last time my Mom saw me run. I wish I could have won. I tried.

(↑) Run the Tussey Mountain 50, US National Championships in State College, Pennsylvania.

On October 16, 2010 at 49, I ran the Tussey Mountain 50 in 7:41:17. I finished 3rd in my age group. At the early morning start, the race director shouted: "For how many of you is this your first ultra?" Many hands went up and newbies shouted excitedly. People clapped. Things quieted down, and I shouted: "For how many of you is this your last ultra?" My hand shot up. Everyone laughed. I smiled. To date, I don't have plans to race another ultra. This was my last.

(↑) Cover the ultra-marathon distance in a day more than 250+ times.

(↑↓) Win an ultra-marathon.

When the race directors switched the Nugget 50 to a 36-mile race from the original 50-mile distance, I tied for 1st in the 36 miler with ultra-running legend Brian Purcell.

(↓) Run sub-6 hours for a 50-mile race.

I never came close to improving on Kim's time.

(↓) Break 24 hours at the Angeles Crest 100.

This race has 46,310 feet of elevation change. I realize that I won't be able to accomplish this goal. On my best day, I believe that I could have done it, but the stars didn't align right.

(↓) Break 24 hours at the Wasatch Front 100.

The same comments from the Angeles Crest 100 apply here.

(↑) Run across the state of Maryland on the Appalachian Trail in one day.

When I thru-hiked the Appalachian Trail, I added this item to my bucket list. I did this run with Colin Smith, my student from the Naval Academy. We ran 43 miles. Colin's Dad did a great job supporting us.

(↑) Finish on the podium in my age group at the US 50-mile championships.

At the US 50-mile championships in 2010, I finished 3rd in my age group.

(↑) Complete a 50+ mile run in the White Mountains of New Hampshire.

I lived in New Hampshire for about ten years. The first mountains that I ever saw or hiked in were the White Mountains. People told me you can't do a 25-mile day in the White Mountains. I added a 50 miler to my bucket list. My favorite training run there was a mountainous 38 miler. On a few occasions, I went 50+ miles. During my time in New Hampshire, I covered the majority of trails in the White Mountains.

(↑) Finish in the top 10 at the US National 100K Championships.

I finished 10th in 1998.

(↑) Unsupported and in one day, run 75 miles between Snoqualmie and Stevens Passes in Washington State.

When I read about the longest hike in my Washington State hiking guide, I added it to my bucket list. The book recommended five to seven days. I decided to do it in one. To complete this run, Randy "Gumby" Day and I skipped a day of classes while in graduate school at the UW. The weather that weekday was perfect, whereas the weekend weather was miserable. Word in the now Paul G. Allen School of Computer Science & Engineering is that we parked a car at each pass, met in the middle, exchanged car keys, continued on running alone, and then drove back to the UW separately to attend morning classes.

Gumby and I actually drove separately to Stevens Pass and dropped my car there (the old Toyota Corolla with the crumbling dashboard); drove to Snoqualmie Pass together and left Randy's pickup truck there; ran to Stevens Pass together and picked up my car; drove to Snoqualmie Pass from Stevens Pass together to get Randy's truck; and drove back to Seattle separately. While stuck in Seattle's morning rush hour, we honked at one another in an effort to remain awake. Then we went to class.

On my PCT thru-hike years later, I would cover this beautiful stretch again, taking two days with my friend Paul who came out to hike with me during the final week.

(↓) Run the London to Brighton Ultra-marathon.

With some of the best runners in the world competing, the London to Brighton 54 miler plus 198 yards was a top race on the ultra-running calendar. I added it to my bucket list. When I was ready to run, the race had been discontinued. The final year of the original race was in 2005.

(↑) Compete in 25 ultra-marathons.

I didn't finish three of the 100-mile races that I entered, but in those cases I dropped out at 59, 61, and 76 miles. So in a way, they were ultras as well. They were certainly harder efforts than my 50 milers. My feet often decided how well I ran in ultras. I competed before the trail-running shoe had been invented, and my feet would have benefited from more support. Given the limitations of my feet, I ran best at the 50-mile and 100K distances.

(↑) Complete the grand slam of ultra-running.

I finished the Western States 100, Leadville Trail 100, Angeles Crest 100, and the Wasatch Front 100. These four trail races make up the "grand slam" of ultra-running. I completed the grand slam over several years, but there are runners who complete the grand slam in a single year.

(↓) Run a sub-24 hour time at each of the 100-mile trail runs in the grand slam of ultra-running.

Although I went sub-24 hours at Western States 100 and the Leadville Trail 100, at the Angeles Crest 100 and the Wasatch Front 100, I couldn't break 24.

Chapter 32
Road/Shorter Trail Races

I focused on running ultra-marathons and marathons, but along the way I ran shorter races as speed work. While in high school, I ran cross-country. My best mile is a 4:38, and my best 10K a 34:31. My fastest half marathon is my split from the 2005 Tucson Marathon, where I went through in 1:18:00. As I get older, I'll focus more on shorter distances. In total I spent the equivalent of two full years hobbling around, struggling to go down stairs after endurance events. The beauty of shorter races is they're over quickly, and you don't develop debilitating soreness. They're easier. There are more options. Entry fees are less.

This portion of my bucket list isn't comprehensive. I don't have my results for events prior to 1992.

(↑) Finish the Crystal Mountain Summit Run in Washington State.

Gumby took me to the Crystal Mountain Summit Run. I vividly remember the pain in my lower back during the 3,100-foot climb to the summit, and this race took place in the 1980s! I hadn't trained for the run, but Gumby assured me it would be fun. I'm still debating.

(↓) Run a sub-4:30 mile.

Although I dreamed of a fast mile, it never happened.

(↑) Run a lap on the track at the Olympic Stadium in Athens, Greece.

(↑) Run the New England Athletics Congress 10M Championships in Newburyport, Massachusetts.

On July 28, 1992 at age 31, I ran the New England Championships in 1:03:15.

(↑) Run the Seven Sisters 12 Mile Trail Run in Amherst, Massachusetts.

On April 25, 1993, I ran the Seven Sisters Trail run in 2:23:54 and finished 10th. It's a beautiful and difficult course, having a steeply uphill start. I went anaerobic after 30 seconds. I guess the 9th place runner was far ahead of me, as I got lost several times. The course is an out-and-back with seven hills each way. The trail is rocky, and if you take risks on the downhills, there's a good chance of falling. In 1994 I ran a 2:06:55 and improved to 5th.

(↑) Run the New England Half Marathon Championships in Newport, Rhode Island.

On September 30, 1996 at age 35, I ran a 1:22:56. Back on home soil, this was a solid run. It works out to about 6:20 pace per mile.

(↑) Run the Market Square 10K in Portsmouth, New Hampshire.

On June 14, 1997, I ran the Market Square 10K in 37:51. It was a 6:05 pace per mile.

(↑) Run the Derry 16 Miler in Derry, New Hampshire.

On January 25, 1998, I ran the Derry 16 Miler in 1:54:02.

(↑) Run the Mount Washington Road Race up Mount Washington, New Hampshire.

On June 20, 1998, I ran the 7.6 miles up Mount Washington in 1:18:17. Entries for this race are limited. I was lucky to get a number in the lottery. They say this is a race with only one hill. There's an elevation gain of 4,650 feet with an average gradient of 12%. The steepest section touches 18% and is called the Raymond Grade. I ran well and finished just behind Olympic-gold medalist and former marathon world-record holder Joan Benoit Samuelson. My goal was to avoid walking, and I achieved it.

(↑) Run the Armstrong Atlantic State University (AASU) Homecoming 5K in Savannah, Georgia.

On January 30, 1999 at age 37, I ran the AASU 5K in 17:59 and finished 3rd. In 2000 I ran an 18:38. In 2001 I ran an 18:27 and finished 1st. On January 26, 2002 at age 40, I ran an 18:46 and finished 2nd.

(↑) Run the Shamrock 5K in Savannah, Georgia.

On March 12, 1999, I ran the Shamrock 5K in 17:53. This time equates to a 5:46 pace per mile. In 2001 I ran an 18:04. In 2002 I ran an 18:46.

(↑) Run the Savannah Bridge Run 10K in Savannah, Georgia.

On May 1, 1999, I ran the Savannah Bridge Run in 39:04 and finished 24th out of 1,591. The course has two big hills, going over the Savannah Bridge toward South Carolina and returning. In 2000 I ran a 39:43 and improved to 22nd. In 2001 I ran a 39:45 and finished 29th. In 2002 I ran a 39:37 and finished 26th. In 2003 at age 42, I ran a 38:36 and finished 17th overall and 3rd Master. I won $100.

(↑) Run the Akranes Half Marathon in Akranes, Iceland.

My friend Olaf from Reykjavik added his hometown race to my bucket list. On June 12, 1999, I ran the Akranes Half Marathon in 1:26:09 and finished 4th.

(↑) Run the Tybee Half Marathon in Tybee Island, Georgia.

On February 3, 2001 at age 39, I ran the Tybee Half Marathon in 1:22:23 and finished 19th.

(↑) Run the Azalea 10K in Savannah, Georgia.

On March 24, 2001 at age 39, I ran the Azalea 10K in 37:46 and finished 8th. On March 27, 2004 at age 42, I ran a 41:02 and finished 3rd. When I was leading, I made two wrong turns.

(↑) Run the High Mountain Institute 25K in Leadville, Colorado.

On July 13, 2002 at age 40, I ran the High Mountain 25K in 2:23:28 and finished 3rd overall and 1st Master. This is a hilly and tough race run at high altitude.

(↑) Run the Trick or Trot 10K in Savannah, Georgia.

On November 1, 2002, I ran the Trick or Trot 10K in 37:40 and finished 2nd overall and 1st Master.

(↑) Run the Run for the Children 10K in Savannah, Georgia.

On September 21, 2003 at age 42, I ran the Run for the Children 10K in 41:10 and finished 6th overall and 1st Master. The course was long.

(↑) Run the Governor's Cup Half Marathon in Columbia, South Carolina.

On October 15, 2005 at age 44, I ran the Governor's Cup Half Marathon in 1:25:26 and finished 12th overall. I was 1st in my division and 2nd Master.

(↑) Run the Skidaway Institute of Oceanography 10K on Skidaway Island, Georgia.

On October 22, 2005 at age 44, I ran the Skidaway Institute 10K in 39:47 and finished 3rd overall and 1st Master.

(↑) Run the Eastern States 20 Miler in Kittery, Maine.

On March 29, 2009 at age 47, I ran the Eastern States 20 in 2:22:06. This event was added to New England's running calendar as a tune-up for the Boston Marathon. The race took place on a cold and rainy early spring day.

(↑) Run the Annapolis 10 Miler in Annapolis, Maryland.

On August 29, 2010 at age 49, I ran the Annapolis 10 Miler in 1:10:27.

(↑) Run the Doi Suthep 11K in Chiang Mai, Thailand.

On February 5, 2012 at age 50, I ran the Doi Suthep 11K in 54:15 and finished 2nd in my age group. The Thai word 'Doi' means 'mountain.' This run ascends to the Doi Suthep temple. It's uphill the entire route, climbing a total of 2,238 feet.

(↑) Run the Phuket Mini-Marathon 11.4K in Phuket, Thailand.

On May 12, 2013 at age 51, I ran the Phuket Mini-Marathon. In a torrential rain over a flooded course, I paced my friend to a 1:26.

(↑) Run the Phayao Lake 26K in Phayao, Thailand.

On May 29, 2016 at age 54, I ran the Phayao Lake 26K in 2:09:15. The race is one lap around Phayao Lake in a lovely mountain setting.

(↑) Run the TuphaLap Half Marathon in San Kamphaeng, Thailand.

On July 24, 2016 at age 54, I ran the TuphaLap Half Marathon in 1:42:46. The course was 13.33 miles, which is .23 miles longer than a standard half marathon. The course is an out-and-back with two long, steep climbs.

(↑) Run the Udon Thani Half Marathon in Udon Thani, Thailand.

On May 7, 2017 at age 55, I ran the Udon Thani Half Marathon in 1:43:30. I cycled 700 miles in the week leading up to this race, including a 100-mile ride the day before. In hot and humid conditions, although my legs were fatigued, I felt strong the entire race. This run was part of my buildup for the Swissman Extreme Triathlon.

(↑) Run the Run for Heart Nakornping Hospital Mini-Marathon 12K in Chiang Mai, Thailand.

On September 17, 2017 at age 56 while pacing a friend, I ran the Run for Heart 12K in 1:17:00.

(↑) Run the Follow King Number 9 9.9K in Udon Thani, Thailand.

On October 8, 2017 while pacing a friend, I ran the Follow King Number 9 race in 57:15. The long-serving Thai King Rama IX was extremely ill. Many Thais, including non-runners, came out to show their love for him. It was an emotional start and finish.

(↑) Run the Lanna Half Marathon in Chiang Mai, Thailand.

On November 19, 2017 while pacing a friend, I ran the Lanna Half Marathon in 2:11:12.

(↑) Run the Chiang Mai Half Marathon in Chiang Mai, Thailand.

On December 25, 2017 at age 56, I ran the Chiang Mai Half Marathon in 1:43:12 and finished 69th out of 1,978.

(↑) Run the Asia Justice Half Marathon in Chiang Mai, Thailand.

On December 9, 2018 at age 57, I ran the Asia Justice Half Marathon in 1:47:14 and finished 10th.

(↑) Run a sub-35 minute 10 km.

❑ Run a sub-1:40 half marathon after age 60.

(↑) Win a 5K road race.

I won the AASU Homecoming 5K in 2001.

❑ Complete 100 road races that are shorter than a marathon.

I only started keeping track of my road races after age 30. I ran about 40 races so far, which is far fewer than my number of marathons. I want to keep running 10 kms and half marathons. They pound the body far less than the marathon.

❑ Run a sub-2:00 half marathon after age 70.

(↑) Win the Masters division in a road race.

I accomplished this goal many times.

❑ Run a sub-1:00 10 km after age 80.

Chapter 33
Multi-Sport and Triathlon

I always loved to run and ride a bicycle. When I was 14, I joined a swim team. My passion for swimming developed under my friend Peter's influence, but I took to the water more slowly than to land-based sports. When I learned about triathlon in the 1980s, I immediately added it to my bucket list. As a young boy, I often rode my bicycle to our Swim & Tennis Club, swam, played tennis and basketball, went for a run, and then cycled home.

Combining three sports came naturally to me. Although I thought I was a better runner than swimmer or cyclist, in the triathlon world, I fared better in the swim. When I took up cycling seriously, my running suffered. I was still competitive in the swim though. After completing a swim workout, I always feel invigorated. The workouts are easier on my joints and help increase flexibility. When training at an indoor pool, the weather isn't a factor. At my job it was usually easy to sneak in a swim at lunchtime.

I focused on endurance races. I never competed in a triathlon as short as the Olympic distance—1.5K swim, 40K bike, and 10K run. It isn't on my bucket list. My first triathlon was a half Ironman (check), and from there I immediately graduated to the Ironman distance—2.4-mile swim, 112-mile bike, and a 26.2-mile run (check). Note that because the Ironman was developed in the US, its distances are expressed in imperial units.

After completing a number of Ironman-distance events (checks), I set a goal of a sub-10 hour performance. My best swim time in the Ironman is a 54:14; my best bike split is a 5:18:02; my best run is a 3:52:36. Combining all three and adding five minutes for transitions gives me a theoretical Ironman time of 10:09:52. I still need to find ten minutes.

In addition to problems such as crashing during the bike segment, a broken zipper on my wetsuit, broken goggles, a loose headset on my bike, aid stations running out of supplies, and getting lost on the run, I always entered Ironman races with hot and humid conditions and/or ones with hilly or mountainous courses. The weather and course undulations were simply the nature of the Ironman races that I was able to enter. The Ironman wasn't designed to be easy; it was designed to be hard. The founders pit endurance athletes from three different disciplines against one another to find out which sport—swimming, cycling, or running—had the better-conditioned athletes.

In the early days of triathlon, of course, few races existed. It was and still is difficult to gain entry. One needs to enter a race a year in advance. And, on the day of signup, one must be ready at the keyboard, as soon as registration opens. Due to bad timing, I missed out on several bucket-list items. It was frustrating being fit to race but being unable to secure an entry for one of the limited slots. The demand far exceeds the available positions, especially for the more popular events.

There are fast courses on my bucket list that I never got a chance to race, for example, the Roth Challenge in Germany and Ironman Western Australia. After I set the goal of a sub-10 hour Ironman, I pushed myself harder in training than I would have otherwise. My goal left me striving to improve. In 2021 I got into the best triathlon shape of my life, as I prepared for Ironman Estonia. Unfortunately, I wasn't able to get vaccinated for the coronavirus in Thailand, where I was training. I felt terribly disappointed to have to withdraw.

Next I provide my best splits for half-Ironman and full-Ironman distance races.

- Best splits in the half Ironman:
    - Swim: 25:00
    - Bike: 2:43:36
    - Run: 1:23:41

- Best splits in the Ironman:
    - Swim: 54:14
    - Bike: 5:18:02
    - Run: 3:52:36

Note that in the Ironman my bike spilt of 5:18:02 divided in half is 2:39:01. This is faster than I ever went in the half Ironman. In fact I once went through the half-Ironman distance on the bike in the full Ironman in 2:30:00. I never held back on the bike. Following are my best finishes in multi-sport and triathlon events:

- 5th place Wildman Biathlon, 1997
- 14th overall Tupper Lake Tinman (half-Ironman distance), 1997
- 5th place Espirit Triathlon (Ironman distance), 2001
- 1st place age-group Chesapeake Man Endurance Festival (now Ironman Maryland), 2011
- 1st place swim age-group Ironman Taiwan, 2016
- 1st place bike age-group Ironman Taiwan, 2016
- 5th place overall age-group Ironman Taiwan, 2016
- 1st place age-group Swissman Extreme (Ironman distance), 2017
- 1st place age-group swim, Laguna Phuket Triathlon, 2020

- 1st place age-group bike, Laguna Phuket Triathlon, 2020
- 1st place age-group overall, Laguna Phuket Triathlon, 2020

Next I provide my bucket list for multi-sport and triathlon competitions.

(↑) Compete in the Black Hills Triathlon in Olympia, Washington.

In August 1988 at age 27, I competed in the Black Hills Triathlon. The distances were a 1-mile swim, 58-mile bike, and 13.1-mile run. My time was 4:51:00 with the following splits: 25:00, 2:55:00, and 1:30 for the swim, bike, and run, respectively. This is one of the world's oldest triathlons. The weekend before the race, I went out and completed the entire course, so I knew what to expect. I became hooked on triathlons.

(↑) Compete in the Bay State Triathlon in Medford, Massachusetts.

On August 13, 1990 at age 29, I competed in the Bay State Triathlon. The distances were a 1.2-mile swim, 42-mile bike, and 10-mile run. My time was 3:30:09 with the following splits: 27:48, 1:53:14, and 1:08:27 for the swim, bike, and run, respectively. I finished 22nd in my age group.

(↑) Compete in Ironman Canada in Penticton, British Columbia, Canada.

On August 26, 1990 at age 29, I competed in Ironman Canada. The distances were 2.4-mile swim, 112-mile bike, and 26.2-mile run. My time was 11:05:01 with the following splits: 58:32, 6:03:13 (both transitions), and 4:03:16 for the swim, bike, and run, respectively. I'd entered the 1989 race, but due to a patella-tendon injury, I withdrew. I planned to race in the Ironman before I'd even run a marathon. During the fall of 1989, I was able to recover enough to run my first marathon. When I took on the Ironman, I had one road marathon under my belt. I was one of the least experienced competitors.

The Ironman wasn't well-known in 1990. I felt like a champion for having finished. The Wide World of Sports TV show had built up the Ironman as one of the hardest endurance tests in the world, which is why I added it to my bucket list. No one in my circles had ever heard of the Ironman. I kept my achievement to myself. From that moment on though, I was an Ironman. I'd done what many consider impossible. Completing this race was a defining moment in my life and athletic career.

On August 28, 1994 at age 33, I completed the course in 10:33:42 with the following splits: 59:41, 5:41:25 (both transitions), and 3:52:36 for the swim, bike, and run, respectively.

(↑) Compete in the Endurance Triathlon in Sunapee, New Hampshire.

On September 9, 1991 at age 30, I competed in the Endurance Triathlon. The distances were a 2.4-mile swim, 112-mile bike, and 26.2-mile run. My time was 11:19:12 with the following splits: 54:14 (8th out of the water), 6:02:37, and 4:16:52 for the swim, bike, and run, respectively. I finished 33rd. My friend Peter and I checked off this bucket-list item together.

The bicycle course was five loops around Lake Sunapee on an extremely hilly circuit. Back then, there was no GPS. According to my research, one loop has 1,532 feet of climbing and the maximum gradient is 9.5%. The race had about 8,000 feet of climbing in the form of sharp, steep hills. Due to stop signs, traffic, and 90° turns, many of the climbs were tackled without the advantage of a good-rolling start. I ran well but due to being misdirected on the course, I ran an extra 2.5 miles.

(↑) Compete in the Tupper Lake Tinman Triathlon in Tupper Lake, New York.

On July 19, 1997 at age 35, I competed in the Tupper Lake Tinman. The distances were 1.2-mile swim, 56-mile bike, and 13.1-mile run. My time was 4:45:05 with the following splits: 31:23, 2:50:01 (both transitions), and 1:23:41 for the swim, bike, and run, respectively. I finished in 14th. My friend Paul and I checked off this bucket-list item together.

(↑) Compete in the Wildman Biathlon in Shelburne, New Hampshire.

On August 9, 1997 at age 36, I competed in the Wildman. The distances were a 6.2-mile run, 22.3-mile bike, and 3-mile run. My time was 2:32:00 with the following splits: 39:00, 1:11:00, and 42:00 for run 1, the bike, and run 2, respectively. I finished 5th. The second run is on a trail up the steep ski-slope of Wildcat Mountain. My parents drove up to New Hampshire from Rhode Island to watch me race. They took the gondola up Wildcat Mountain. At the finish Mom was on the verge of tears, seeing me nauseous from my effort. The elevation of Wildcat is 4,422 feet. We enjoyed good views. My friends Paul and Patrick checked off this bucket-list item with me.

(↑) Compete in the New England Triathlon Festival in Sunapee, New Hampshire.

On August 23, 1997 at age 36, I competed in the New England Triathlon Festival. The distances were a 1-mile swim, 44-mile bike, and 9-mile run. My time was 3:30:05 with the following splits: 23:30, 2:07:41 (both transitions), and 58:55 for the swim, bike, and run, respectively.

(↑) Compete in the Greater Floridian Triathlon in Clermont, Florida.

On October 24, 1998 at age 37, I competed in the Greater Floridian. The distances were a 2.4-mile swim, 112-mile bike, and 26.2-mile run. My time was 11:10:49 with the following splits: 1:03:31, 5:42:36, and 4:14:36 for the swim, bike, and run, respectively. I spent about five minutes in each transition. I finished 95th.

The middle of Florida is hilly. It's hot and humid. When I put my face in the Floridian lake for the first time, I couldn't see anything. It's like putting your head into a black abyss. The water is jet black from tannic acid leaching organic matter. When my face was in the water during the swim, I found myself closing my eyes. With my eyes shut, it wasn't any darker. I felt more comfortable. While turning my head to breathe, I opened my eyes. I could see land. That helped. I could see sky. I avoided a panic attack and drowning.

The following year I returned. My time was 11:37:37 with the following splits: 1:07:07, 6:22:41, and 3:55:24 for the swim, bike, and run, respectively. I improved my placing to 74th despite the slower time, as the conditions were much tougher. I spent an extra few minutes in transition as well.

(↑) Compete in the Sea-to-Summit Triathlon from New Castle Island to Mount Washington, New Hampshire.

On July 29, 2000 at age 39, I competed in the Sea-to-Summit. My friend Paul added this item to my bucket list, and we competed together. The distances were a 12-mile kayak, 90-mile bike, and 8.5-mile run. My time was 9:27:51 with the following splits: 2:00:58, 5:00:00 (includes both transitions), and 2:26:53 for the kayak, bike, and run, respectively. I finished 11th. The race was by invitation only, and it had a select field of top athletes. The roads were open to traffic. The race finished on the summit of Mount Washington. I'd never done any serious kayaking before, so in preparation I took a lesson from a Navy SEAL.

During the kayak segment of the race, I paddled well. I was in a borrowed touring kayak. I chose a good line through the wide open Great Bay. One needed to be careful of shallow water and getting stuck, due to the tides. The Piscataqua River is known for some of the strongest currents on the East Coast. Those with racing kayaks gained an advantage. I expended a lot of energy trying to keep pace.

When I mounted my bicycle, my hands were numb. My shoulders and arms ached. I stretched my back. I tried to brake. I couldn't. I shook out my hands. After a while, I regained feeling. Because the roads weren't closed to traffic, having braking ability was critical. I rode well on the hilly course. I ran a steady pace up the rocky trail to the summit of Mount Washington.

(↑) Compete in the Esprit Triathlon in Montreal, Canada.

On September 8, 2001 at age 40, I competed in the Esprit Triathlon. The distances were a 2.4-mile swim, 112-mile bike, and 26.2-mile run. My time was 10:53:25 with the following splits: 1:03:23, 5:18:02, and 4:25:34 for the swim, bike, and run, respectively. I finished 6th. Although it poured rain and we experienced major thunderstorms, I put in my fastest bike split in an Ironman-distance race. Due to the slick track, there were many crashes. I almost went down a number of times. I avoided numerous incidents, where riders fell directly in front of me.

The day broke the record for the highest temperature ever recorded in Montreal, and the heat index rocketed to over 135°F. The humidity was 100%, with steam rising off the pavement throughout the race. My Mom and brother were there to support me. They searched out shade. On a ridiculously hot day, the good swim and fast bike allowed me to break 11 hours. Due to the weather conditions and bike crashes, many racers dropped out.

(↑) Compete in Ironman Arizona in Tempe, Arizona.

On November 23, 2008 at age 47, I competed in Ironman Arizona. The distances were a 2.4-mile swim, 112-mile bike, and 26.2-mile run. I didn't finish. My swim split was a 1:11:29 and bike split a 5:41:35. I dropped out of the run at mile 18. While trying to reach my bucket-list goal of a sub-10 hour Ironman, I overcooked the bike and first part of the run. When I became badly dehydrated and cramped, I decided it was safest to withdraw. By then, my time goal was far out of reach.

(↑) Compete in the Pumpkin Man Triathlon in South Berwick, Maine.

On September 12, 2010 at age 49, I competed in the Pumpkin Man. The distances were a 1.2-mile swim, 56-mile bike, and 13.1-mile run. My time was 5:06:39 with the following splits: 31:31, 1:29, 2:43:36, and 1:44:54 for the swim, hill climb, bike, and run, respectively. I jumped into this race on the spur of the moment to check off this bucket-list item with my friends Paul and Patrick.

(↑) Compete in Ironman Louisville in Louisville, Kentucky.

On August 28, 2011 at age 50, I competed in Ironman Louisville. The distances were a 2.4-mile swim, 112-mile bike, and 26.2-mile run. My time was 12:21:24 with the following splits: 1:05:30, 5:44:36, and 5:14:12 for the swim, bike, and run, respectively. I finished 755th out of 2,437, which was a huge field. I had a fair swim and an okay bike, but I fell apart on the run. The high heat and humidity affected me, as I overcooked things on the hilly bike course.

(↑) Compete in the Chesapeake Man Endurance Festival in Cambridge, Maryland.

My friend Marjorie has a house in Cambridge, Maryland, so I added the nearby race to my bucket list. Race-day logistics never were as simple. On September 24, 2011 at age 50, I competed in the Chesapeake Man. The distances were a 2.4-mile swim, 112-mile bike, and 26.2-mile run. My time was 11:15:29 with the following splits: 1:10:23, 5:32:50, and 4:19:41 for the swim, bike, and run, respectively. I spent almost 15 minutes in transitions. I won my age group and finished 33rd overall.

This race is now Ironman Maryland.

(↑) Compete in Ironman Taiwan in the Penghu Islands, Taiwan.

On October 2, 2016 at age 55, I competed in Ironman Taiwan. The distances were a 2.4-mile swim, 112-mile bike, and 26.2-mile run. My time was 13:59:14 with the following split times: 1:02:13, 5:48:41, and 6:51:41 for the swim, bike, and run, respectively. I spent 16:37 in transitions. In my age group, I finished 1st in the swim, 1st in the bike, and 5th overall.

I hadn't raced a triathlon for five years. I prepared extremely well for this event and again had the goal of breaking ten hours. This was the inaugural event for Ironman Taiwan. They were working through logistical issues. I pushed the swim and came out of the water near the front of the pack. I hammered the first half of the bike in 2:30. I was on pace. The problem was that the heat index reached 115°F, and already by mile 40 my legs were cramping.

At the aid stations, the organizers ran out of supplies and fluids. On the multi-loop course, there were crowds of racers lining up to obtain water. Due to this issue, I slowed dramatically during the second part of the bike segment. I would have slowed anyway, but severe dehydration exacerbated my problems. Although the organizers tried to solve the logistical nightmare, they weren't able to do so in real-time. I suffered, as did other competitors.

Because I was covered in salt, badly dehydrated, and overheated, in an effort to recover, I soft pedaled the last ten miles of the bike. My plan didn't work. I'd been without fluids far too long. I went too deep. The tank was empty. I ate and drank while in the transition area, but I couldn't recover. During the run, I wasn't competing. I was surviving. I walked much of the marathon.

(↑) Compete in the Swissman Extreme Triathlon in Ascona, Switzerland.

On June 24, 2017 at age 55, I competed in the Swissman Extreme Triathlon. The distances were a 2.4-mile swim, 112-mile bike, and 26.2-mile run. The race has 17,500 feet of climbing. My time was 17:47:00 with the following splits: 1:04:00, 9:00:00, and 7:06:00 for the swim, bike, and run, respectively. I spent 37 minutes in transition.

The race organizers screen entries. Due to the narrow roads and demanding nature of the course, the field is limited to 250 experienced athletes. I felt lucky to receive an entry. My goal was to finish. I didn't have a specific-time goal in mind. I had a solid swim.

When I descended the first mountain pass on my bike, I noticed a loose headset. My bicycle wobbled badly, but I regained control. Throughout the bike segment, I feathered my brakes on descents and couldn't descend full gas. There were two fatal accidents on the bike course, where I was significantly delayed. The people who died weren't affiliated with the race, but one of them was cycling in a tunnel that I needed to transit. After a long delay, I walked over the dead man's blood to get through the tunnel. Riding wasn't permitted. The loss of life made me sick.

My crew member Shagg learned that ahead they wouldn't be able to support me because of blocked roads caused by the accidents. The police weren't letting vehicles through the tunnels. With 37 miles remaining on the bike, I needed to carry a backpack with my running gear and any supplies that I could manage. I received no support for the remainder of the bike course. I didn't know when I would meet my crew next.

In the bike-to-run transition area, I spent about 25 minutes telephoning my crew and instructing them where to pick up my bicycle. There are no bike racks in this race, as normally the rider hands the bike off directly to a crew member. However, in this case most crews weren't able to get to the bike-to-run transition ahead of their athletes.

Before ending our call, my enthusiastic crew gave me valuable words of encouragement. I remained positive. We hoped for the best and a quick rendezvous. A number of triathletes whom I spoke to planned to drop out there because they didn't have their running shoes. I was lucky Shagg found out about the crewing problem early. When I set off on the run, I left my cycling gear and bicycle unattended. After struggling to get going and a few painful strides, my concern about gear quickly vanished. I focused on running the brutal course.

My team finally caught up to me at mile 16 of the mountainous run course. Without support for five hours, I'd bonked. I was deeply relieved to see my crew and vice versa. I ate and drank like a wild man. Unable to exercise any self-restraint, I over did it. For the final climb up to the high-altitude Kleiner Scheidegg, pacers are mandatory. Shagg and I carried required survival gear. We reached the finish line together.

I finished well within the original time limit. Similar to my case, many racers were delayed for a couple hours and had to carry on without support. Race organizers extended the cutoff. Despite my long delays, I didn't need to take advantage of the extra allotted hours. There were seven entrants as old as me, four of them finished. The closest one to me was 54 minutes behind. In a sense I won my age group. At the Swissman the organizers don't keep track of placings.

(↑) Compete in the Laguna Phuket Triathlon in Phuket, Thailand.

On November 22, 2020 at age 59, I competed in the Laguna Phuket Triathlon. The distances were a 1.8K swim, 51K bike, and 12K run. My time was 3:20:56 with the following splits: 33:51, 1:36:47, and 1:04:30 for the swim, bike, and run, respectively. I spent about six minutes in transitions. In my age group, I was 1st in the swim, 1st in the bike, and 1st overall.

This is the oldest and most competitive triathlon in Asia. The bike course is technical and has steep gradients over 20%. In the tropical jungle, moss has turned the roads green. The asphalt behaves like ice when wet. It was critical to preview the course. During the race, the roads aren't closed to automobile traffic. You can't swing wide on any of the hairpins. Although some competitors rode their TT bikes, for safety I chose my road bike.

On race day the heat index reached 100°F. I swam well and felt good coming off the bike. I hung tough on the run. The skies opened up after the race. The violent storm cancelled the last half of the awards ceremony, and I was disappointed not to receive my trophy on stage. The beautiful-beach start in Phuket and the unique nature of the two-segment swim, the technical circuit and steep hills on the bike course, and the hilly, winding run make for a wonderful adventure. The heat and humidity guarantee challenging conditions.

❑ Compete in the Ironman World Championships.

For many years this goal wasn't on my bucket list. Now I see that was a mistake. When I had the opportunity, I wish I had gone to Hawaii to compete in the world championships. I'm not sure if that opportunity will ever come again. If it does, I'll take it the second time around.

(↑) Finish in the top-10 overall at an Ironman-distance race.

I checked this bucket-list item off in 2001 in Montreal, where I finished 6th.

❑ Compete in Ironman Estonia in Tallinn.

(↑) Win my age group at an Ironman-distance race.

I checked this bucket-list item off in 2011 at the Chesapeake Man in Cambridge, Maryland. I was first in my age group at the Swissman Extreme Triathlon in 2017, too.

(↓) Compete in the Ironman-distance race the Roth Challenge in Germany.

Although there was a time when I wanted to race in the Roth Challenge, my desire isn't there now. The race has become so popular that the course is very crowded.

(↑) Compete against one of the "big four" triathletes of my time: Scott "The Terminator" Molina, Scott "ST" Tinley, Mark "The Grip" Allen, or Dave "The Man" Scott.

I raced against The Terminator and ST. They both beat me soundly.

❑ Compete in Ironman Western Australia in Busselton.

The course in Busselton is considered one of the fastest in the world. I added it to my bucket list to try to set a PR.

(↓) Run under 3:30 in the marathon at the end of an Ironman-distance race.

❑ Compete in a half-Ironman or full Ironman-distance race in five decades: 1980s, 1990s 2000s, 2010s, and 2020s.

To check this box, I need to complete a half Ironman within the next nine years. Although in the best triathlon shape of my life in 2021, as I mentioned, I withdrew from Ironman Estonia due to the COVID-19 pandemic.

(↑) Break five hours in a half Ironman-distance race.

❑ Break 10.5 hours in an Ironman-distance race.

My PR is a 10:33 on the tough course at Ironman Canada.

(↑) Run under 1:30 in the half marathon at the end of a half Ironman-distance race.

I ran a 1:23 at the Tupper Lake Tinman in 1997.

❑ Break ten hours in an Ironman-distance race.

This bucket-list item is slipping away. I may take one more shot if I can get an entry into a race with a fast course. Although the entry fees are a whopping $700, the races fill up 12 months in advance, only a few hours after registration opens.

(↑) Break 55 minutes in the Ironman-distance swim of 2.4 miles.

❑ Compete in an Aqua Man Race that involves just the swimming and cycling portion of an Ironman-distance race.

(↑) Complete at least ten Ironman-distance triathlons.

Although fit enough to take part in Ironman-distance triathlons for many of the past 30 years, for reasons previously mentioned, I didn't compete too often.

❑ Compete with friends as a relay team in an Ironman-distance triathlon.

(↑) Compete in multi-sport events that don't involve just swimming, bicycling, and running.

I competed in the Sea-to-Summit race in New Hampshire that involved kayaking 12 miles.

Chapter 34
Cycling

As a child, I learned to ride a bicycle. I grew up in a neighborhood in Rhode Island, where it's safe to ride. When I was 13, I paid a visit to my grandmother's house with my parents. She lived about 30 miles away. I asked her if it would be okay if my friend John "Spooky" Allen and I rode over to her house sometime. Although Mémé thought I was joking, Spooky and I completed the ride the very next day. Check. My Mémé was shocked. After a good night's sleep, we rode back home. Check.

I completed my first one-day, 200-mile ride with my friend Peter at age 15. Check. We rode from Riverside, Rhode Island to Provincetown, Massachusetts, and back to Onset. While attending Pomona College in Southern California, I rode in outstanding weather both for enjoyment and general transportation. I often rode to the Ice Station on Mount Baldy, Huntington Beach and back, and to Lake Big Bear. Checks. My friend Grant "Minnow" Mason and I rode from San Francisco down the Pacific Coast Highway to the LA area. Check. While attending graduate school at the UW in Seattle, I cycled in the windy, rainy Pacific Northwest. Doug Wiebe and I rode many centuries together. Checks. When I took up the Ironman triathlon, I increased my riding volume.

When I lived in New Hampshire, Georgia, and Maryland, I continued as an avid cyclist. But, when I relocated to Thailand for part of each year, I started riding more and farther, much farther. During my biggest training year, I covered the distance around the earth: 24,800+ miles. Check. I love riding in the big, steep, remote mountains of Thailand. My book *The Hazards of Cycling in Thailand* discusses the dangers of riding in The Land of Smiles. There the heat and humidity challenge all long-distance riders.

I discovered quiet routes throughout Thailand. I found steep, paved roads with gradients up to 28%. As my rides became one- to two-week solo forays, the Race across America (RAAM) entered my consciousness again. While in graduate school, I'd ridden a fundraising century to support Cheryl Marek's RAAM ride. I added RAAM to my bucket list. I increased my training volume further. I remember the head of the RAAM organization Fred Boethling saying to me: "Don't underestimate the difficulty of RAAM." I took Fred's admonishment seriously.

With this background, let me review a few facts about my cycling. I begin by presenting the number of times that I rode various distances or farther within 24 hours or less:

- 100 miles: 1,181
- 200 miles: 57
- 300 miles: 12
- 350 miles: 7

I estimate that one third of my century rides exceeded 150 miles and about 20% of them over 175 miles, but less than 200. This means I rode more than 175 miles in a day over 300 times. During the COVID-19 lockdown, I learned that the majority of the men's pro peloton had never ridden this far in a single day. Because races were postponed, some pro riders did longer training rides in 2020. People on social media gushed over such "long" rides.

I present my bucket-list rides over 500 miles. I follow this by my cycling races. The chapter concludes with general cycling bucket-list items.

(↑) Crossing the USA from Provincetown, Massachusetts to San Diego, California.

From April 28 to June 4, 2011 at age 49, I pedaled 3,477 miles from Provincetown to San Diego. I checked this bucket-list item off with my friend Peter. I rode my Trek Madone 5.5 road bike. We spent 36 days on our trip. We rode unsupported. On our east to west crossing of the continent, we joined the RAAM route in northern Maryland.

Before we left Provincetown, I let Adrian "Aceman" Plante know that we would be arriving at his place in San Diego at 3:00 PM on June 4. When we showed up at 3:30 PM on the designated day, he quipped: "You're half an hour late." We laughed ourselves silly. Due to road closures and a terrible sand storm in Arizona, we rode about 35 miles of the trip from west to east. We needed to hitch-hike forward at the end of one day. Then we rode back to where we hitch-hiked from, and due to horrendous blowing sand, after some discussion, we hitch-hiked back to where we'd started that day.

We deviated from the RAAM route in Southern California because our destination was San Diego not Oceanside. There were no gaps in our route. We averaged just under 100 miles per day for our first ride over 3,000 miles.

(↑) Ride the Euro Velo 6 from Budapest, Hungary to Constanta, Romania.

From May 23 to June 5, 2012 at age 50, I pedaled 680 miles from Budapest to Constanta. I checked this bucket-list item off with my friend Paul. I rode a Hungarian hybrid bicycle, which I purchased in Budapest. We spent 13 days on our trip.

We rode unsupported through Hungary, Croatia, Serbia, Bulgaria, and Romania. We maintained a blog, and it's linked in from my website. We averaged 50 miles per day and one beer for every 10 miles.

(↑) Ride from Chiang Mai to Phuket, Thailand roundtrip.

From April 14 to April 23, 2013 at age 51, I pedaled 2,010 miles from Chiang Mai to Phuket and back. I rode alone. I used my Specialized S-Works Roubaix road bike. The trip took 9 days and 11 hours. This ride was part of my RAAM training.

I traveled far west of Bangkok through Kanchanaburi—the place where the Bridge over the River Kwai is located. I reversed my route on the way back. My ride was unsupported. April is the hottest month in Thailand with a heat index often well over 120°F. I learned that riding during the Songkran water festival is the most dangerous time to ride in the country. Many people drink and drive. I saw many bad accidents.

I averaged just over 210 miles per day.

(↑) Ride from Chiang Mai to Bueng Gan, Thailand roundtrip.

From May 5 to May 11, 2013 at age 52, I pedaled 1,044 miles from Chiang Mai to Bueng Gan roundtrip. I rode alone. I used my Specialized S-Works Roubaix road bike. The trip took 5 days and 10 hours. I rode unsupported. I consulted a map to determine my route. It was entirely new to me. I decided to go Chiang Mai, Lamphun, Lampang, Phrae, Uttaradit, Phitsanulok,

Loei, Nong Bua Lamphu, Udon Thani, Nong Khai, and Bueng Gan. I reversed my course on the way back. I especially enjoyed riding along the border with Laos—in the mountains and along the Mekong River. I averaged 190+ miles per day.

In the winter of 2014, I completed a similar ride in seven days. My ride was a bit longer. I took a route via Chiang Mai, Lamphun, Lampang, Phrae, Nan, Uttaradit, Phitsanulok, Loei, Nong Khai, and Bueng Gan. I reversed my course on the way back. While crossing Thailand this time, I rode through Nan province. I call this the *hard mountainous route* as there are many steep climbs in Nan and down through Uttaradit and Phitsanulok, especially along the Laotian border. I averaged 150 miles per day.

In the fall of 2014, I rode 1,048 miles from Chiang Mai to Bueng Gan roundtrip. I average 150 miles per day. In the fall of 2015, I completed this same ride again. I averaged 143 miles per day. In the winter of 2016, I did the same ride. I averaged 116 miles per day. In the spring of 2016, I rode the hard mountainous route. I averaged 113 miles per day. In the fall of 2016, I rode the hard mountainous route. I averaged 100 miles per day.

In the winter of 2017, I rode the hard mountainous route on my Specialized Epic Carbon mountain bike. I averaged 105+ miles per day. I repeated the same ride from April 28 to May 8, 2017. Again, I averaged 105+ miles per day in brutally hot conditions. From October 5 to October 10, 2017, I completed 611 miles of this route, while averaging 103 miles per day.

(↑) Ride from Chiang Mai to Phuket, Thailand partial return.

In the spring of 2014 at age 52, I rode 1,400 miles from Chiang Mai to Phuket and part of the way back. I rode alone. I used my Specialized S-Works Roubaix road bike. The trip took 9 days. I averaged 156 miles per day.

In the spring of 2015 at age 52, I rode 1,200 miles from Chiang Mai to Phuket and part of the way back. I rode alone. I used my Specialized S-Works Roubaix road bike. The trip took 10 days. I averaged 120 miles per day.

(↑) Ride from Chiang Mai to Bueng Gan to Ubon Ratchathani, Thailand return.

In the spring of 2016 at age 54, I rode 1,426 miles in 14 days from Chiang Mai to Bueng Gan to Ubon Ratchathani and back to Chiang Mai. I rode alone and unsupported. I used my Specialized S-Works Roubaix road bike.

I rode a route via Chiang Mai, Lamphun, Lampang, Phrae, Nan, Uttaradit, Phitsanulok, Loei, Nong Khai, Bueng Gan, Sakon Nakhon, Mukdahan, Amnat Charoen, Ubon Ratchathani, Si Saket, Surin, Buriram, Chaiyaphum, Phetchabun, Phitsanulok, Uttaradit, Phrae, Lampang, Lamphun, and Chiang Mai. I covered a lot of new territory, especially along the Thai-Cambodian border. The road surface was rough for the Roubaix. I averaged 100+ miles per day.

(↑) Ride from Chiang Mai, Thailand to Hanoi, Vietnam.

From February 17 to March 6, 2017 at age 55, I rode 700 miles from Chiang Mai to Hanoi with my friend Paul. I used my Specialized Epic Carbon mountain bike. The trip took 18 days. We rode unsupported.

We took a route via Chiang Mai, Fang, Chiang Rai, Chiang Khong, Houay Xai, Pak Tha, Pak Beng, Xayaboury, Luang Prabang, Pak Mong, Muang Lai, Muang Mai, Dien Bien Phu, Tuan Giao, Muong Lay, Lai Chau, Phong Tho, a middle route across Vietnam, and Hanoi.

The route involved long sections of dirt roads and was remote.

At one point we squeezed past a jackknifed semi, which dangled over a precipice. For several days no vehicles passed us from behind. When word spread about the blocked road, few vehicles came toward us either. It was an adventure—finding and following the route that I'd mapped out online, securing accommodations, and obtaining supplies. We had limited mobile service. The guesthouses are beautiful in Laos.

Paul's rear tire suffered a big gash. It took several days to find a replacement. We moved his rear tire to the front, so he could steer the gash around sharp rocks. When my pump failed, we negotiated to buy one from a villager. My Thai-language skills came in handy. In dense fog we rode up and down mountains, while avoiding livestock on the roads. The part labeled 'middle route across Vietnam' in my route description is where we deviated from our planned route, when Paul developed severe bronchitis. On riding days we averaged 50+ miles.

(↑) Ride from Chiang Mai, Thailand to Luang Prabang, Laos return.

From April 12 to April 22, 2018 at age 56, I rode 803 miles from Chiang Mai to Luang Prabang. I rode alone. I used my Specialized Epic Carbon mountain bike. The route had 42,147 feet of climbing. The trip took nine days of riding.

I rode a route via Chiang Mai, Lamphun, Lampang, Phrae, Den Chai, Uttaradit, Nam Pat, Pu Soi Dao (detour from Phuu Duu border), Pu Soi Dao, Tha Li, Xayaboury, Luang Prabang, Na Mor, Huay Xai, Chiang Khon, Chiang Rai, Fang, Chiang Dao, and Chiang Mai. Temperatures reached 108°F (42°C) on most days. Although Thais and Laotians are allowed to cross the border at Phuu Duu, others aren't. I wasn't aware of this fact. I completed a long detour to Tha Li to reach the next border crossing with Laos. In record-setting heat, I averaged 90 miles and a vertical mile per day.

(↑) Ride from Chiang Mai, Thailand to Vientiane, Laos partial return.

From April 28 to May 17, 2018 at age 56, I rode 1,370 miles from Chiang Mai to Vientiane and nearly back. I rode alone. I used my Specialized Epic Carbon mountain bike. The route had 46,609 feet of climbing. The trip took 16 days of riding.

I rode a route via Chiang Mai, Lamphun, Lampang, Long (Phrae), Den Chai (Phrae), Uttaradit, Chat Trakan (Phitsanulok), Nakhon Thai (Phitsanulok), Dansai (Loei), Tha Li (Loei), Kean Thao (Loei, border), Na Phor (Laos), Xayaboury, Nan City, Kasi, Hin Hoeup, Vang Vieng, Vientiane, Nong Khai, Bueng Gan, Si Chiang Mai (Nong Khai), Tha Li, Chat Trakan, Uttaradit, Phrae, and Lampang.

From Muang Nan to Kasi, there's an hors catégorie (meaning too hard to be categorized) climb of about six miles at 14% average gradient. The road climbs to 6,000 feet. The area is considered dangerous because over the years, Hmong rebels have killed a number of tourists in the region. The descent is exceptionally dangerous, especially in wet conditions such as I experienced. Three semis remained vertically on end after crashing. I worried about the descent far more than the Hmong rebels.

Temperatures exceeded 104°F (40°C) on most days. The high was 110°F (43+°C) with humidity. The heat index surpassed 150°F. There was a terrible lightning storm on the last day, so I picked up in Lampang. On riding days I averaged 86 miles.

(↑) Ride the Trans America Trail (TAT) from Astoria, Oregon to Yorktown, Virginia.

From May 27 to July 8, 2018 at age 56, I rode 4,326 miles from Astoria to Yorktown. I used my Specialized Epic Carbon mountain bike. I rode with my friend Andy for 20 days and solo for the remainder. The trip took 42.5 days.

We rode unsupported. We maintained a blog, and it's linked in from my website. Many details can be found there. I loved riding the TAT. I averaged 102 miles per day for six weeks. I didn't take any rest days. The longest day was 150 miles.

(↑) Ride from Chiang Mai to Ubon Ratchathani to Nakhon Phanom to Chiang Mai, Thailand.

From November 4 to November 28, 2018 at age 57, I rode 2,079 miles from Chiang Mai around Northern Thailand and back. I rode alone. I used my Specialized Epic Carbon mountain bike. I rode for 19 days.

I rode a route via Chiang Mai, Lamphun, Lampang, Sukhothai, Phitsanulok, Phichit, Phetchabun, Chaiyaphum, Nakhon Ratchasima, Buriram, Surin, Si Saket, Ubon Ratchathani, Amnat Charoen, Mukdahan, Nakhon Phanom, Bueng Gan, Nong Khai, Loei, Phitsanulok, Uttaradit, Nan, Phayao, Chiang Rai, and Chiang Mai. I covered new ground on this ride.

Near Cambodia I broke a rim on my mountain bike. It caused six mysterious flats and a three-day delay. I acquired a new rim in Ubon Ratchathani, but to make a wheel, we needed to reuse my old spokes. I averaged 110 miles per day, which is a lot on a fully loaded mountain bike, especially with all my flats.

From October 21 to November 24, 2021 at age 60, I rode 2,567 miles from Chiang Mai around Northern Thailand and back, using a fairly similar extended route from the one described above. I rode alone. I used my Specialized Epic Carbon mountain bike. I cycled 25 days. I completed my ride on Doi Ang Khang in northern Chiang Mai. After an 850-mile week, riding up the brutally steep Doi Ang Khang the following day was difficult. I had support for about nine days. I rode one century in 5:18 and had a biggest day of 150 miles.

(↑) Ride from Chiang Mai around Northern Thailand through 33 provinces and back.

From August 2 to October 19, 2020 at age 59, I rode 4,556 miles around Northern Thailand. I rode alone. I used my Specialized Epic Carbon mountain bike. The trip involved 58 days of riding. I rode unsupported.

During the COVID-19 pandemic, I completed this ride in rainy season. When my GPS got wet on day three, I lost my maps. I got two flats, 14 wasp/bee stings, two new chains, two new sets of brake pads, new clothes, and new tires. I climbed Phu Chi Fah nonstop via Route 4018 from Chiang Rai. I descended via Thoeng. That out-and-back ride was 127 miles (205K). The climb up Route 4018 is hors catégorie with long stretches well over 20%. I feared coming down Route 4018 without a dropper seat-post, which is why I rode a much longer route back via Thoeng.

I rode 26 centuries with a biggest day of 175 miles—a long way on a fully loaded mountain bike. My route was via Chiang Mai, Lamphun, Lampang, Sawankhalok, Sukhothai, Phitsanulok, Wang Tong, Phetchabun, Lomsak, Chaiyaphum, Chum Pae, Khon Kaen, Maha Sarakham, Kalasin, Sakon Nakhon, Nakhon Phanom, Ban Phaeng, Seka, So Phisai, Bueng Gan, Nong Khai, Udon Thani, Ban Phaeng, Nakhon Phanom, Mukdahan, Yasothon, Amnat Charoen, Ubon Ratchathani, Khong Chiam, Si Saket, Surin, Buriram, Prakhon Chai, Aranyaphrathet, Sa Kaeo, Chantaburi, Trat, Ban Hat Lek, Chantaburi, Soi Dao, Prachin Buri, Sa Kaeo, Cabin Buri, Chok Chai, Nakhon Ratchasima, Buriram, Maha Sarakham, Mancha Kiri, Khon Kaen, Maha Sarakham, Kalasin, Som Det, Kalasin, Sakon Nakhon, Phong Khon, Udon Thani, Nong Khai, Bueng Gan, Nong Khai, Sang Kham, Pak Chom, Chiang Khan, Loei, Tha Li, Na Haeo, Phitsanulok, Uttaradit, Ban Khok, Na Noi, Nan, Phayao, Chun, Thoeng, Chiang Rai, Phayameng Rai, Phu Chi Fah, Thoeng, Chiang Rai, Phayameng Rai, Chiang Klong, Chiang Rai, Mae Suai, Fang, Chiang Dao, and Chiang Mai.

Due to the pandemic, finding accommodations was challenging. Although I'd been in country for months, locals (not privy to this fact) were afraid of me. I was turned away at numerous hotels. Numerous resorts/hotels were out of business. At the time, others were closed temporarily. I intentionally rode over 4,500 miles to check off a bucket-list item. I experienced heavy rain on most days. I averaged 80 miles per day.

(↑) Ride from Chiang Mai to Nakhon Phanom, Thailand return.

From February 4 to March 5, 2021 at age 59, I rode 1,625 miles from Chiang Mai to Nakhon Phanom roundtrip. I rode alone, except Bueng Gan to Nakhon Phanom return with Kig. I used my Specialized Epic Carbon mountain bike. The trip took 30 days with 19 days of riding. The ride was unsupported.

I completed this ride during the COVID-19 pandemic. I rode a route via Chiang Mai, Lamphun, Lampang, Phrae, Den Chai, Uttaradit, Phitsanulok, Nakhon Thai, Loei, Pak Chom, Nong Khai, Si Kai, Bueng Gan, Pak Khat, Bueng Gan, Seka, Nakatae, Nakhon Phanom, Ban Phaeng, Bueng Gan, Nong Khai, San Kom, Loei, Thai Li, Na Haeo, Dan Sai, Nakorn Thai, Chat Trakan, Phitsanulok, Uttaradit, Phrae, Rong Kwang, Ngao, Phayao, Chiang Rai, Mae Suai, Fang, and Chiang Mai.

Over the course of the ride, I put in six days of running, nine centuries, and a biggest day of 134 miles. This was Kig's first multi-day trip. She rode 300+ miles on my old mountain bike. While riding together, we averaged 65 miles per day. On riding days, including those with Kig, I averaged 86 miles.

(↑) Race the Adirondack 540 in Wilmington, New York.

From September 13 to 14, 2012 at age 51, I raced the Adirondack 540. I added it to my bucket-list due to its RAAM-qualification status. I used my Trek Madone 5.5 road bike. As the name indicates, the race takes place in the Adirondack Mountains in New York State. The Adirondack 540 has 31,000+ feet of climbing in 544 miles. I couldn't assemble a crew in time, so I drove to the race from Maryland alone and competed unsupported. I booked a hotel near the course, so I could visit my room during the four-lap race without losing too much time.

I rode great. The varying terrain and steep climbs required constant shifting. After 365 miles and 20,000 feet of climbing, I broke my rear-derailleur's shift lever. I called the race director John Ceceri. He drove to meet me and tried to help. Although he had a full set of tools, John was unable to fix my shift lever. Without the use of gears, I couldn't ride the climbs. The circumstances dictated that I withdraw.

I returned to the race on September 13, 2013 at age 52. My friends Peter and Nonglak "Oum" Treethummakul crewed for me. I rode my Specialized S-Works Roubaix road bike and won the 544-mile race in 41 hours and 27 minutes. This time I got through the 31,000+ feet of climbing without any mechanical issues. My crew did a remarkable job supporting me.

John Ceceri made the 2014 edition of the Adirondack 540 the race of champions. At age 53 I returned to Wilmington, New York on September 12. I rode my Specialized S-Works Roubaix road bike. Race day brought cold, rain, and fierce winds. I completed the first 272 miles in 17 hours and for most of that was leading the race by a comfortable margin. However, I lost vision in my left eye. I took a break and put in eye drops, but my vision didn't improve. I felt disappointed to drop out of a race that I was winning. I couldn't see. There was no choice. I didn't finish.

(↑) Race the Florida Cycling Challenge in Daytona Beach, Florida.

On November 11, 2012 at age 51, I raced in the Florida Cycling Challenge. I added it to my bucket-list due to its RAAM-qualification status. I raced on my Trek Madone 5.5 road bike. Although frequently lost, I completed the race in 27:39:00 and finished 5th. It was only the second bike raced that I ever entered.

(↑) Race in the Doi Inthanon Climb in Chiang Mai, Thailand.

On February 3, 2013 at age 51, I raced the Doi Inthanon Climb over a distance of 30.1 miles. I used my Trek Madone 5.5 road bike. I climbed 7,720 feet to complete the race in 3:08:00. I finished 53rd out of 700. The 8,415-foot high Doi Inthanon, which is the highest mountain in Thailand, is considered one of the hardest climbs in Asia. By some sources, it ranks in the top-100 hardest climbs in the world. The climb via Route 1009 gains almost one and a half vertical miles. Near the finish the road pitches to 23%. There are long sections with gradients over 17%. Many riders end up walking. It's the only bicycle race I rode which wasn't an individual time trial. This race allowed drafting.

(↑) Race in the Race across America (RAAM) from Oceanside, California to Annapolis, Maryland.

From June 12 to June 23, 2013 at age 51, I rode 2,962 miles from Oceanside to Annapolis. I used my Trek Madone 5.5 and Specialized S-Works Roubaix road bikes. I climbed 160,000+ feet and completed the ride in 12 days, 1 hour, and 57 minutes. I finished unofficially in 23rd, as I missed the 12-day cutoff. My crew consisted of a group of five great friends.

Riders encounter extreme heat in the desert with temperatures in the shade exceeding 120°F. I developed hot spots on my feet. The absurdly high temperatures in the desert caused swelling. A crumbling section of road in California being readied for repaving was responsible for the start of my bloody saddle sores. They bled all the way to Annapolis. The roof of my mouth sunburned. Due to low humidity, I suffered bloody noses. My knees ached. Whenever we stopped, I iced. One time everyone fell asleep while I was icing. I woke up with frozen knees. I worried.

My crew did a remarkable job. Sleep deprivation pushed us to our limits. Several storms battered us, where I wasn't able to ride due to nearby lightning strikes, gale-force winds, and flooding. Throughout the race, my crew remained in close contact with race headquarters. My team told me that I was going to finish on time. When I crossed the line in Annapolis, they exclaimed: "You finished RAAM, Ray!" Those words were music to my ears. My crew was so proud of me and vice versa. Team Greenlaw finished RAAM. We were in the house in the nick of time.

Although exhausted beyond human limits, we felt satisfied. We did it. We made it. We achieved our goal. In order to surmount all obstacles, we'd slept little for 12 days. Relieved, every-one hugged and backslapped. We were giddy. Shortly thereafter, a race director approached me. I awaited his congratulations. I smiled. He told me I hadn't finished. I didn't ask why. My crew had convinced me that I was an official finisher. We were all heartbroken.

I gave everything to the race. Although I wanted to be an official finisher, I had to be satisfied with my maximum-effort performance. I felt bad for my crew; they felt bad for me. No one who races RAAM wants to be given anything, ever. It's a cruel event. The racers are the strongest, toughest, and most dedicated people whom I've met. The race is legendary, as are its stories of human endurance, commitment, and suffering.

More details about the race can be found in my RAAM 2013 blog, which is linked off my website.

On June 11, 2014 at age 52, I returned to race RAAM a second time. The course was longer at 3,020 miles. I used my Specialized S-Works Roubaix road bike and Specialized Shiv time-trial bike. I completed the route with 160,000+ feet of climbing in 11 days, 22 hours, and 45 minutes. I finished 23rd.

After my experience at RAAM in 2013, few people thought I would return a year later. Costing me about $50,000 to participate, the expense was a financial burden. I didn't want to trouble my crew again, as they already had made great sacrifices. They pushed beyond their limits in 2013. I never wanted them to dig that deep again. My bike mechanic and friend Brad "Wrench" Phillips, my crew chief Peter, my dear friend Oum, and Andy returned for a second attempt with me at RAAM. They wouldn't have missed this opportunity for anything. They went all in and wanted me to become an official finisher. I added many other friends to my crew as well.

On the last day in Maryland, I had no time to spare. When I got two flat tires, my dream faded. I was terribly exhausted, and I needed a rest, as did my crew. At the final checkpoint, I told the crew that I needed to sleep a couple hours. I had been weaving all over the road. After what seemed like only 15 minutes, they woke me up and assured me I'd been down for two hours. I carried on like a zombie and made it to the finish line with just over an hour to spare. This time I thought that I'd finished officially, and I had.

I owe a great debt of gratitude to my crew, especially those team members who came back a second time and believed in me. Everyone did a remarkable job. A few years later I was told that I'd slept for only 15 minutes at the last RAAM checkpoint. When I learned this fact, I shook my head. If the team had allowed me the sleep that I craved, I would have missed the cutoff. Their white lie kept me in the game. It was an incredible team effort. I thanked my crew member for revealing this secret. We laughed.

When I meet people in bicycle shops and other cyclists around the world, they tell me excitedly: "I never thought that I'd meet a RAAM finisher." I'm one of about 40 men over age 50 to complete RAAM in under 12 days. I have scars on my ass, numbness in my hands, and nerve damage in my feet to remind me. The experience and what I gained from RAAM is far more important than what I lost. I don't ever plan on doing anything as hard as RAAM again. It was almost a bridge too far. I suppose that's the point.

More details about the race can be found in my RAAM 2014 blog, which is linked off my website.

(↑) Race the World Time Trial Championships in Borrego Springs, California.

On November 5, 2016 at age 55, I raced the World Time Trial Championships. I rode my Specialized Shiv time-trial bike. I completed 117.6 miles in 6 hours. I finished 2nd in my age group and 6th overall.

My race started at noon, and it was hot in the Anza-Borrego Desert. The course consisted of two distinct loops—a hilly loop of 19 miles and a short loop of 4.8 miles. Only full loops, which are completed within six hours, are counted. After four and a half hours, riders move from the big to the small loop. Because of problems with my water-bottle cage, I carried insufficient fluids and became progressively dehydrated.

As I returned for the final time, I heard that there was adequate time to complete another short loop. I pushed hard to make sure my last loop counted. I knew it would. Nearing the finish, the 24-hour world-record holder, five-time RAAM champion, and RAAM course-record holder Christoph Strasser passed me. He was finishing the 24-hour race and had started 18 hours earlier than me!

I couldn't believe how fast Christoph flew by me. The great man averaged 23.5 mph for the entire 24-hour race. I pressed on even harder, inspired by this magnificent athlete. On the last loop, I finished a few seconds behind Christoph and exactly two seconds over the time limit. None of my last 4.8 miles counted. Christoph had motored in and his last lap counted.

Although my final lap wasn't counted, the memory of Strasser flying be me is one that I won't forget. I won't forget the times that he passed me at RAAM either. RAAM riders start at one-minute intervals in decreasing order of their numbers, which are assigned for life.

(↑) Race against Christoph Strasser—the greatest ultra-cyclist of all-time.

I competed against Strasser at RAAM twice (2013 and 2014) and at the World Time Trial Championships in Borrego Springs, California in 2016.

(↑) Be an official finisher in the Race across America (RAAM) from Oceanside, California to Annapolis, Maryland.

❑ Cycle the Green Velo in Poland.

While traveling in Poland, I met a couple who were riding the Green Velo. At that moment I added it to my bucket list. The 1,250+ mile route starts in the north at Elbląg and finishes in Końskie. There are many possible variations of the course to explore.

(↑) In a one-year period ride my bicycle the distance of a circumnavigation of the Earth: 24,800+ miles.

(↑) Visit the Cycling Museum Our Lady of Ghisallo in Magreglio, Italy above Lake Como.

The museum is a shrine that all serious cyclists would love to visit.

(↓) Ride the 370-mile Mae Hong Son loop in Thailand's Chiang Mai and Mae Hong Son provinces in under 24 hours.

This difficult, mountainous ride has many long, steep climbs with grades up to 25%. The loop has 29,000+ feet of climbing. There are more than 50 climbs with gradients over 10%. While training for RAAM, I rode this loop almost weekly. I set off at all times of day—10:00 PM, 5:00 AM, noon, and 4:30 PM—to see if I could complete the entire loop in under 24 hours. Even while in great shape, I couldn't quite make it. Riding unsupported in the middle-of-nowhere with many harassing dogs and descending mountains at high speed in the dark probably wasn't smart.

I reluctantly gave up this bucket-list item. If I couldn't do it back then, I can't realistically ever do.

❏ Cycle from northern Alaska to Punta Arenas, Chile.

(↑) Complete RAMROD (Ride around Mount Rainier in One Day) in Washington State.

I completed one of the first editions of this event back in the 1980s. It's a 154-mile ride with about 10,000 feet of climbing around beautiful Mount Rainier. I finished RAMROD in just over eight hours. I'm lucky to have survived some of the descents that I raced down. Several times I lost control and almost flew off road into trees. Some fellow riders did crash and were taken away in ambulances.

(↑) Own a Specialized S-Works Roubaix with Dura-Ace components.

❑ Everest on a bicycle.

To Everest on a bicycle means to complete a one-day ride having 29,032+ feet of elevation gain—the height of Mount Everest. I may have done this on the Mae Hong Son loop, but I need to verify the elevation gain. In setting the Everesting FKT, a rider repeated the same hill 76 times and covered a distance of just 78 miles, whereas the Mae Hong is 370 miles. When I attempt to Everest, I'll find an appropriate hill to repeat.

(↑) Ride from Claremont, California to the ski lifts at Mount Baldy return.

While attending Pomona College from 1979-83, I did this beautiful ride frequently.

❑ Serve as a volunteer at the Race across America.

I would like to give something back to the Race across America and the amazing riders who take on this extreme challenge.

(↑) Complete a ride over 4,500 miles.

❏ Cycle across Africa from south to north, or vice versa.

I would take a route between Cairo, Egypt to Cape Town, South Africa.

(↑) Win a bike race.

I won the Adirondack 540 in Wilmington, New York.

❏ Cycle the 2,696-mile long Great Divide Mountain Bike Route.

(↑) Ride 1,000+ centuries.

As of this writing, I rode 1,181 centuries. A *century* is a 100-mile ride. Many of these rides were farther than 100 miles.

❏ Ride the Milan San Remo Gran Fondo in Italy.

The Milan San Remo bicycle race is the first of five monuments in the professional-cycling season. The monuments are the five oldest, most prestigious, one-day, cycling races in the world. The day before the professional race, amateur riders can ride the same 180-mile route.

❏ Spectate the Milan San Remo bicycle race in Italy.

(↑) Ride my bicycle 200 miles (a double century) in one day.

(↑) Ride 50+ double centuries.

As of this writing, I rode 57 double centuries.

❏ Ride the Tour of Flanders Gran Fondo in Belgium.

The Tour of Flanders bicycle race is the second of the monuments. The day before the professional race, amateur riders can ride the same 142-mile course.

❏ Spectate the Tour of Flanders bicycle race in Belgium.

(↑) Ride my bicycle 300 miles (a triple century) in one day.

❏ Do a double climb up Doi Inthanon in Thailand.

I haven't attempted it yet.

❏ Ride a triple Samoeng Loop in Chiang Mai, Thailand.

The Samoeng Loop, as I ride it from downtown Chiang Mai and back, is 56 miles in length. It's a classic ride in northern Thailand. I rode this loop frequently in training. The route has 5,000 feet of climbing with the steepest gradients around 17%. My best time for this ride is three hours and 45 minutes, but with traffic slowing you down, it isn't fair to compare two different rides. One day I thought: "Why not do a triple Samoeng?" I skipped right over the idea of doing a double.

When I started out, I completed the first loop easily. I completed the second loop without too much trouble either. I had the legs for a third loop, but my motivation failed me. I packed it in after two loops and eight hours of riding. I don't know if anyone has ever done a triple Samoeng Loop. I'm not sure that I ever will.

(↑) Ride 10+ triple centuries in one day.

As of this writing, I rode 12 triple centuries.

❑ Spectate the week-long World Cycling Championships.

(↑) Ride my bicycle 350 miles (a triple century and a half) in one day.

❑ Complete the Taiwan KOM Challenge.

Chapter 35
Scuba Diving

In this chapter I list bucket-list items related to scuba diving and snorkeling. I should point out that *Scuba* stands for Self-Contained Underwater Breathing Apparatus. *PADI* stands for the Professional Association of Diving Instructors; *NAUI* stands for the National Association of Underwater Instructors; *SSI* stands for Scuba Schools International. *BCD* stands for buoyancy control device. I make use of these diving acronyms here.

I completed my first-ever dive from a beach entry in Rhode Island. My brother Rob dressed me in a BCD and weight belt. While handing me a regulator, he said: "Here, breathe normally through this." Of course at that time, I didn't know what a regulator was. I followed his instruction. There was only one. It was a solo dive. We only had one set of gear. Luckily I survived. My friend Paul added organized scuba diving to my bucket list. I was certified in beautiful Turks and Caicos. Check. The PADI course focused on safe diving. When I dove "with" my brother, I never realized all the things that could go wrong. As of this writing, I logged 338 dives.

I dove in many different conditions: cold water, low visibility, strong currents, rough seas, and so forth. Repeated checks. I dove with many different divers from all over the world, having a wide range of experience. Check. I dove/snorkeled with many different creatures, including sharks on feeding dives at Stuart's Cove in the Bahamas, manta rays in Yap, thresher sharks in the Philippines, whale sharks in Thailand, seals and marine iguanas in the Galapagos, giant clams in Australia's Great Barrier Reef, and big sharks in the Gulf Stream. Checks. I dove with all sorts of different entries from jumping off rocks on Bonaire's shore to squeezing into caves and cenotes in Mexico to rolling out of bamboo-made catamarans in the Philippines to swimming through cracks leading to springs in Florida. Checks.

I dove at all hours of the day and night. I dove on a wide variety of dive sites. I dove fresh-water lakes. Checks. I dove on and penetrated many wrecks, including commercial aircraft, fighter planes, warships, helicopters, submarines, cargo ships, pirate ships, ancient sailing vessels, ferries, and scuttled ships. Checks. I dove many sites that are considered to be in the top-ten dive sites in the world, places such as the Blue Corner in Palau, the Great Blue Hole in Belize, and Richelieu Rock in the Andaman Sea. Checks. My Mount Everest of diving is Chuuk Lagoon. Check. The deepest I dove is 185 feet.

My friend Paul and I completed many diving certifications together. Checks. The majority of courses were taken in remote, exotic diving locations. Most scuba certifications involve course work, land-based training, and diving. Some require a completion of a certain number of dives before attaining a given level. Less-involved courses can sometimes be completed in a day. Others may require weeks.

A good diver learns new tricks of the trade constantly. Equipment and techniques evolve. It's important to remain current. I dive on a regular basis. I start off by providing a list of my diving certifications. Following this I provide a list of my diving/snorkeling locations. Many of these are remote, and they involve extensive travel to get there, for example, Reunion Island, Micronesia, Vanuatu, and the Maldives.

When I review the list of sites, I see that I spent about two full years of my life on diving trips, meaning 730 days. In other words for someone to follow in my footsteps and visit all these locations, if they were dedicated full-time to this pursuit, they would require two entire years. If it weren't for diving I probably wouldn't have checked some of these destinations off my bucket list. Diving opened up many new adventures and opportunities.

My bucket-list items for scuba-diving certifications follow.

(↑) Become certified as a PADI Dive Instructor.

My friend Paul and I completed this course together in Phuket, Thailand.

(↑) Become certified as a PADI Specialist Instructor (SI) as an Oxygen Provider.

(↑) Become certified as a PADI SI for Project Aware.

(↑) Become certified as a PADI SI for Project Aware: Coral Reef.

(↑) Become certified as a PADI SI for Peak Performance Buoyancy.

(↑) Become certified as a PADI SI for Nitrox.

(↑) Become certified as an Emergency First Responder.

(↑) Become certified as an Instructor for Emergency First Responder.

(↑) Become certified as a NAUI Dive Master.

My friend Paul and I completed this course together with our instructor Jeff Toorish in Palau, Micronesia.

(↑) Become certified as an SSI Master Diver.

I completed all my SSI courses with Paul, having Jeff Toorish as an instructor.

(↑) Become certified as an SSI Rescue Diver.

(↑) Become certified as an SSI Advanced Open Water Diver.

(↑) Become certified as an SSI Deep Diver.

(↑) Become certified in SSI Underwater Navigation.

(↑) Become certified as an SSI Nitrox Diver.

(↑) Become certified as an SSI Underwater Photographer.

(↑) Become certified as a PADI Wreck Diver.

I enjoy diving on and learning about the history of wrecks. I took this course in Truk Lagoon, Micronesia with my friend Patrick Carroll and our instructor Dar.

(↑) Become certified as a PADI Open Water Diver.

The list of certifications shows that I'm a NAUI Dive Master but became a PADI Dive Instructor. The conversion from the NAUI to the PADI system was a real challenge. I learned the SSI, NAUI, and PADI systems, which gives me a greater depth of knowledge. However, I had to fill in many gaps along the way, as the systems don't follow the same methods and styles. This path was challenging, especially because I never worked as a dive professional.

In what follows I organized my diving and snorkeling locations alphabetically by continent. In most of these places, I visited numerous locations and dive sites. When diving with others, they often added new sites to my bucket list. I checked all these places off my bucket list.

(↑) Dive and snorkel in Africa:

I went to the following locations:
- Egypt (Sharm El Sheik)
- Reunion Island
- South Africa

(↑) Dive and snorkel in Asia:

I went to the following locations:
- Bahrain
- Georgia
- Indonesia (Bali)
- Kazakhstan
- Kyrgyzstan
- Maldives
- Oman
- Philippines (Bohol, Boracay, Cebu, Dukit, Gato, Leyte, Malapapsuca, Negros, Palawan, Panglao, Siquijor, and Tubbatha)
- Sri Lanka
- Thailand (Koh Bayu, Koh Bon, Koh Chang, Koh Ha, Koh Hin Pousar, Koh Kai, Koh Klang, Koh Lanta, Koh Miang, Koh Nang Yuan, Koh Payu, Koh Ri, Koh Samui, Koh Similian, Koh Surin Nuea, Koh Surin Tai, Koh Tao,

Koh Tachai, Krabi, Phuket, Similian Islands, and Surin Islands)
- Turkmenistan

(↑) Dive and snorkel in Europe:

I went to the following locations:
- Croatia
- Cyprus
- Greece
- Italy
- Romania
- Switzerland

(↑) Dive and snorkel in North America:

I went to the following locations:
- Antigua and Barbuda
- Bahamas (Freeport and Nassau)
- Barbados
- Belize
- Bermuda
- California
- Dominican Republic
- Florida (Boynton Beach, Ginny Springs, many locations in the Keys, and West Palm)
- Grand Cayman
- Grenada
- Hawaii (Kauai and Oahu)
- Jamaica
- Maine
- Maryland
- Massachusetts
- Mexico (Baja, Cancun, Cozumel, Pinto Point, and Yucatan)

- New Hampshire
- North Carolina
- Oregon
- Rhode Island
- St. Lucia
- St. Maarten
- St. Thomas
- Saint Vincent and the Grenadines
- South Carolina
- Tobago
- Turks and Caicos
- US Virgin Islands
- Virginia
- Washington

(↑) Dive and snorkel in Oceania:

I went to the following locations:
- Australia (Great Barrier Reef)
- Chuuk (see Truk below)
- Cook Islands
- Federated States of Micronesia
- Fiji
- Guam
- New Caledonia
- New Zealand
- Palau
- Truk/Chuuk: engine-room penetrations on the Heian Maru, Kensho Maru, Nippo Maru, Shinkoku Maru, and Yamagiri Maru. San Francisco Maru.
- Vanuatu
- West Carolines
- Yap

(↑) Dive and snorkel in South America:

I went to the following locations:
- Aruba
- Bonaire
- Brazil
- Columbia
- Galapagos

(↑) Dive on a sunken U-boat.

❏ Dive Ningaloo Reef in Western Australia.

(↑) While there were still 8,000,000 jellyfish, snorkel in Jellyfish Lake in Palau.

The experience at Jellyfish Lake was so awesome that my friend Paul and I snorkeled there twice.

❏ Dive the SS President Coolidge wreck off the coast of the island Espiritu Santo in Vanuatu.

When in Vanuatu, I added the SS President Coolidge dive to my bucket list. The steamship is huge, having many different dive sites. Even from Efate though, it's not cheap to reach the Coolidge.

(↑) Dive in Ginny Springs, Florida.

Ginny Springs is world-renowned for its crystal-clear water and caves. I enjoy entering dive sites from the surface: small fissures, holes, and the like.

❏ Average at least one dive per month until I'm 75 years old.

(↑) Dive the cenotes in the Yucatán Peninsula of Mexico.

I made numerous diving trips to the cenotes with my friend Paul. They're peaceful and beautiful. They offer a wide range of diving experiences.

❏ Dive on a one-week long live-aboard trip to the Solomon Islands.

(↑) Dive and snorkel with whale sharks in the wild.

❏ Go ice diving.

(↑) Dive in the Black Sea.

❏ Become a certified cavern diver.

I dove in many caverns and some caves. I should obtain this certification.

❏ Dive Lake Baikal in Russia.

(↑) Dive with thresher sharks.

❏ Scuba dive the Atlanta Aquarium.

While visiting the Atlanta Aquarium, I added this item to my bucket list.

(↑) While diving, penetrate into a helicopter wreck.

Helicopters are small and contain many sharp objects, so great care must be exercised.

❏ Dive on a giant head at Easter Island far off the coast of Chile.

(↑) Dive in the Red Sea.

❏ Dive on a live-aboard trip for a week in Myanmar.

(↑) Dive the Great Barrier Reef in Australia.

❏ Dive with hammerhead sharks.

(↑) While diving, penetrate into an airplane wreck.

❏ Accumulate 500 scuba dives.

(↑) Dive in a quarry.

❏ Dive in Mozambique.

(↑) Dive with giant manta rays.

Chapter 36
Mountaineering

When I was 14, in an effort to meet girls, my friend Peter and I joined a religious youth group on their trip to climb Mount Monadnock in New Hampshire. I didn't fall in love with a girl, but I did fall in love with mountains. After that experience I began climbing in the White Mountains of New Hampshire. I feel at home and at peace in mountains. When I possessed the financial resources to travel freely, I started climbing bigger mountains. I traveled around the world to climb high peaks. I did many climbs in the Swiss and Italian Alps, often with my friend Paul. I became a decent climber, honing my skills on steep, snowy slopes and icy glaciers.

I climbed about 1,500 mountains across seven continents. Examples are Pico de Orizaba in Mexico, the Matterhorn on the border of Switzerland and Italy, Mount Olympus in Greece, and Mount Rainier in Washington State. I climbed the highest mountain in many countries and US states. In the adventure chapter, I listed my goal of climbing the seven summits. I start here with those six peaks and continue with other mountaineering bucket-list items.

(↑) Climb the highest mountain in Europe.

I climbed Mount Elbrus at 18,481 feet with my friend Paul on July 24, 2001.

(↑) Climb the highest mountain in South America.

I climbed Aconcagua at 22,840 feet on July 9, 2002.

(↑) Climb the highest mountain in Africa.

I climbed Mount Kilimanjaro at 19,339 feet on August 3, 2002.

(↑) Climb the highest mountain in Australia.

I climbed Mount Kosciusko at 7,310 feet with the **Göransson** family on March 17, 2003.

(↑) Climb the highest mountain in Antarctica.

I climbed Vinson Massif at 16,067 feet with Peter and Paul **Göransson and John Rust** on January 10, 2005.

(↑) Climb the highest mountain in North America.

I climbed Mount McKinley at 20,320 feet with Rainier Mountain Guides on May 26, 2009.

❑ Go to Mount Everest base camp.

Even if I never climb Mount Everest, I want to visit its base camp.

(↑) Get a view of Mount Everest.

On one of my trips to Nepal, I got a look at Mount Everest.

(↑) At midsummer's night take a snowmobile to the top of the glacier Snæfellsjökull in Iceland.

In the Jules Verne's novel *A Journey to the Center of the Earth*, Snæfellsjökull is the location where the group began their journey.

❑ Climb Peak Lenin in the Gorno-Badakhshan Autonomous Region on the border of Kyrgyzstan and Tajikistan in Central Asia.

On a trip to Central Asia, when I saw Peak Lenin, I added it to my bucket list. The summit is 23,406 feet high. Although the climb isn't technical on the normal route, the altitude and weather are significant obstacles to overcome to reach the summit.

(↑) Watch the sunrise from the top of Mount Sinai in Egypt.

❑ Continue to climb mountains in my 70s and 80s.

(↓) Climb Nanga Parbat in Pakistan.

Ever since I read Hermann Buhl's account—*Nanga Parbat Pilgrimage: The Lonely Challenge*—of his first ascent of this 26,660-foot peak, this Himalayan mountain fascinated me. It's one of the hardest to climb in the world and many have died trying. I never reached the level of mountaineering required to think seriously about going to Nanga Parbat. It's in an extremely remote part of Pakistan. There was a massacre at the Nanga Parbat base camp in 2013, when Taliban militants murdered ten climbers and a local guide. If the climbing community feels the area is safe, I would like to go to Nanga Parbat base camp.

(↑) Run non-stop to the top of Mount Si, which is located near North Bend, Washington.

Back in 1980s, Mt. Si wasn't crowded. I often did summit runs while encountering only a couple hikers. The vertical gain is 3,200 feet. My fastest time was well under an hour for the 7.5 miles to the base of Haystack, located just below the 4,167-foot summit.

(↑) Climb the highest peak in Mexico.

I summited Pico de Orizaba with my friend Paul and Oso (bear in Spanish), our Mexican guide. Orizaba is the third highest mountain in North American with an altitude of 18,491 feet.

❑ Climb an 8,000-meter peak.

Eight-thousand meters is 26,247 feet. This elevation is termed the "Death Zone," as there's insufficient oxygen to sustain human life. There are 14 peaks over 8,000 meters high in the world. Cho Oyo (6th highest mountain in the world) on the Tibetan/Nepalese border and Broad Peak (12th highest) in Karakoram region of Pakistan are considered two of the safer and easier ones. Both are difficult climbs.

(↑) Climb the 14,690-foot high Matterhorn on the border of Switzerland and Italy.

From the moment I set eyes on the Matterhorn, I added it to my bucket list. My friend Paul and I both summited. A rock avalanche fell 75 feet away from me and almost ended my life.

❑ Climb the six highest peaks in Mexico.

I climbed Orizaba (number 1) at an elevation 18,491 feet, Nevado de Toluca (4) at 15,354 feet, and La Malinche (6) at 14,501 feet. I attempted Iztaccíhuatl (3) at 17,126 feet, but without proper acclimatized, I failed. I descended from 15,500 feet. I went from sea-level to this elevation in a single day. I haven't gone to Sierra Negra (5) at 15,026 feet. It's forbidden to climb Popocatépetl (2) at 18,045 feet because the mountain is an active volcano. So I may never get to check this box.

(↑) Climb the 9,573-foot high Mount Olympus in the northeast of Greece.

I free-climbed Mount Olympus with Constanza Ceruti.

❑ Climb the 20,564-foot high volcano Chimborazo in Ecuador.

(↑) Climb the 14,410-foot high Mount Rainier in Washington State.

Having attended graduate school in Seattle, I looked at Mount Rainier often. I added it to my bucket list. The snow-capped peak fascinated me. I climbed it 20 years after I graduated from the UW.

(↑) Climb the 6,288-foot high Mount Washington in northern New Hampshire in the middle of winter.

On a day with wind chills touching −65°F, my friend Paul and I reached the summit of Mount Washington. We didn't see anyone else on the mountain. We'd climbed the mountain together previously, so despite the extreme conditions, we felt reasonably safe. About 150 people have died on Mount Washington.

❑ Climb the 19,347-foot high volcano Cotopaxi in Ecuador.

(↑) Complete a non-stop run up the 5,633-foot high Granite Mountain in Washington State.

When I lived in Seattle, I climbed Granite Mountain throughout the year. It has a 3,800-foot vertical gain. On winter ascents there's a high danger of avalanches.

❏ Climb the ten highest mountains in Thailand.

This bucket-list item is described further in the Thailand's mountains chapter.

Chapter 37
Hiking

I always enjoy walking in a forest, through the mountains, alongside a river, or on a seashore. I even enjoy walking around town. I haven't owned a vehicle for many years. I took countless day hikes all over the world, and many shorter backpacking/day trips, especially in the states where I lived: Rhode Island, California, Washington, New Hampshire, Georgia, and Maryland. These states border 17 different ones and two countries. I had easy access to 23 states, Mexico, and Canada. When I met other hikers, they added items to my bucket list.

(↑) Thru-hike the Appalachian Trail (AT).

Distance: 2,169 miles
Dates: May 11 to August 16, 1995 (97 days)

I hiked the AT with my friend Peter whose trail-name is Fish-out-of-Water, or Fish for short. We flew to Atlanta together. For many years I'd been trail running along the AT in Maine, Vermont, and New Hampshire. While I was living in New Hampshire, each fall season in spectacular New England foliage, I would meet northbound thru-hikers on their way to the northern terminus of the AT—the majestic Mount Katahdin. They all had a certain glint in their eyes. They were all hungry. Other than sore feet, their stress levels were down, and they seemed genuinely happy. They would be finishing their thru-hikes soon.

The northbound hikers whom I met seemed fulfilled, and most were in great shape. They possessed a sense of achievement and exuded confidence. Some hikers said: "Once you complete the AT, you can do anything." Many believe this statement to be true. The hikers who weren't enjoying their hikes dropped out before reaching Vermont. My hiker conversations reached a tipping point, where I wanted to do what the thru-hikers were doing and get that glint in my eyes. I added the AT to my bucket list. My typical nine-month contract allowed me 90 days off during the summer. In this case I stretched it to 100.

The southbound thru-hikers whom I met in late spring and early summer didn't convince me to hike the AT. They were in rough shape from hiking through a swampy Maine, starting out with too heavy a pack, enduring terrible biting flies and mosquitoes, and lacking the fitness for the steep, rocky climbs. I guess most of those folks didn't make it to Springer Mountain. I'm sure the successful hikers who were entering Georgia, while hiking from Maine, possessed a wonderful glint in their eyes.

Fish and I went northbound. We reached an important milestone after a few weeks, when we threw away our return airplane tickets to save weight. Back then, it was cheaper to purchase a round-trip fare. Shredding those tickets showed commitment and confidence. A few weeks later I sustained a serious ankle injury. I took a number of rest days, and Fish reluctantly forged ahead. With trepidation, I started hiking again. I pushed through my pain and hiked the remainder of the trail solo.

I hiked the trail pure, meaning that I covered the entire white-blazed, designated AT without deviation.

This meant if I got lost and missed a section of trail, I returned to where I unintentionally had deviated. I took seven rest days, mostly related to my bad ankle. Fish completed his thru-hike as well. Although my injury forced us to split up, we both found ways to see our dreams through to the end. That ability to adapt helped me to complete many activities on my bucket list. After our thru-hikes, Fish and I got together to celebrate our successes and share trail stories. Whenever we meet, we reminisce about the good old days on the AT.

My biggest day on the AT was 45 miles. On hiking days I averaged 24.1. In memory of my hike on a sidewalk in the small town of Damascus, Virginia, there's a decorated brick with my trail-name Wall painted on it. During my ride of the Trans America Trail, I visited my brick. Fond memories came flooding back. The brick empowered me for the remainder of my bicycle ride across America.

❑ Walk across Africa.

This hike would either be from east to west: from Zanzibar Island off the coast of Tanzania to Walvis Bay, Namibia, or from north to south from Cairo, Egypt to Cape Town, South Africa. I hope to talk one of my hiking buddies into joining me.

(↑) Thru-hike the Pacific Crest Trail (PCT) in a FKT.

Distance: 2,659 miles
Dates: May 12 to August 2, 2003 (83 days)

Due to work constraints, I drew up an ambitious schedule to hike the PCT in 88 days. I ran my draft by my friend Fiddlehead because he's an expert on the PCT. My schedule was two days shy of the world record for the fastest hike of the PCT (the Fastest Known Time, FKT), so Fiddlehead suggested that I try and set the FKT. I took his suggestion and added this goal to my bucket list. I sat down with my Excel Spreadsheet again. In 45 minutes I trimmed three days.

I ended up setting the FKT by an additional two days. Most of the time I walked alone. I went northbound. I hiked the trail pure without any navigational aids. Fish joined me for about ten days in California, and my friend Paul hiked with me for the final week in Washington State. He was inspired and added the PCT to his bucket list. While I'm writing this, at age 67 Paul (whose trail-name is Tarman—total-ankle replacement man) just finished his section hike of the PCT. He also thru-hiked the AT.

My book *The Pacific Crest Trail: Its Fastest Hike* describes my hike. Setting the FKT for the PCT required a great commitment and a huge physical effort. I took risks. My record has long since been broken and conditions have changed. The PCT became a popular trail. Many hikers rely on software applications (such as Guthook Guides) and GPS units. This makes hiking safer and simpler. When I hiked the trail, such tools weren't available. Fiddlehead told me: "Just follow footsteps in the sand." We laugh about that now but in the deserts of California, I wasn't laughing.

My biggest day was 48 miles. My biggest week was 325 miles. I averaged 32+ miles of trail per day. I often needed to walk long distances off trail and back for resupplies. I got lost many times, as the trail wasn't as well marked or worn, as it is now. The PCT taught me many lessons. It was far more remote and much higher than the AT.

❏ Thru-hike the Pacific Northwest Trail.

(↑) Take a backpacking trip in Torres del Paine National Park in Chile's Patagonia region.

❏ Thru-hike the Arizona Trail.

(↑) Thru-hike the Continental Divide Trail (CDT) in 100 days or less.

Distance: 2,800 miles
Dates: April 25 to August 2, 2015 (100 days)

I went northbound from the Mexican border, following the Ley Route. My friend Shagg hiked with me for the first week. We only saw a couple of other hikers. After Shagg departed, I continued alone. I missed him. When I arrived near the Colorado border, due to avalanche danger and flooding, many sections of the CDT were closed. I learned about which ones from Fish. Groups of strong hikers were forced to retreat after attempting to push north of the New Mexico-Colorado border. I altered my plans.

    I drove north to South Pass City, Wyoming. I walked south for two weeks across the windy Great Basin. Then I drove back to the point where I'd left off near Chama, New Mexico. Due to trail closures and high snow levels, I did a lot of road walking in Colorado. When I reached the Colorado-Wyoming border again, because eight feet of snow had melted, I didn't recognize the area. From there I drove past the southern Wyoming section that I'd hiked already. From where I'd gone south at South Pass City a month earlier, I went north toward the border with Canada.

    Because the vast majority of thru-hikers traveled to the US-Canadian border from the New Mexico-Colorado border to avoid the Colorado snow, I went weeks without seeing anybody. I was probably the only thru-hiker that year who went north for the bulk of the trail. Once through part of Montana, I began encountering old friends. They were heading south. We greeted each other by trail-name but with some uncertainty, as our appearances and dispositions had changed significantly in a matter of weeks. We shared stories and helpful information. I walked around several large fires in Montana.

For the most part, I followed the Bear Creek Route, except where there were trail closures. I relied on road-atlas maps, the Ley maps, the Guthook Guides, Yogi's book, and my GPS. On many days I didn't encounter any other hikers. My friend Marjorie sent me a handful of mail drops. Whenever I received a package, it was very meaningful. I completed a continuous north-bound walk, except for the two weeks where I went south. The entire route was an uninterrupted, continuous, border-to-border hike.

Completing the CDT meant finishing the Triple Crown of hiking. Check. At that time less than 200 hikers claimed to be Triple Crowners. The trail itself was cold, hot, high, snowy, dry, remote, poorly marked, beautiful, difficult, peaceful, full of wildlife, and spectacular. The CDT taught me many lessons. It was more difficult than the AT or PCT. I would love to hike the CDT again. It stimulates personal growth. It's by far my favorite trail, as Fiddlehead had told me it would be.

My biggest day was 40 miles. I averaged 28 miles per day. I think of the CDT daily.

(↑) Hike in Africa and climb Mount Kilimanjaro.

(↑) Hike in the Snowy Mountains of Australia.

❑ Thru-hike the Ice Age Trail in Wisconsin.

(↑) Go trekking in Nepal.

(↑) Thru-hike the Via Dinarica White Trail (VDWT).

Distance: 780 miles
Dates: July 4 to August 24, 2017 (52 days)

Fiddlehead and I completed one of the first thru-hikes of the GPS route for this (at the time) new trail through Slovenia, Croatia, Bosnia-Herzegovina, Montenegro, and Albania. There were many places where it appeared as if no one had ever hiked the route, even though we were on a published GPS track. The route seemed designed by someone sitting in an office. We were lost frequently and bushwhacked through exceptionally rugged terrain, where there was no trail. When frustrated, we often said: "The Via Dinarica, it's not for everybody."

We hiked past mine fields. When off trail bushwhacking, we would say: "You go first." The other would reply: "Naw, you go ahead." The challenges of being on foreign soil, being unable to speak Russian and local languages, and crossing borders in places without official crossings made this hike a rewarding adventure. The route has since been extended, hopefully via a real trail. I'm sure this beautiful trail will develop and become better marked over time. Through our blogging, documentation, and discussions with others, I hope we made it easier and safer for hikers to complete the trail.

Our hike was prior to the route being extended into Kosovo. We hiked the trail in the middle of summer. Finding water is a serious problem in the karst. We relied on cisterns. I hope as the trail develops that these cisterns will become more obvious and available to hikers. Our biggest day was 25 miles. We took a number of rest days. I was terribly sick with vomiting and diarrhea for five days. We averaged 20 miles per day on the days that we hiked.

(↑) Hike on the island of Vanuatu.

(↑) Hike through the Okefenokee Swamp on the border with Georgia and Florida.

❑ Hike the Annapurna Circuit.

(↑) Hike in the area around Uluru (Ayers Rock) in Australia.

(↑) Take a multi-week expedition to Vinson Massif in Antarctica.

(↑) Take a multi-week trip into the Andes Mountains in Argentina.

❑ Hike across Mongolia.

(↑) Hike in Hawaii, including Waimea Canyon.

(↑) Hike around Iceland.

(↑) Hike in the Caucasus Mountains in Russia.

(↑) Thru-hike east to west 725 miles across Thailand in a FKT.

Distance: 725 miles
Dates: March 12 to April 3, 2018 (22 days and 9 hours)

Starting at the PK Riverside Resort, Ubon Ratchathani, I hiked alone from the easternmost point of the mainland of Thailand to its westernmost point, reaching the Salawin River View Point at Mae Sam Laep, Mae Hong Son. My hike got off to a rough start, as I suffered from terrible blisters that plagued me throughout. I completed a hot walk, meaning my hike was done during the hottest months in Thailand. I was fully supported by Kig and her eight-year old daughter Jennie. I only carried snacks and water.

The challenges of this hike are the heat and humidity, its remoteness, the fact that it's on roads, dogs, snakes, insects, traffic, and pollution. My shoes melted along the way, and I acquired new ones at a store in the middle-of-nowhere. The selection for size 12 is limited in Thailand. The hike is detailed in my book *The Fastest Hike across Thailand*. My biggest day was 37 miles, and I averaged 32.4 miles per day. This average is identical to my daily PCT mileage from 15 years earlier.

(↑) Hike in the rugged mountains of Réunion Island, located in the Indian Ocean.

❑ Hike the 335-mile long Lycian Way from Fethiye to Antalya, Turkey.

After I met a Turkish fellow who marked the trail, I added this item to my bucket list.

(↑) Hike on Cable Beach in Australia.

(↑) Hike on Grand Terra in New Caledonia, located in the South Pacific.

(↑) Hike in the Pitons on Saint Lucia, located in the Caribbean.

I traveled to all the countries in the Caribbean and been fortunate to hike in most of them. They have lovely beaches for hiking, as well as some rugged mountains. The views of the sea are amazing.

❑ Hike the traditional El Camino de Santiago in Spain.

Although the reviews are mixed about this hike, I want to experience it for myself.

(↑) Hike in the French, Swiss, and Italian Alps.

I hiked in the Alps and climbed many of the highest peaks there.

❑ Complete a second thru-hike of the Continental Divide Trail.

(↑) Hike in the high mountains of the country of Georgia near the Russian border.

(↑) Section hike the Long Trail in Vermont.

(↑) Hike in the Black Forest in Germany.

❑ Hike the Great Divide Trail between Alberta and British Columbia.

(↑) Hike in the mountains of the Stans.

I hiked in Kazakhstan, Kyrgyzstan, Tajikistan, Turkmenistan, and Uzbekistan.

(↑) Hike in the Zhangjiajie National Forest Park of China.

The grand canyon of China is located in this beautiful park. Parts of the movie Avatar were filmed there. The formations in the mountains are spectacular. Prior to Avatar, the area wasn't crowded.

(↑) Hike across the Grand Canyon in Arizona.

❑ Hike across Mongolia.

(↑) Hike in the jungles of Malaysia.

(↑) Take a one-year backpacking trip around the world.

In 2019 and into 2020, I completed a 53-week, 120,000+ mile trip around-the-world, stopping in and visiting 67 countries and territories. I backpacked through these places. Many of the miles were covered by airplane, going between continents.

(↑) Hike up and around the volcanoes in Bali, Indonesia.

(↑) Hike in the Greek islands.

Part IV
Professional Activities

The final part of the book includes bucket-list items for professional activities. There are chapters on career, computing books, speaking engagements, journal papers, and conference papers.

Chapter 38
Career

I spent the bulk of my career as a professor of computer science and cybersecurity: teaching and conducting research with my students and colleagues, and providing service to my institutions and disciplines. I worked primarily at three institutions: the UNH in Durham, New Hampshire; AASU in Savannah, Georgia; and the USNA in Annapolis, Maryland. I was fortunate to have many outstanding students and colleagues.

I also worked as a visiting professor at the following institutions: the Universitat Politècnica de Catalunya in Barcelona, Spain; the University of Iceland in Reykjavík, Iceland; the University of Tokyo in Tokyo, Japan; the Wilhelm-Schickard-Institut für Informatik, Universität in Tübingen, Germany; the Università degli Studi di Roma La Sapienza in Rome, Italy; Chiang Mai University (CMU) in Chiang Mai, Thailand; and the Management and Science University (USM) in Shah Alam, Malaysia. I visited 85+ universities internationally and double that in the US.

As noted earlier in Part I, I formed two businesses: ABET Consulting Services and Roxy Publishing. I consult with universities and assist them with their accreditation needs, particularly in the areas of computing, engineering, technology, and applied sciences. In computing, I help institutions with cybersecurity, computer science, information technology, information systems, software engineering, and computer engineering. My publishing company publishes books on a wide range of topics.

In this chapter I list general professional goals. In later chapters I discuss publications and speaking engagements.

(↑) Work as a Senior Software Engineer for Paul Allen, co-founder of Microsoft Corporation.

In 1985 I worked as a Senior Software Engineer for Paul Allen at Asymetrix Corporation in Bellevue, Washington. Our team programmed in the alpha release of Microsoft Windows. Paul threw house parties for the company's ten employees. He usually hired a band. Bill Gates frequently attended. Paul spared no expense with food and drinks. RIP, Paul.

(↑) Teach 10+ different subject areas within my discipline.

(↑) Write textbooks for 5+ courses.

(↑) Serve as a consultant to assist universities in developing their computing programs to achieve ABET accreditation.

ABET is the recognized world leader in accrediting computing, technology, engineering, and applied science programs. Through my consulting company, I worked with many colleges and universities to improve their programs to the point where they could seek and attain ABET accreditation.

(↑) Have my textbooks used by students in 150+ universities and colleges.

(↑) Write one of the first textbooks about the Internet and World Wide Web.

(↑) Develop a PhD degree program.

I helped develop and implement the PhD program in computer science at the UNH.

(↑) Develop a Masters degree program.

I helped develop and implement the Masters program in computer science at AASU.

(↑) Develop one of the first fully online undergraduate degrees.

While at AASU in 2003-4, I was part of a team in the University System of Georgia that developed and implemented the first fully online undergraduate program in the State of Georgia—a Bachelor of Science in Information Technology. The program became a model for other institutions and disciplines.

(↑) Help develop, implement, and get accredited the Bachelor of Science in Cyber Operations at the USNA.

I wrote the first draft of the ABET Self-Study for the Bachelor of Science in Cyber Operations and led the accreditation efforts. When I retired from the USNA, Allen Parrish took over my work. The program received one of the country's first ABET cybersecurity accreditations.

(↑) Develop and implement a Bachelor of Science in Information Technology.

I proposed the curriculum for and got approved a Bachelor of Science in Information Technology at AASU. We implemented my curriculum.

(↑) Help develop a regional engineering program.

I was part of the Georgia Tech Regional Engineering Program in Georgia.

(↑) Develop a Bachelor of Science in Cybersecurity.

I developed curriculum for and proposed a Bachelor of Science in Cybersecurity at AASU in 2003. The program was far ahead of its time and misunderstood by administrators. They failed to grasp the importance of cybersecurity. Later this material helped me with the development of the Bachelor of Science in Cyber Operations at the USNA.

(↑) Develop a Bachelor of Science in Gaming.

Along with my colleague Ben Page, I developed curriculum for and proposed a Bachelor of Science in Gaming at AASU in 2003. The program was far ahead of its time and misunderstood by administrators. They failed to grasp the importance of computer gaming.

(↑) Develop a Bachelor of Science and Master of Science in Health Management Information Systems.

I helped develop a proposal and curriculum for a Bachelor of Science and Master of Science in Health Management Information Systems at AASU.

(↑) Develop international exchange programs.

I wanted to create opportunities for my students to study abroad, as well as for international students to study at my university. I created and implemented three international-exchange programs: with the USM in Shah Alam, Malaysia; with the University of Koblenz/Landau in Koblenz, Germany; and with CMU in Chiang Mai, Thailand.

(↑) Bring the Yamacraw Project to AASU.

The year before I was hired at AASU, they failed in an effort to bring the Yamacraw Project—a $100,000,000 technology initiative in the State of Georgia—to campus. As a newbie, I made a bold proposal to the Academic Vice President Frank Butler that I independently write the proposal alone. Frank agreed. My proposal was accepted by the University System of Georgia. I became the Regional Coordinator for the Yamacraw Project. AASU received nearly $3,000,000 of funding through my efforts. After that, Frank and I collaborated on a number of other big initiatives.

(↑) Develop an Associate of Engineering degree.

(↑) Serve as a journal editor.

I served as an editor for several journals.

(↑) Be part of the ABET pilot visits for Information Technology and Cybersecurity.

(↑) Serve as an ABET program evaluator for computer science, information systems, information technology, and cybersecurity.

I'm one of the only (if not the only) person to have gone on visits for ABET for all four of these disciplines—computer science, information systems, information technology, and cybersecurity—demonstrating a wide range of expertise in computing topics and accreditation.

(↑) Supervise masters students.

(↑) Supervise doctoral students.

(↑) Receive $1,000,000+ in grant funding from the National Science Foundation.

(↑) Organize and host a conference.

While at AASU, I proposed, organized, and hosted numerous conferences.

(↑) Develop a computing game show for high-school students.

Through my team at AASU, led by Chris McCarthy, I sponsored a successful Jeopardy-style game show.

(↑) Receive $5,000,000+ in total grant funding from various industry and government sources.

(↑) Develop and run a Distinguished Speaker Series.

While at AASU, I ran a Distinguished Speaker Series for many years. My friend Paul was a regular speaker.

(↑) Serve as an endowed, distinguished professor.

For three years I served as the Leighton Endowed Distinguished Professor of Information Technology at the USNA. It was a true honor to serve at this great institution.

(↑) Obtain early tenure at UNH.

(↑) Serve as a distinguished Chair.

I served for three years as the Office of Naval Research Distinguished Chair in the Center for Cybersecurity Studies at the USNA. It was a true honor to serve three additional years at this great institution.

(↑) Attain the rank of full professor by age 40.

(↑) Serve as a Department Chair and successfully develop a computer-science program.

(↑) Serve as an academic Dean.

I worked as an academic Dean for six years.

(↑) Learn to program in a wide range of programming languages.

I programmed in APL, C, C++, Java, FORTRAN, Pascal, PL1, Lisp, Ada, BASIC, COBOL, Python, parallel versions of some of these, and a variety of other languages (some proprietary).

(↑) Found my own school.

I founded the School of Computing at AASU, where I hired 35+ professors and staff members.

(↑) Mentor faculty.

I wanted to give back to my colleagues. I served as a mentor to 30+ faculty members.

(↑) Win a Fulbright Fellowship.

I won four Fulbrights: Spain, Iceland, Thailand, and Namibia.

(↑) Win a Humboldt Fellowship.

(↑) Win a Sasakawa Fellowship.

(↑) Propose and help lead the development of ABET-accreditation criteria for the discipline of cybersecurity.

(↑) Present 200+ invited lectures throughout the world.

(↑) Perform 12+ ABET site visits.

(↑) Serve on the ABET Executive Committee.

(↑) Serve as Chair of the ABET Training Committee.

(↑) Work for one of the United States service academies.

I worked at the USNA.

(↑) Publish 15+ academic books.

My academic books are described in detail in the chapter on computing books.

(↑) Have my books translated into multiple languages.

(↑) Have my books used at my alma maters.

Both Pomona College, where I was an undergraduate, and the UW, where I was a graduate student, have used my books in courses.

(↑) Have my books used by someone other than myself at the schools at which I taught.

My books were used at the UNH, AASU, the USNA, and CMU. I consider this a great accomplishment and honor.

(↑) Win a Japanese Society for the Promotion of Science Fellowship.

(↑) Work at the University of Tokyo in Tokyo, Japan.

The University of Tokyo is the top-ranked institution in Asia and one of the foremost in the world.

(↑) Become recognized as the world's leading expert on P-completeness theory.

(↑) Publish 100+ academic items: books and research papers.

(↑) Provide scholarships to 200+ students.

Through National Science Foundation grants, my colleagues and I accomplished this bucket-list item. Many of the scholarships covered full tuition for multiple years.

(↑) Sell 25,000+ copies of a book.

My Internet book with Ellen Hepp and published by McGraw-Hill sold well over 25,000 copies.

(↑) Provide service to my institutions at the departmental, college, university, and system levels.

I wanted to thoroughly understand the workings of an institution. As such, I volunteered or was appointed to 60+ different committees in my career. My committee work got me involved in many aspects of the institutions where I worked. This knowledge served me well.

I was able to make contributions in many different areas.

❑ Sell 100,000+ copies of a book.

If I include used copies of my Internet book with Ellen, we probably achieved this total.

(↑) Participate in a successful Southern Accreditation for Colleges and Schools (SACS) reaccreditation.

(↑) Give an invited lecture at Cambridge University.

❑ Give an invited lecture at Oxford University.

Even though Oxford University Press published one of my books, I never had the opportunity to give a talk there.

(↓) Fully retire by age 50.

At age 48 I reduced my work commitment to four months per year. I fully retired at age 54. Although I loved my job and worked with some of the best and most dedicated students in the country at the USNA, I decided that there were many other bucket-list items that I wanted to pursue.[6] I loved working at the Naval Academy and serving my country. It was a difficult decision to retire.

(↑) Participate in successful ABET accreditations.

I wrote numerous Self-Studies for successful ABET accreditations: for computer science, information technology, and cybersecurity.

---

[6] This book provides the evidence.

(↑) Find a good balance and blend among teaching, research, and service throughout my academic career.

(↓) Become a professor emeritus at the USNA.

Although this achievement would have been a great honor, the rules require that someone serve at the Academy for many years before being granted this status.

Chapter 39
Computing Books

I describe bucket-list items pertaining to computing books in this chapter. In many cases I wrote a book for a course I was teaching. I did this for three main reasons: 1) the subject matter was novel and no textbooks existed, 2) I felt that I could improve upon the best existing book, and 3) it forced me to become an expert in the subjects I was teaching. In other cases I wrote books as a service to the computing community. Because of the widespread adoption of my books, I was able to reach more students. I became an authority on many topics and influenced computing education throughout the world.

(↑) Write a research monograph that explains the theory of P-completeness and also categorizes all-known P-complete problems.

With Jim Hoover and Larry Ruzzo, I wrote *Limits to Parallel Computation: P-Completeness Theory*. This research monograph took us ten years to write. It contains a comprehensive catalogue of both old and new problems that are *inherently sequential*, meaning problems that don't benefit significantly from being solved by massively parallel computers. The book describes and advances P-completeness theory itself. We published the book with Oxford University Press.

Our book is regarded as the go-to source for parallel computation. Twenty-five years later, I still receive frequent emails from professors around the world asking for my input on their research in parallel computation. We received many kudos for the book from top computer scientists around the world, including Donald Knuth, Richard Karp, Stephen Cook, David Johnson, Albert Meyer, Juris Hartmanis, Richard Lipton, and so forth.

(↑) Write an introductory textbook for a course on the theory of computation.

Jim Hoover and I enjoyed collaborating on our first book. We decided to work together on a college textbook about computation. We wrote *Fundamentals of the Theory of Computation: Principles and Practice.* Morgan Kaufmann published our book. It has a nice illustration of the traveling-salesman problem on its cover. We took several unique approaches in the book. One such innovation involved introducing undergraduates to the deterministic theory of P-completeness as a lead in to the more abstract theory of NP-completeness.

(↑) Write a textbook about the Internet and World Wide Web (WWW).

I began teaching a new course about the Internet and WWW in 1996. When registration opened, it immediately reached its capacity of 100 students. I developed the course from scratch. The material I taught was cutting edge. It wasn't available in any textbook. There was a need for a textbook for such a course, as student demand was great and few professors had the expertise to develop such a course on their own. Without an available, suitable textbook, some schools couldn't offer a course about the Internet.

I had a clear picture of the book that I wanted to write. Colleagues suggested additional material and topics. Due to the magnitude of the task, I asked my graduate student Ellen Hepp to collaborate with me on the project. Through my advising, she knew my writing style. I helped to develop hers. We wrote *In-line/On-line: Fundamentals of the Internet and the World Wide Web*. Back then, it took a long time for a webpage to load. This is where the title originated.

Our book was one of the first college textbooks written about the Internet and WWW. McGraw-Hill published it. At that time no one really understood the significance the Internet and WWW would play in human history. We knew the Internet was exploding in size, and webpages were becoming ubiquitous. Many students were excited to learn about the Internet and WWW. They wanted to develop their own websites. Our book filled this demand, too.

In-line/On-line became a bestseller. Many professors taught classes based on our book. Because few were experts, they requested supporting materials from McGraw-Hill. We developed resources to accompany our book, including some of the first websites ever associated with a college course. For each chapter in the book, we provided extensive supplementary online-material. We broke a lot of new ground.

Where we taught, the Internet course was in high demand. Our institutions offered many sections. They all filled. We used our book. Students enjoyed learning from it. The book was translated into Italian and Chinese. It was adopted widely in the US and internationally. We received thanks from many professors and students. We were excited to be on the cutting-edge of technology and pedagogy.

(↑) Develop supporting materials for *In-line/On-line: Fundamentals of the Internet and the World Wide Web*.

Because of the cutting-edge nature of Ellen's and my book *In-line/On-line: Fundamentals of the Internet and the World Wide Web*, many instructors were overwhelmed by the volume and newness of the material. Because of the popularity of the book, McGraw-Hill requested additional resources to support instructors. So we wrote the *Instructor's Resource Guide to Accompany In-line/On-line: Fundamentals of the Internet and the World Wide Web*. We provided lecture notes and other supplemental materials. The book gave professors the assistance they needed to teach a successful course about the Internet and WWW.

(↑) Write an introductory textbook about the Internet for engineering students.

McGraw-Hill asked Ellen and me to write a version of our popular Internet book for engineering students. The Internet touched all disciplines, including technical ones. We wrote the *Introduction to the Internet for Engineers*. We got under the hood more concerning the workings of the Internet and algorithms relating to the World Wide Web, as engineering students had stronger scientific and mathematical backgrounds than liberal-arts students.

(↑) Develop supporting materials for the book *Introduction to the Internet for Engineers*.

When Ellen's and my Internet book for engineers became popular, McGraw-Hill asked us to develop an instructor's manual for it. We wrote the *Instructor's Manual to Accompany Introduction to the Internet for Engineers*. We provided lecture notes and other supplemental materials. The book gave engineering professors the support they needed to teach a successful course to engineering students about the Internet and WWW.

(↑) Develop supplemental materials to support student learning about the Internet and WWW.

When Ellen's and my Internet and WWW book became popular, McGraw-Hill requested a solutions manual for the exercises. We wrote the *Student Solutions Manual to Accompany In-line/On-line: Fundamentals of the Internet and the World Wide Web*. To a non-technical audience, the manual explained how to think computationally. We illustrated ways to view and understand computing, as well as various problem-solving methodologies.

(↑) Through a second edition bring Ellen Hepp's and my Internet textbook up to date.

Because of the dynamic nature of the Internet, McGraw-Hill requested that Ellen and I update and revise our popular Internet book. We added 150+ pages of new material and updated the content in remainder of the book. The tome came in at 720 pages. The second edition necessitated revising our instructor's-resource guide (392 pages) and our student-solutions manual (192 pages).

(↑) Develop test and quiz materials to support Ellen Hepp's and my Internet and WWW book.

Due to the booming Internet and the popularity of courses taught using Ellen's and my book, McGraw-Hill requested a quiz book to support instructors teaching from our book. We wrote a *Quiz Book to Accompany In-line/On-line: Fundamentals of the Internet and World Wide Web*. It's 160 pages.

(↑) Collaborate with Jim Leisy on another writing project.

Jim Leisy liked my writing style. We banter around various topics. We settled on an introductory book about the UNIX operating system. I wrote *Understanding Practical UNIX*. The book was published by Jim's company Franklin, Beedle & Associates.

(↑) Develop supporting materials for my operating-systems textbook.

As my UNIX book became popular, professors requested supporting materials from Jim. I asked my friend Greg Geller to help me write this book. We wrote the *Instructor's Resource Guide to Accompany Understanding Practical UNIX* and published it with Franklin, Beedle & Associates. The supplemental materials helped instructors teach a successful operating-systems course using my book.

(↑) Develop supplemental materials for student learning for my UNIX book.

Greg Geller and I collaborated again to satisfy Jim Leisy's request for a student-solutions manual. We wrote the *Student Solutions Manual to Accompany Understanding Practical UNIX*. In the book we provided problem-solving strategies for the operating-systems domain.

(↑) Co-author a book with Geir Agnarsson.

Geir and I enjoy working together. He's a mathematician. I'm a computer scientist. We decided to write a textbook on graph theory—a fundamental topic spanning the fields of mathematics and computing. We spent several years writing *Graph Theory: Modeling, Appli-*

cations, and Algorithms. Our book includes the fundamental results in graph theory, as well as (at the time) cutting-edge material on web graphs. For a number of algorithms presented in the book, we included Java programs. We published the book with Prentice-Hall. It's been adopted at many universities. Geir has taught from it. Unfortunately, I never had the opportunity to teach a course using our book.

(↑) Collaborate on a book with my friend Paul.

I met Paul when he enrolled in my graduate algorithms class at UNH. We became best friends. We checked off many bucket-list items together. Long after Paul completed his PhD, we added co-authoring a book to our bucket lists to complement our sporting adventures. We wrote *Secure Roaming in Wireless 802.11 Networks*. The book (at the time) described many cutting-edge security issues. It was highly technical. We published the book with Elsevier. The book has found favor in networking circles.

(↑) Share my knowledge and experience in technical writing, presentation, and online communication with others.

Having published 10,000+ pages of technical material, given 225+ invited lectures all over the world, and developed a plethora of material for online teaching, I wanted to share my knowledge and experience with others. I wrote *Technical Writing, Presentation Skills, and Online Communication: Professional Tools and Insights*. I published the book with IGI Global.

The book fell short of my ambitions. The difficulty was with publishing a book that spanned two or more disciplines. The book didn't belong in an English department because of its technical nature. It didn't belong in a computing, engineering, or scientific program because it focused on writing. Few English professors had the technical knowledge to use my book, and few scientists took a deep dive into writing. I scaled back the topics in my book. Rather than producing the comprehensive 500+ page book in my vision and outline, I wrote a 250-page book to satisfy my reviewers.

I take some solace in knowing that I (positively) influenced the writing styles of students whom I taught and professors with whom I collaborated. They continue to pay it forward. So I have reached a wide audience.

Chapter 40
Speaking Engagements

I have much enthusiasm for my bucket-list items. Having worked so hard to gain knowledge and experience, I felt obligated to share it with others—a prehistoric tug to story tell. The opportunities that I took advantage of, others might never know. For those following in my footsteps, I could deflect common pitfalls and clear up misconceptions. I could add items to my audience members' bucket lists. I could help them stay the course. Here I list talks that I gave professionally or as a service to a community.

I divide the talks into four groups: invited distinguished speaker, panels and workshops, conferences, and invited talks. Within each section, the talks are in chronological order. I made 225+ presentations. It's interesting to skim the titles and locations of the talks. I elaborate on the content and provide anecdotes for selected talks. As this book is for a general reader, I stay out of the weeds and don't get into too many technical details.

Invited Distinguished Speaker—in these talks I gave keynote lectures to either open or close a conference.

(↑) Present keynote lectures at the Summer School on Complexity Theory in Barcelona, Spain.

By age 33 I established myself as one of the world's leading experts in parallel complexity theory. Institutions throughout the world invited me to lecture on the subject. In 1994 I gave a talk titled: "Topics in Parallel Complexity Theory." I spoke about my research in parallel computation. I researched problems and determined how much they could benefit by being solved on a massively parallel computer, as opposed to a single-processor one. Parallel computing was a hot topic in the 1990s. It's become a hot topic again, as the problems humans seek to solve become computationally more complex.

At the same summer school, I gave a talk titled: "P-Complete Problems." At that time my research specialty was *P-complete problems,* which are a class of problems that are notoriously difficult, if not impossible, to parallelize well. In layman's terms, using more computers in parallel to try and solve such a problem more efficiently bears little fruit. The problem's solution can't be sped up by throwing more processors at it, no matter how those processors are utilized. This contrasts the ditch digger's problem, where the more people whom you have digging, the faster a ditch can be dug, assuming their shovels don't interfere.

(↑) Present a keynote lecture at the *12th Clemson Mini Conference on Discrete Mathematics* in Clemson, South Carolina.

In 1997 I presented the keynote lecture at the Clemson Mini Conference. I spoke about my research in parallel computation in a talk titled: "Topics in Parallel Computation and P-Completeness Theory."

(↑) Present a keynote talk at the USM in Shah Alam, Malaysia.

In 2004 I gave a talk titled: "Parallel Algorithms in Graph Theory" at the USM. By using many processors, I devised new ways of solving graph-theory problems efficiently.

(↑) Present a keynote talk at the *Leadership, Education, and Development (LEAD) Conference* at AASU in Savannah, Georgia.

In my popular talk—"The Fastest Hike: A Lesson in Leadership"—I tied in leadership skills to the mentality and fortitude required to set the FKT for the PCT. People left the talk feeling hungry.

(↑) Present an invited Two-Day Seminar on Parallel Computing at CMU in Chiang Mai, Thailand.

In 2006 I gave the following talks at a seminar dedicated to my research:

> (a) "Parallel Computation and P-Completeness Theory: Part I."
> (b) "On Accreditation of Computing Programs."
> (c) "Parallel Computation and P-Completeness Theory: Part II."
> (d) "Parallel Algorithm Design for Problems on Trees: Part I."
> (e) "Ten Breakthroughs in Computer Science."
> (f) "Parallel Algorithm Design for Problems on Trees: Part II."
> (g) "Ten Interesting Computer Scientists."

As the only speaker at the seminar, I gave four to six hours of talks each day. With my colleague Chris Williams, I developed talks (e) and (g) for less technically oriented students.

(↑) Present keynote lectures at the *Conference on Computer Science and Software Engineering* at King Mongkut's Institute of Technology in North Bangkok, Thailand.

King Mongkut is the Thai king from the film The King and I. The movie is banned in Thailand. The university is named after him. In 2006 I gave three keynote lectures there at conference. Talks (e) and (g) from the talks I gave at CMU above, and a third talk: "Sequential and Parallel Algorithms for Some Problems on Trees." For numerous interesting problems on *trees*, the latter talk considered the best-known sequential algorithm for solving a particular tree problem and determined whether by using a parallel computer one could do better. A tree is a special type of graphical structure that computer scientists study.

(↑) Present the opening speech at the Savannah Ogeechee Regional Science and Engineering Fair in Savannah, Georgia.

In 2007 in a talk titled: "On the Importance of Science," I inspired young scientists in the audience by relaying the important role science played in my life. When I passed around my Rensselaer Science Medal that I won in high school, students became excited. Early on in my career, I learned the impact of using a prop in a lecture. After my presentation, I answered many student questions.

(↑) Present a keynote lecture at the *22th Clemson Mini Conference on Discrete Mathematics* in Clemson, South Carolina.

In 2009 I was invited back to Clemson University for another distinguished lecture. I presented: "The Complexity of the Evolution of Graph Labeling," which was a talk about my latest research.

(↑) Present the opening keynote lecture at the conference *Breaking Boundaries: Multidisciplinary Computing and Innovation* in Chiang Mai, Thailand.

In the late 2000s, I consulted for my friend Paul's company Elbrus Networks. In an independent effort from Fitbit, we developed a similar application. Because Paul and I enjoyed running together so much, once I moved out of New England, we wanted a way to continue running together virtually. As such, his company was developing a device and app that would allow people with similar interests to train together remotely. At that time this was cutting-edge technology.

My presentation—"Social Networking, Wellness, and Algorithms"—focused on using social networking, which was exploding in popularity, to help people maintain their wellness via the ability to interact online with people having similar interests. I developed some of the first matching algorithms for social networks to group people together who shared similar fitness abilities and training goals. My algorithms matched a number of other parameters as well. Now, of course, such algorithms are used in online-dating sites to match like-minded people.

Panels and Workshops—in these talks I sat with a group of other experts and we discussed a particular topic and fielded questions, or I presented an in-depth discussion about a particular topic.

(↑) Present a workshop at the *Complexity, Logic, and Recursion Conference* at the Universitat Politècnica de Catalunya in Barcelona, Spain.

In 1996 I presented a workshop titled: "Hamiltonian Paths and Circuits in Interval Graphs." It discussed my research on efficiently finding a route through a restricted type of computing structure.

(↑) Present an overview of the Yamacraw Project at the *Wireless Computing Symposium* in Savannah, Georgia.

After getting AASU involved in the $100,000,000 economic-development Yamacraw Project, I was appointed regional coordinator for Georgia. In 2001 I conducted a workshop titled: "Yamacraw Applications in Southeast Georgia" with the goal of sparking interest in the project in Southeast Georgia. I was successful.

(↑) At the *Best Assessment Processes Symposium* in Terre Haute, Indiana in 2003, present a how-to accreditation workshop.

At the Rose-Hulman Institute of Technology, I shared my expertise about the required documentation for an accreditation visit. My workshop was titled: "Accurate and Efficient Accreditation Documentation Preparation."

(↑) In 2005 present a workshop on "Faculty Evaluation" in Savannah, Georgia.

(↑) At the *ABET Symposium* in Las Vegas, Nevada, present a workshop about accrediting online programs.

In 2010 I served on ABET's *first* accreditation team to evaluate an online program. We broke ground on many fronts for accreditation issues for online, multiple-site programs, including the use of statistical sampling. We created the process and guidelines for the evaluation of online programs. We described our methodology in a workshop titled: "Accreditation in Online and Hybrid Learning Environments." The workshop became a training session for future evaluators of online programs. For those administering online programs, our session provided insights into the evaluation process for online and hybrid (partially online) programs.

(↑) With Kay Schulze present a workshop to the Divisions of Engineering & Weapons and Mathematics & Science at the USNA in Annapolis, Maryland.

I contributed to the revision of ABET-accreditation criteria. Institutions need to understand and adjust for such revisions in their preparations for an accreditation visit. In 2011 my friend Kay Schulze and I gave a workshop titled: "ABET's Harmonized Criteria." We brought administrators and professors at the Naval Academy up to speed on the recent, sweeping changes made to ABET's Criteria. We highlighted required program, data-collection, and reporting adjustments needed. Our workshop helped many programs with their reaccreditation efforts.

(↑) In 2013 present a workshop on "Graduate Education Opportunities" at the *Naval Academy Science and Engineering Conference* in Annapolis, Maryland.

(↑) In Memphis, Tennessee at the *Special Interest Group on Computer Science Education Symposium (SIGCSE)*, present a workshop describing the development of ABET cybersecurity Program Criteria for accrediting programs in cybersecurity.

SIGCSE is the premier symposium in computing education. The Program Criteria for cybersecurity accreditation allows institutions to seek ABET accreditation for their programs in cybersecurity, cyber forensics, information assurance, network security, and other similarly named programs.

My friends, Andy Phillips and Allen Parrish, and I were three of the leaders in pushing for the development of Program Criteria for the emerging discipline of cybersecurity. Initially, we encountered many skeptics. We kept pushing forward to address this important issue—critically important because of national-security concerns. In 2016, as part of our Cyber Education Project, we gave a workshop at SIGCSE titled: "Validating the Draft Cybersecurity Accreditation Criteria."

In our workshop we described the cybersecurity Program Criteria. We responded to all concerns expressed by skeptics. We convinced them of the importance of Program Criteria for cybersecurity. Our efforts reached a favorable tipping point. We succeeded in developing ABET Program Criteria for cybersecurity, putting it on the same ABET footing as computer science, information technology, software engineering, information systems, and computer engineering.

Our work shaped the field of cybersecurity education because programs seeking ABET accreditation must satisfy our curriculum requirements. My work on this effort is one of the most important contributions of my career. As Chair of the Accreditation Committee for the Cyber Education Project, I wrote the first draft of the Program Criteria for cybersecurity. I participated in one of the first pilot visits for ABET to test the Program Criteria for cybersecurity accreditation. Once the Program Criteria for cybersecurity became official, after a four-year process, I evaluated one of the first programs to seek this accreditation. I also helped the USNA achieve this accreditation for its cyber-operations program. These were proud moments. Because of the leadership role I played in the development of the Program Criteria for cybersecurity, I'm in demand as a consultant by programs seeking accreditation in this and similarly named disciplines.

(↑) In Hollywood, Florida at the *ABET Symposium*, present an opportunity for the computing community to provide input on our developing ABET Program Criteria for cybersecurity.

In 2016, in a similar vein to the previous item, Andy Phillips, Allen Parrish, myself, and others shared with the computing community our accreditation Program Criteria for cybersecurity in a workshop titled: "An Interactive Workshop: Draft Program Criteria for Cyber Sciences." We sought the audience's input, answered their questions, and received support for our work. After addressing all concerns, as noted in the previous item, we succeeded in getting Program Criteria for cybersecurity approved by ABET.

Conferences—in these talks I disseminated my latest research to professors and graduate students. Because the field of computing advanced so rapidly, it was important to make other researchers aware of the latest cutting-edge results in a timely fashion. The ability of computer scientists to share their work so quickly helped innovation in the field progress at a fast rate.

(↑) Disseminate my research on search algorithms at the *IEEE Symposium on Parallel and Distributed Processing* in Dallas, Texas in 1990.

I presented a talk titled: "The Parallel Complexity of Stack versus Queue Breadth-First Search."

(↑) Disseminate my research on the development of parallel algorithms from existing sequential ones at the *International Conference on Computer Science* in Santiago, Chile in 1991.

I presented a talk titled: "Towards Understanding the Effective Parallelization of Sequential Algorithms." When possible, I submitted my research to top-quality conferences in interesting destinations. This helped me check off some bucket-list items related to travel as well.

(↑) Disseminate my research on groundbreaking, interdisciplinary work combining the fields of computer science and physics to quantify the complexity of pattern-formation problems.

The material was presented at the *Canada-France Conference on Parallel Computing* in Montreal, Canada in 1994. I gave a talk titled: "The Parallel Complexity of Algorithms for Pattern-Formation Models." This talk was the first of many I gave describing my work with the physicist Jonathon Machta. Our research combined the fields of computer science and physics in unique ways. It helped advance the field of computational physics.

(↑) Disseminate my research on the complexity of growth models at the *European Symposium on Algorithms* in the Netherlands in 1994.

I presented a talk titled: "The Parallel Complexity of Eden Growth, Solid-on-Solid Growth, and Ballistic Deposition." Of all my talks, perhaps this one has the most erudite-sounding title. Jon Machta and I continued our fruitful collaboration.

(↑) Disseminate my research on parallel algorithms at the *Discrete Mathematics and Theoretical Computer Science Symposium* in Auckland, New Zealand in 1999.

I presented a talk titled: "Computing Prüfer Codes Efficiently in Parallel."

(↑) Disseminate my research on online education at the *Valdosta State University Mathematics Technology Conference* in Valdosta, Georgia in 1999.

When I developed my Internet course in 1996, it was one of the first courses at any level of instruction to go digital. I broke new ground. Professors wanted my guidance and advice. To that end, I presented a talk titled: "In-line/On-line: One Tested Approach to Offering a Paperless Course." Now there are online courses and even online degrees—I helped develop the first fully online degree in the University System of Georgia—but in the mid-1990s, this work was truly innovative and pioneering.

(↑) Disseminate my research on parallel algorithms at the *Combinatorics and Algorithms Seminar* in Reykjavik, Iceland in 1999.

I presented a talk titled: "On Computing Prüfer Codes and Their Corresponding Trees Optimally in Parallel." This talk led to my career-long collaboration with Geir Agnarsson and also a collaboration with Magnus Halldórsson. I ended up hiring Geir to come work at my university in Georgia. We became great friends. We wrote a book together and numerous research papers. This example illustrates the importance of visiting other institutions to meet potential collaborators. Of course, not everyone has the ambition and energy level required to make such trips.

(↑) At the *Yamacraw Conference* in Savannah, Georgia in 2000, share my knowledge about hiring faculty members.

When there was a dearth of PhDs in computer science in the 1990s, I successfully hired many new professors and built a School of Computing from the ground up. Administrators wanted me to talk about my recruitment strategy. I presented a talk titled: "Hiring Faculty in Computer Science."

At the time, the majority of PhDs in computer science went to work in industry, where they were granted stock options and a higher salary than in academia. During this time of intense hiring competition between academia and industry, recruiting faculty members became an art—one that I mastered. Nationally, many academic positions went unfilled for years. Whenever I had an open position, I successfully filled it that same year. I helped my counterparts at other institutions in the University System of Georgia improve their recruitment processes.

(↑) Disseminate my research on parallel algorithms at the *Journées de l'Informatique Messine Conference* in Metz, France in 2000.

I presented a talk titled: "On Computing Prüfer Codes and Their Corresponding Trees Optimally in Parallel." My colleagues and I continued to advance our research on computing Prüfer codes in parallel, eventually developing what became my favorite parallel algorithm. In the algorithm we employed many known parallel techniques in innovative ways, as well as introducing new methods. The complex algorithm beautifully illustrates important parallel-programming techniques and how they can be combined successfully.

(↑) At the *Best Assessment Processes Symposium* in Terre Haute, Indiana in 2004, share my knowledge about preparing accreditation materials for an ABET site visit.

I presented a talk titled: "Leading a Self-Study Preparation."

(↑) Disseminate my research on clustering algorithms at the *Electronics, Computer, Telecommunications, and Infor-*

mation Technology Conference in Chiang Rai, Thailand in 2007.

I presented a talk titled: "Bottom-Up Hierarchical Clustering is CC-Complete." In this research we identified a new CC-complete problem. Very few problems are known to have this computational complexity. Our work helped expand the small class of such problems. When I read these titles now, I recall that some of my research addressed complex mathematical subjects.

(↑) Disseminate my research on wireless networking at the *International Conference on Interdisciplinary Mathematical and Statistical Techniques* in Shanghai, China in 2007.

I presented a talk titled: "A Mobility Model for Studying Wireless Communications." After this conference I became fascinated with China and its people. I added many items to my bucket list. I made a handful of trips to China in rapid succession to check off those items.

(↑) At the *Best Assessment Processes Symposium* in Atlanta, Georgia in 2008, share my knowledge about utilizing advisory boards in the ABET-accreditation process.

I presented a talk titled: "Utilizing an Industrial Advisory Board in the Accreditation Process." I geared it toward adding practical feedback to academic programs through interactions with industry. We didn't want there to be a gap in the skills and knowledge of graduating students from what industry was expecting and needing from them. During this period, the computing industry evolved rapidly. I explained how academia and industry could be more tightly coupled. This helped students obtain employment and industry meet its goals.

(↑) At the *Best Assessment Processes Symposium* in Indianapolis, Indiana in 2009, share my knowledge about industrial advisory boards.

I presented a talk titled: "Setting Up and Maintaining a Strong Industrial Advisory Board." This work piggybacked on the previous presentation. I gave guidance on how to connect industry with academia.

(↑) At the *International Conference on Learning and Teaching* in Bangkok, Thailand in 2009, on an international scale, share my knowledge about accreditation.

Worldwide from 2005 or so onward, colleges and universities started heavily recruiting international students for a host of reasons—the primary one being to boost enrollments for their own financial gain and the secondary one being to meet workforce needs. It became important for specialized programs at such institutions to become accredited, providing (some sort of) validation of their legitimacy and quality. This issue was especially true for disciplines competing for top-notch students. The institutions could point to their program's accreditation status, as a way to prove to students, parents, and industry that the school had a good program, or at least one that met a set of internationally recognized standards.

I gave talks illustrating how a program could move in the direction of becoming ABET accredited. I presented my talk titled: "Accreditation in Applied Science, Computing, Engineering, and Technology." I explained to administrators and faculty members how to improve their programs. I went into details of what the programs needed to do in order to become compliant with accreditation standards. In some cases, programs didn't have the resources necessary to come into compliance with international standards. Overall though, the number of internationally accredited programs by ABET soared during this period.

At that time several factors combined to shift the focus in academia to the science, technology, engineering, and mathematics (STEM) disciplines. The technology wave meant there were a tremendous number of high-paying jobs available in STEM fields. Due to the rapid expansion of the technology industry, there was always a shortage of qualified workers. Students who sought high-paying, salaried positions realized that they greatly increased their chances of success of being hired if they had a degree from an accredited program in a STEM discipline.

In some cases liberal arts institutions that were struggling to stay afloat migrated their focus to the STEM areas, too. In order to be viewed as legitimate and improve their chances of increasing enrollments, such schools needed to seek accreditation for their emerging technology-related programs. As an expert in ABET accreditation and a well-known speaker, what this meant was that administrators and faculty members wanted to hear from me about accreditation and how to achieve it.

(↑) At the *ABET Symposium* in Las Vegas, Nevada in 2010, share my knowledge about the ABET-accreditation process.

I presented my talk titled: "ABET-Accreditation Timeline." This talk continued in the theme of my presentation given in 2009 in Bangkok. The upper-level administration at many universities exerted pressure on their departments to achieve ABET accreditation for their programs. Because of this urgency, deans and department heads took a keen interest in the timeframe required to achieve ABET accreditation.

(↑) At the *International Conference in Electronics, Computer, Telecommunications, and Information Technology* in Chiang Mai, Thailand in 2010, present my research on matching algorithms for social networks.

As mentioned, I consulted for my friend Paul's company Elbrus Networks. At that time and a few years prior, we worked on developing something like Fitbit—which didn't yet exist. I worked on the matching algorithms to pair up compatible users. Unfortunately, Fitbit beat us to the punch. I presented my talk titled: "An Activity Profile Model and Dynamic-Matching Results for Social Networks Regarding Wellness Applications." It dealt with issues confronting early matching algorithms for social networks.

(↑) At the *Careers in Cyber Security Workshop* in Columbia, Maryland in 2011, share my knowledge about the development of materials for a cybersecurity curriculum.

My colleagues and I pioneered a cybersecurity curriculum at the Naval Academy in the form of a degree in cyber operations. Other institutions wanted to learn our methodologies. We were on the cutting edge. With Derek "Mouth" Snyder, I developed and taught the introductory course in our new degree program at the USNA. I explained lessons learned and pitfalls to avoid. I presented my talk titled: "Cybersecurity at the United States Naval Academy."

(↑) At the *Royal Golden Jubilee International Congress* in Pattaya, Thailand in 2012, disseminate my research on matching algorithms relating to wellness and social networking.

I presented my talk titled: "Dynamic Matching Problems in the Context of Wellness and Social Networking."

(↑) At the *Conference on Innovation and Technology in Computer Science Education* in Haifa, Israel in 2012, disseminate my knowledge about curriculum development in cybersecurity.

I presented my talk titled: "Anatomy, Dissection, and Mechanics of an Introductory Cybersecurity Class's Curriculum at the United States Naval Academy." In Israel there's great interest in cybersecurity from both military and civilian perspectives. Other institutions wanted to know how we taught cybersecurity at the Naval Academy. The course I developed with Mouth was on the cutting edge. The materials we taught went immediately into practice in the US Navy.

(↑) At the *National Institute for Standards and Technology's Shaping the Future of Cybersecurity Education Workshop* in Gaithersburg, Maryland in 2013, share my knowledge about a general introductory course in cybersecurity.

In 2011 the Naval Academy rolled out an introductory cybersecurity course. Every single student at the institution was required to take that course. This was reminiscent of when institutions required all students to take a course in computer literacy. I taught the course in its first instantiation and developed materials for the dean. I believe the Naval Academy was the first to impose a cybersecurity requirement on all students. Others institutions wanted to know how the Naval Academy achieved this goal. I presented my talk titled: "On a University-Wide Required Cybersecurity Course," which highlighted the key issues involved and the major hurdles to overcome. Many were amazed by what we had accomplished at the USNA in such a short timeframe. It's a great course, and I learned a lot by teaching it.

Invited Talks—in these talks I was invited to speak at an event or institution about a topic of interest to a particular audience. In some cases, people were interested in hiring me. As a form of recruitment, they invited me to their location to give a presentation. I presented numerous talks at multiple venues. I provide anecdotes in a few cases. In earlier parts of this chapter, I explained the contents of related talks in more detail.

(↑) Present "Problems that Are Hard to Parallelize" at the Department of Computer Science, University of Oregon in Eugene, Oregon in 1989.

As a new PhD, I went on a speaking tour explaining my research to others in academia.

(↑) Present "The Complexity of Parallel Computations" at the Department of Computer Science, University of Pittsburgh in Pittsburgh, Pennsylvania in 1989.

I received a job offer from the University of Pittsburgh.

(↑) In 1989 present "Identification of Inherently Sequential Algorithms" at the following institutions:

1. Department of Computer Science, Colorado State University in Fort Collins, Colorado.
2. Department of Computer Science, University of Rhode Island in South Kingstown, Rhode Island.
3. Department of Computer Science, Tufts University in Medford, Massachusetts.
4. Department of Computer Science, UNH in Durham, New Hampshire.

I received job offers from all four institutions. At UNH, I accepted my first faculty position.

(↑) Present "Search Problems that are P-Complete" at the Department of Computer Science, University of Rhode Island in South Kingstown, Rhode Island in 1990.

The University of Rhode Island invited me back to give another talk. I took the opportunity to explore the university further and visit my family in Rhode Island.

(↑) Present "The Parallel Complexity of Approximation Algorithms for the Maximum Acyclic Subgraph Problem" at the Department of Computer Science, University of Maine in Orono, Maine in 1991.

(↑) Present "Optimal Edge Ranking of Trees in Polynomial Time" at the Department of Computer Science, University of Massachusetts at Amherst in Amherst, Massachusetts in 1992.

During my visit to Amherst, I met Jon Machta. We began our long-term collaboration at that time.

(↑) Present "Tree Ranking" at the Department of Computer Science, Boston University in Boston, Massachusetts in 1993.

I frequently got invited to nearby universities to talk about my research.

(↑) Present "The Parallel Complexity of Algorithms for Pattern Formation Models" at the Department of Computer Science, University of Hong Kong in Hong Kong in 1994.

I also got invited to far-away universities to talk about my research. Although I couldn't always accept such invitations, if they came in the summer or winter breaks, I tried to accept. I enjoyed meeting researchers from around the world and visiting their institutions. I found new collaborators. I always tried to bring back some useful ideas to share with my colleagues and my home institution. In this case I checked off the bucket-list item of visiting Hong Kong.

(↑) Present "Tree Ranking Results" at the Department of Computer Science, University of Hong Kong in Hong Kong in 1994.

(↑) Present "Parallel Computation and P-Complete Problems" at the Department of Computer Science, University of Iceland in Reykjavik, Iceland in 1994.

(↑) Present "Tree Ranking Results" at the Departament de Llenguatges i Sistemes Informàtics, Universitat Politècnica de Catalunya in Barcelona, Spain in 1995.

While on my Fulbright Fellowship to Spain, I gave this talk.

(↑) In 1996 present "Node and Edge Ranking of Trees" at the following institutions:

1. Fakultät für Informatik, Universität Ulm in Ulm, Germany.
2. Institut für Informatik, Der Technischen Universität München in Munich, Germany.
3. Wilhelm-Schickard-Institut für Informatik, Universität Tübingen in Tübingen, Germany.
4. Dipartimento di Scienze dell'Informazione, Università degli Studi di Roma La Sapienza in Rome, Italy.

While in nearby Spain, the European Fulbright Commission supported my travel to give lectures in Germany. I made an effort to give lectures at other institutions in Europe. In Italy I met Rossella Petreschi. We became friends and long-term collaborators.

(↑) In 1996 present "Topics in Parallel Computation and P-Completeness Theory" at the following institutions:

1. Wilhelm-Schickard Institut für Informatik, Universität Tübingen in Tübingen, Germany.
2. Departamento de Ingenieria de Sistemas Telemáticos, Universidad de Madrid in Madrid, Spain.

(↑) Present "A Compendium of Problems Complete for Symmetric Logarithmic Space" at the Departament de Llenguatges i Sistemes Informàtics, Universitat Politècnica de Catalunya in Barcelona, Spain in 1996.

(↑) Present "Node and Edge Ranking" at the Department of Computer Science, Tennessee Technological University in Cookeville, Tennessee in 1997.

I was offered a job at Tennessee Tech.

(↑) Present "Topics in Parallel Computation and P-Completeness Theory" at the Dipartimento di Scienze dell'Informazione, Università degli Studi di Roma La Sapienza in Rome, Italy in 1998.

I visited Italy frequently to work with my friend Rossella and give talks about my research. She visited me at the UNH, too. Later I hired one of her colleagues. He came to work with me in Georgia.

(↑) Present "Node and Edge Ranking of Trees" at the Department of Computer Science, AASU in Savannah, Georgia in 1998.

AASU made me a job offer. I accepted it.

(↑) Present "Topics in Parallel Computation and P-Completeness Theory" at the Department of Mathematics and Computer Science, Saint Mary's College of California in Moraga, California in 1998.

Saint Mary's College made me a job offer. Although I loved Moraga and got along extremely with the faculty and administration, the cost of living in California made working there as a professor prohibitively expensive.

(↑) Present "Topics in Parallel Computation and P-Completeness Theory" at the Department of Computer Science, University of North Carolina at Wilmington in Wilmington, North Carolina in 1998.

The University of North Carolina made me a job offer.

(↑) Present "Node and Edge Ranking of Trees" at the Department of Computer Science and Quantitative Methods, Winthrop University in Rock Hill, South Carolina in 1998.

Winthrop University made me a job offer.

(↑) Present "Topics in Parallel Computation and P-Completeness Theory" at the Department of Computer Science, University of Central Florida in Orlando, Florida in 1998.

The University of Central Florida expressed an interest in hiring me. When I worked at AASU, I ended up hiring several of their graduate students as faculty members.

(↑) Present "Computing Prüfer Codes Efficiently in Parallel" at the Department of Computer Science, University of Central Florida in Orlando, Florida in 1998.

I worked with a couple professors in the Department of Computer Science at the University of Central Florida. I used my visits there as faculty-recruitment trips.

(↑) Present "Topics in Parallel Computation and P-Completeness Theory" at the Department of Computer Science, University of New Mexico in Albuquerque, New Mexico in 1998.

The University of New Mexico made me a job offer. Although I got along well with the faculty, I wasn't interested in moving to the Albuquerque area.

(↑) Present "Computing Prüfer Codes Efficiently in Parallel" at the Department of Computer Science, UNH in Durham, New Hampshire in 1999.

(↑) Present "Fundamental Results in Parallel Computation" at the Department of Computer Science, University of Iceland in Reykjavik, Iceland in 1999.

At that time, I loved visiting Iceland. Few tourists had discovered the country.

(↑) In 1999 present "On Computing Prüfer Codes and Their Corresponding Trees Optimally in Parallel" at the following institutions:

1. Department of Computer Science, University of Central Florida in Orlando, Florida.

2. Department of Computer Science, Southern Polytechnic State University in Marietta, Georgia.
3. Department of Mathematics and Computer Science, Georgia Southern University in Statesboro, Georgia.

(↑) Present "Parallel Algorithms and Prüfer Codes" at the Human Genome Center, Institute of Medical Science, University of Tokyo in Tokyo, Japan in December 1999.

I was fortunate to win a Japanese Society for the Promotion of Science Fellowship and work at the prestigious University of Tokyo. It's considered the top institution in Asia and one of the best in the world. It was an honor to work in the Human Genome Center with my colleague Satoru Miyano. We collaborated on P-completeness research.

(↑) In 2000 present "Parallel Algorithms and Prüfer Codes" at the following institutions:

1. Department of Informatics, Kyushu University in Fukuoka, Japan.
2. Department of Computer Science, University of Georgia in Athens, Georgia.
3. Department of Computer Science, Brandeis University in Waltham, Massachusetts.
4. Department of Computer Science, Pomona College in Claremont, California.

In item (3), I checked off a bucket-list item by giving a talk at my friend Paul's alma mater. In item (4), it was a great pleasure to be invited to my alma mater to give a research presentation. Check. After 17 years, my former professors whom I encountered in the hallways still remembered my name.

(↑) Present "A Real Walk through the Woods" as part of the Robert Ingram Strozier Lecture Series, AASU in Savannah, Georgia in 2000.

I modified the title of Bill Bryson's popular book for my talk. Most people aren't nearly as interested in someone who actually completed a successful hike, as they are in someone who failed miserably. There are fewer things to poke fun at when someone does things correctly. My audience was amazed at my thru-hike of the AT. They only knew me as a brainy professor. They left the room hungry.

(↑) Present "Parallel Algorithms and Prüfer Codes" at the Department of Computer Science and Information Systems, Kennesaw State University in Kennesaw, Georgia in 2000.

(↑) In 2000 present "Yamacraw in Southeast Georgia" at the following Georgia institutions:

1. Department of Mathematics and Computer Science, Georgia Southern University in Statesboro.
2. Department of Computer Engineering Technology, Savannah State University in Savannah.

(↑) Present "Tree Ranking Algorithms" at the Department of Informatics, Kyushu University in Fukuoka, Japan in 2000.

(↑) In 2001 in Washington State, present "Sequential and Parallel Algorithms for Some Problems on Trees" at the following institutions:

1. Department of Computer Science and Engineering, UW in Seattle.

2. Department of Computing and Software Systems, UW Tacoma in Tacoma.
3. Department of Computing and Software Systems, UW Bothell in Bothell.

It was a great honor to be invited to my alma mater to give a research presentation. They arranged for me to give talks at two branch campuses as well. My former professors wanted me to run the programs at the branch campuses, and I was offered jobs at both of them.

(↑) Present "Yamacraw Project Overview" at the Landings Kiwanis Club on Skidaway Island, Georgia, in 2001.

(↑) In 2001 present "Sequential and Parallel Algorithms for Some Problems on Trees" at the following institutions:

1. Department of Computer Science, University of Central Florida in Orlando, Florida.
2. Department of Computer Science, University of Montreal in Montreal, Canada.

(↑) Present "Introduction to Parallel Computation" at the Department of Computer Science, Northern Arizona University in Flagstaff, Arizona in 2002.

Northern Arizona University offered me a job. I loved Flagstaff and visited it many times over the years.

(↑) Present "The School of Computing's Explosive Growth" at the following Georgia venues:

1. AASU Alumni Association on Wilmington Island in 2002.

2. Landings Rotary Club on Skidaway Island in 2003.

I founded the School of Computing at AASU. Alumni and locals were eager to hear how I brought about such great changes so rapidly.

(↑) Present "A Regional Center for Cyber Security Education and Training" at the Business and Education Technology Alliance Meeting in Savannah, Georgia in 2003.

At that time we were on the cutting edge of cybersecurity education in the world. I'd proposed a new degree in cybersecurity to the University System of Georgia, but it was too far ahead of its time. Now I'm sure they wished we'd implemented the degree back then. It would have been one of the first of its kind in the world. Partly because of my work in cybersecurity, the Naval Academy ended up hiring me away from AASU. They understood the critical importance of cybersecurity in nearly all aspects of society, including the military.

(↑) Present the following talks at the USM in Shah Alam, Malaysia in 2003:

   1. "Curriculum Issues in Information Technology and Computer Science."
   2. "Parallel Computing in Engineering."
   3. "An Introduction to Parallel Computation."
   4. "An Overview of the Yamacraw Initiative."
   5. "Fundamentals of Parallel Algorithms."
   6. "Research Issues in Computer Science and Information Technology."
   7. "An Introduction to Parallel Computation."
   8. "P-Complete Problems."
   9. "Technical Writing in Computer Science."

10. "Careers in Computer Science and Information Technology."

I held a visiting professorship at the USM for 15+ years. I gave many talks there. When at the USM, I usually spoke to very large audiences, several hundred students, faculty members, and administrators.

(↑) Present "Algorithms for Tree Problems" at the Indian Institute of Technology (IIT) Kharagpur in Kharagpur, India in 2004.

While visiting my friend Rimili Sengupta, I gave a talk at this prestigious institution in India. Another friend of mine Therese Araneta gave me a button that reads: "I've survived DAMN near everything." When I look at that button, I think of my bike ride in Kolkata, which I went on after my talk. That ride is one of the most dangerous things that I ever did. I survived.

(↑) Present the following talks at the USM in Shah Alam, Malaysia in 2004:

1. "Introduction to Graph Theory."
2. "Fundamental Results in Graph Theory."
3. "Trees and Forests in Graph Theory."
4. "Graph Theory Applications."
5. "Technical Writing."

(↑) Present "Leadership" at AASU in Savannah, Georgia in 2004.

(↑) Present "Sequential and Parallel Algorithms for Some Problems on Trees" at the Department of Mathematics and Computer Science, Saint Mary's College of California in Moraga, California in 2004.

I visited Saint Mary's College again. They offered me a job again. I wanted to work there. The problem was the high cost of living in California.

(↑) In 2004-8 present "The Fastest Hike: A Lesson in Leadership" at the following venues:

1. UNH in Durham, New Hampshire.
2. Savannah Striders Running Club in Savannah, Georgia.
3. AASU in Savannah, Georgia.
4. Middlebury College in Middlebury, Vermont.
5. Sentient Bean in Savannah, Georgia.
6. Early Alert Support Environment Seminar at AASU in Savannah, Georgia.
7. Wesley Monumental in Savannah, Georgia.
8. Savannah Mission Fund Raiser in Savannah, Georgia.
9. Savannah Methodist Church on Tybee Island in Georgia.

It felt good to have my colleagues invite me back to give a talk at UNH, where I previously worked for ten years.

(↑) In 2004-8 present "Leadership: I Chose to Climb" at the following venues (When no location is specified, the event took place in Savannah, Georgia.):

1. AASU Alumni Association on Wilmington Island, Georgia.
2. Landings Kiwanis Club on Skidaway Island, Georgia.
3. The Rotary Club.
4. Middlebury College in Middlebury, Vermont.
5. AASU, public lecture.
6. Landings Rotary Club on Skidaway Island, Georgia.

7. United States Air Force Academy in Colorado Springs, Colorado.
8. Rotary Club East.
9. AASU, special faculty lecture.
10. United Methodist Church.
11. Savannah Striders Running Club.
12. Rotary West Club of Savannah.
13. Sunrise Rotary Club of Savannah.
14. Richmond Hill Rotary Club in Richmond Hill, Georgia.
15. Kiwanis Club in Statesboro, Georgia.

People from the flatlands in South Georgia were interested to hear about my forays into the mountains of the world, as were people from mountainous regions. I gave radio and talk-show interviews, and appeared on TV. During this period, I got invited to give talks at many different venues. It was an honor to speak at one of the nation's service academies.

(↑) In 2004-5 present "Sequential and Parallel Algorithms for Some Problems on Trees" at the following institutions:

1. Department of Computer Science, Middlebury College in Middlebury, Vermont.
2. United States Air Force Academy in Colorado Springs, Colorado.
3. Universität Koblenz-Landau in Koblenz, Germany.

I was offered a distinguished professorship at the Air Force Academy. It was a great honor.

(↑) Present "AASU and the School of Computing" at the Universität Koblenz-Landau in Koblenz, Germany in 2005.

(↑) Present the following talks at the USM in Shah Alam, Malaysia in 2005:

1. "Parallel Algorithms in Computer Science."
2. "Sequential Algorithms for Graph Theory Problems."
3. "Preparing an Accreditation Self-Study Report."
4. "The Synergy of Mathematics and Computer Science."
5. "Ten Breakthroughs in Computer Science."
6. "Ten Interesting Computer Scientists."

(↑) Present "P-Completeness Theory: A Seminar Series" at CMU in Chiang Mai, Thailand.

(↑) At Khon Kaen University in Khon Kaen, Thailand in 2006, present the following talks:

1. "Topics in Parallel Computation."
2. "Ten Breakthroughs in Computer Science."

(↑) Present "Ten Interesting Computer Scientists" at CMU in Chiang Mai, Thailand in 2006.

(↑) At the Department of Computer Science, Asian Institute of Technology in Bangkok, Thailand in 2006, present the following talks:

1. "Parallel Algorithms and Prüfer Codes."
2. "Parallel Algorithms for Ranking Problems."

(↑) Present "Ten Breakthroughs in Computer Science" at the National Cheng Chung University in Chiayi, Taiwan in 2006.

(↑) At the National Dong Hua University in Hualien, Taiwan in 2006, present the following talks:

1. "Ten Interesting Computer Scientists."
2. "Ten Breakthroughs in Computer Science."

(↑) At the Prince of Songkla University in Hat Yai, Thailand in 2006, present the following talks:

1. "An Introduction to Parallel Computation."
2. "Ten Breakthroughs in Computer Science."
3. "A Lesson in Leadership."
4. "Ten Interesting Computer Scientists."
5. "Overview of Accreditation for Computing Programs."

(↑) Present "Technical Writing in Computer Science" at CMU in Chiang Mai, Thailand in 2006.

(↑) At the Bansomdejchaopraya Rajabhat University in Bangkok, Thailand in 2006, present the following talks:

1. "Ten Interesting Computer Scientists."
2. "A Lesson in Leadership."
3. "Ten Breakthroughs in Computer Science."

(↑) In 2006-7 present "Senior Fulbright to CMU in Thailand" at the following Georgia venues:

1. AASU in Savannah.
2. Savannah Striders Running Club in Savannah.
3. ACM Club, AASU in Savannah.
4. Richmond Hill Rotary Club in Richmond Hill.

(↑) Present "Parallel Computation and P-Completeness Theory" at George Mason University (GMU) in Fairfax, Virginia.

My friend Geir accepted a professorship at GMU and invited me there to give a talk.

(↑) Present "On the Parallel Complexity of Hierarchical Clustering and CC-Complete Problems" at AASU in Savannah, Georgia in 2007.

(↑) At the Kuakarun College of Nursing in Bangkok, Thailand in 2007, present the following talks:

1. "Overview of Computing/Technology."
2. "A Comparison of Thailand and the United States' Educational Systems."
3. "Current Trends in Technology Relating to Medicine."
4. "Time Management."

I co-led a student trip to Thailand to visit a nursing college, and they asked me to give several presentations. I spoke about the reliance of medicine on technology, the advances in medicine based on technology, and the future impact of technology on medicine. I discussed both hardware and software issues. In another presentation I compared Thailand and the United States' educational systems. When impressed by my accomplishments, they asked me to give a talk on time management, too. I managed it.

(↑) At a seminar dedicated to my research, at CMU in Chiang Mai, Thailand in 2007, present the following talks:

1. "On the Parallel Complexity of Hierarchical Clustering and CC-Complete Problems."
2. "Parallel Models of Computation."
3. "Introduction to P-Completeness Theory."

(↑) Present "Parallel Algorithms for Tree Problems" at Chulalongkorn University in Bangkok, Thailand in 2007.

Chulalongkorn University is the most prestigious academic institution in Thailand. It's named after Rama V—the son of King Mongkut. Chulalongkorn is a very popular Thai king. After my presentation, the dean offered me a job. He asked me: "Do you have a Thai wife?" I responded: "No." To which he said: "If we find you one will you take the job?" I smiled. As a dean myself, I knew that such a line of questioning is illegal in the US. I didn't go to work there.

(↑) Present "Rankings and Codings of Trees" at the University of St. Louis in St. Louis, Missouri in 2008.

(↑) Present "Parallel Algorithms" at Cambridge University in Cambridge, England in 2008.

It was a pleasure to give a talk at Cambridge University. They beamed it to the Massachusetts Institute of Technology (MIT), too. I easily answered many questions from the erudite audience. I wrote the book on parallel computation.

(↑) Present the following talks at the USM in Shah Alam, Malaysia in 2008:

1. "Research Methodologies and Current Research Topics in Computing."
2. "Overview of the ABET Process."
3. "Preparing a Self-Study for Accreditation."
4. "ABET's General Criteria for Computing Programs."
5. "On Obtaining a PhD in Computing."
6. "Writing a Dissertation."
7. "On Oral Presentations."
8. "On the Parallel Complexity of Hierarchical Clustering and CC-Complete Problems."
9. "Report Writing."

(↑) Present "The Complexity of Graph Labeling" at CMU in Chiang Mai, Thailand in 2008.

(↑) Present "The Complexity of the Evolution of Graph Labelings" at AASU in Savannah, Georgia in 2008.

(↑) At the Seminar on Higher Education for Science and Technology in Bangkok, Thailand in 2009, present the following talks:

1. "On Industrial Advisory Boards."
2. "Overview of ABET Accreditation."

Later in 2009, as part of the same traveling seminar series, I presented my two talks at the Prince of Songkla University in Hat Yai and at Khon Kaen University in Khon Kaen.

(↑) At CMU in Chiang Mai, Thailand in 2009, present the following talks:

1. "Sequential Algorithms for Problems on Trees."
2. "Parallel Algorithms for Problems on Trees."

(↑) Present "The Complexity of the Evolution of Graph Labeling" at the USNA in Annapolis, Maryland in 2009.

It was an honor to be invited to another of our nation's service academies to give a presentation. After my talk Dr. Reza Malek-Madani, who was the Director of Research and Scholarship at the Naval Academy, came up to me and said it was the best technical talk he'd ever heard. It was an extraordinary compliment. I thanked him. Shortly thereafter, the Naval Academy offered me a job that I happily accepted. I wanted to serve the nation by helping the Academy to build a program in cyber operations.

(↑) Present "A Wellness Profile Model and Dynamic Matching for Social Networks" at CMU in Chiang Mai, Thailand in 2010.

(↑) Present "Social Networking, Wellness, and Complexity" at Chulalongkorn University in Bangkok, Thailand in 2010.

The administrators at Chulalongkorn University tried to hire me again. I rejected their offers of finding me a Thai wife.

(↑) At CMU in Chiang Mai, Thailand in 2011, present a writing seminar consisting of the following sessions:

1. "On Journal Paper Writing."
2. "On Journal Paper Submission."

(↑) In 2011 via an online forum, deliver the presentation "USNA as a Member of CyberWatch" to members of CyberWatch.

(↑) Present "Ten Breakthroughs in Computing" at the Department of Computer Engineering, CMU in Chiang Mai, Thailand in 2011.

(↑) Present "Anatomy and Dissection of an Introduction to Cybersecurity Class" at the United States Air Force Academy in Colorado Springs, Colorado in 2011.

It was an honor to be invited back to the Air Force Academy. They were ramping up their cybersecurity program.

(↑) In 2012 present "On a Cybersecurity Class" at the following Thai institutions:

1. Khon Kaen University in Khon Kaen.
2. Mae Jo University in Mae Jo.
3. Mae Fah Luang University in Chiang Rai.
4. CMU in Chiang Mai.

(↑) In 2013 present "Network Reconnaissance, Attack, and Defense Laboratories for an Introductory Cybersecurity Course" at the following Thai venues:

1. Northern CMU in Hang Dong.
2. Far Eastern University in Chiang Mai.
3. Chiang Mai Rajaphat University in Mae Tang.
4. CMU in Chiang Mai.

(↑) Present "An Assessment Model for Game-Over Components in Cybersecurity Designs and the Model's Complexity" at the University of the District of Columbia in Washington, DC in 2013.

(↑) Present "Hardest Bicycle Race in the World" at the Rotary Club in Portsmouth, New Hampshire in 2015.

I described my experiences at the Race across America. The audience was astonished.

(↑) Present "Via Dinarica White Route" at the Rotary Club in Portsmouth, New Hampshire in 2017.

I described my friend Fiddlehead's and my experience of thru-hiking the Via Dinarica White Route trail in the Balkans.

Chapter 41
Journal Papers

I spent the majority of my career as a researcher. I published my work to advance science in order to contribute to human knowledge. I enjoyed doing groundbreaking research in the fields of computing, physics, and mathematics. I like problem solving. In this chapter I list my non-book and non-conference publications. Conference publications are given in the next chapter. Journal papers are peer-reviewed works. They must be submitted and accepted by an editor prior to publication. I chose journals based on their subject-matter preference, quality, and the style of works they specialized in publishing.

The journal-paper publication process is rigorous, especially with top-notch journals. Papers are peer reviewed by two to five referees. They might reject a work, provide comments or criticisms, or require revisions. If revisions are required, a paper must be edited and resubmitted. Once accepted for publication, a paper needs to be typeset. The typeset pages, called page proofs, are reviewed by the author to correct any errors introduced during the typesetting process. Once page proofs are approved, a paper is ready to appear in print. This entire process takes up to five years for a single publication.

With advances in publishing technology, it became possible to submit papers that were camera-ready. This advance eliminated the tedious process of reviewing typeset page proofs, and errors were no longer inadvertently introduced by the publisher. Camera-ready publishing shortened the time to print by about six months, which is critical for time-sensitive research.

Computer-science journals were the first to accept camera-ready papers, usually in the form of digital *Latex* files. Latex is a typesetting system for mathematics and technical papers. It isn't a WYSIWYG system—what you see is what you get. You code your materials, compile, debug, recompile, and then can view the output. Latex is much harder to master than software such as Microsoft WORD, which is WYSIWYG. Latex requires programming skill. It produces beautiful output. I became an expert in Latex. My colleagues often called on me for assistance.

In my career I worked with some gifted, dedicated researchers. Their names appear in our joint publications. If you fancy a title, you can read that work because these papers are archived in journals. I give their citations. Otherwise, simply enjoy reading the strange titles. Before I even embarked on the five-year publication process, I spent several years solving some of these research problems. Conducting and publishing ground-breaking research isn't for the faint of heart.

(↑) Publish the article "Ordered Vertex Removal and Subgraph Problems." *Journal of Computer and System Sciences,* 39(3):323–342, 1989.

Before the submission of my first journal paper, my PhD advisor Larry Ruzzo reviewed the article for me. He taught me a lot about research and writing. The *Journal of Computer and System Sciences* is one of the top journals in computer science. I was fortunate to publish my first paper there.

(↑) (With Larry Snyder) Publish the article "Achieving Speedups for APL on an SIMD Distributed Memory Machine." *International Journal of Parallel Programming,* 19(2):111–127, 1991.

I got involved with some of the early research in parallel computing and parallel-programming languages. Larry Snyder, who served on my PhD-Dissertation Committee, taught me a lot about research and writing.

(↑) Publish the article "A Model Classifying Algorithms as Inherently Sequential with Applications to Graph Searching." *Information and Computation,* 97(2):133–149, 1992.

This article contains numerous results from my PhD dissertation.

(↑) Publish the article "The Parallel Complexity of Approximation Algorithms for the Maximum Acyclic Subgraph Problem." *Mathematical Systems Theory: An International Journal on Mathematical Computing Theory,* 25(3):161–175, 1992.

This article was the first one that I published completely on my own, meaning that neither my PhD advisor nor anyone else was involved. I remember it being a bit scary. I felt a heavy responsibility to the scientific community.

(↑) Publish the refereed book chapter titled: "Towards Understanding the Effective Parallelization of Sequential Algorithms" for *Computer Science: Research and Applications.* Plenum Press, chapter 30, pages 395–406, 1992.

(↑) (With Pilar de la Torre and Teresa Przytycka) Publish the article "Optimal Tree Ranking is in NC." *Parallel Processing Letters,* 2(1):31–41, 1992.

I never met Teresa Przytycka, as we collaborated entirely online. Pilar de la Torre was my brilliant colleague at the UNH. She had PhDs in both mathematics and computer science. I learned a great deal from working with Pilar. She was an exceptionally dedicated researcher. RIP, Pilar.

(↑) Publish the invited refereed book chapter "Polynomial Completeness and Parallel Computation" for *Synthesis of Parallel Algorithms.* Morgan Kaufmann Publishers, chapter 21, pages 901–953, 1993.

As researchers learned about my work, I got invited to participate in a variety of projects. In this case I was asked to write a book chapter for the booming field of parallel algorithms.

(↑) Publish the article "Breadth-Depth Search is P-Complete." *Parallel Processing Letters,* 3(3):209–222, 1994.

(↑) (With Jonathan Machta) Publish the article "The Parallel Complexity of Growth Models." *Journal of Statistical Physics,* 77(3/4):755–781, 1994.

This article was the start of my long-term collaboration with the well-known physicist Jon Machta.

(↑) (With Pilar de la Torre and Alex Schäffer) Publish the article "Optimal Edge Ranking of Trees in Polynomial Time." *Algorithmica,* 13(6):592–618, 1995.

Algorithmica is one of the leading journals for papers dealing with algorithms.

(↑) (With Rossella Petreschi) Publish the article "Cubic Graphs." *ACM Computing Surveys,* 27(4):471–495, 1995.

While in Rome, I worked with my friend Rossella. We collaborated for many years.

(↑) (With Jonathan Machta) Publish the article "The Computational Complexity of Generating Random Fractals." *Journal of Statistical Physics,* 82(5/6):1299–1326, 1996.

(↑) Publish the article "Subtree Isomorphism is in DLOG for Nested Trees." *International Journal of Foundations of Computer Science,* 7(2):161–167, 1996.

DLOG stands for deterministic logarithmic space. I showed that the subtree isomorphism problem can be computed using very little computer memory. I traded off time for space. In other words I designed an algorithm that recomputes values when they're needed rather than storing them, due to space constraints. If it were possible to store the values, their values could be looked up with no need for recomputation. This research added to knowledge about space-time tradeoffs in computing.

(↑) (With Jonathan Machta) Publish the article "Parallel Computational Complexity and Logical Depth in Statistical Physics." *InterJournal of Complex Systems,* BArticle 57, www.interjournal.org, 1996.

In this work, Jon Machta and I built a bridge between computer science and physics. I excelled in physics in high school. When I entered college, before switching to mathematics, I majored in physics. Jon got me into a branch of physics that I enjoyed.

(↑) (With Kenneth Moriarty and Jonathan Machta) Publish the article "Parallel Algorithm and Dynamic Exponent for Diffusion-Limited Aggregation." *Physical Review*, E55:6211–6218, 1997.

I don't remember who came up with this title, but it describes our paper accurately. Ken was one of Jon's PhD students.

(↑) (With Kenneth Moriarty and Jonathan Machta) Publish the article "Parallel Computational Complexity in Statistical Physics." *InterJournal of Complex Systems*, BArticle 94, www.interjournal.org, 1997.

(↑) (With Rossella Petreschi) Publish the article "Computing Prüfer Codes Efficiently in Parallel." *Discrete Applied Mathematics*, 102:205–222, 2000.

(↑) (With H. James Hoover) Publish the invited refereed book chapter "Parallel Computation: Models and Complexity Issues" for *CRC Handbook of Algorithms and Theory of Computation*. CRC Press, chapter 45, pages 45.1–45.26, 1999.

When opportunities arose, Jim and I collaborated on projects.

(↑) (With Carme Álvarez) Publish the article "A Compendium of Problems Complete for Symmetric Logarithmic Space." *Computational Complexity*, 9:73–95, 2000.

Carme Álvarez and I began this work in 1995, when I was working as a Fulbrighter in Barcelona, Spain. Before our paper appeared, we spent five years going through the usual journal-publishing process.

(↑) (With Geir Agnarsson and Magnus Halldórsson) Publish the article "On Powers of Chordal Graphs and

Their Colorings." *Congressus Numerantium,* 100:41–65, 2000.

While working as a Fulbrighter to Iceland, I conducted research with these brilliant Icelanders.

(↑) (With Chris Williams) Publish the invited article "Parallel Computing in Engineering." *Journal of the University of Technology and Management Malaysia,* 1(2):10–14, 2004.

(↑) (With Chris Williams) Publish the invited article "Ten Computer Science Breakthroughs." *Journal of the University of Technology and Management Malaysia,* 4(2):62–74, 2006.

(↑) Publish the article a "Biography of Dr. Larry Snyder." *Scientific and Practical Computing Journal,* 1(2):71–73, 2007.

Larry Snyder was a mentor of mine at the UW. As I noted earlier, he served on my PhD-Dissertation Committee. I was invited to write this biography to honor Larry. It was my great pleasure.

(↑) (With Sanpawat Kantabutra) Publish the article "On the Parallel Complexity of Hierarchical Clustering and CC-Complete Problems," *Complexity,* Wiley, DOI 10.1002/cplx.20238, 14(2):18–28, 2008.

This article was my first of many with my friend Sanpawat "Bobby" Kantabutra. We met while I was working as a Fulbrighter in Chiang Mai, Thailand. Our long-term collaboration started then.

(↑) Publish the invited special article "An Overview of Some Issues Relating to the Accreditation Process," *Chiang Mai Journal of Science,* 35(3):391–398, 2008.

(↑) (With Chris Williams) Publish the article "Large-Scale Software Systems: Skills and Tools for Developers," *Journal of Management and Science*, 6(2):80–103, 2008.

(↑) Publish the invited article "Setting Up and Maintaining a Strong Industrial Advisory Board." *Scientific and Practical Computing Journal*, 3(2):23–34, 2010.

(↑) (With Sanpawat Kantabutra) Publish the invited book chapter "Introduction to Clustering: Algorithms and Applications" for *Dynamic and Advanced Data Mining for Progressing Technological Development*. IGI Global, chapter 10, pages 224–254, 2010.

(↑) (With Geir Agnarsson and Sanpawat Kantabutra) Publish the article "The Complexity of the Evolution of Graph Labelings," *Thai Journal of Mathematics*, 8(1):21–42, 2010.

(↑) (With H. James Hoover) Publish the invited book chapter "Parallel Computation: Models and Complexity Issues" for the *CRC Algorithms and Theory of Computation Handbook: General Concepts and Techniques*. CRC Press, second edition, chapter 28, pages 28.1–28.28, 2010.

(↑) Publish the invited article "Accurate and Efficient Accreditation Document Preparation," *Journal of Management and Science*, 8(1):113–20, 2010.

(↑) Publish the invited article "Wellness, Social Networking, and Algorithms." *Chiang Mai Journal of Science*, special issue, 38:17–30, 2011.

(↑) (With Sanpawat Kantabutra and Pattama Longani) Publish the invited article "A Mobility Model for Studying Wireless Communication and the Complexity of

Problems in the Model," special issue of *Networks*, 59(3):320–330, 2012.

I was invited to write this article for a special issue of *Networks* in honor of my friend Rossella. I did so with pleasure.

(↑) (With Chris Brown et al.) Publish the article "Anatomy, Dissection, and Mechanics of an Introductory Cybersecurity Class's Curriculum at the United States Naval Academy." *ASEE Computers in Education Journal*, 3(3):63–80, 2012.

I led this effort to get a number of my colleagues at the Naval Academy engaged in educational research. With this article, my co-authors and I shared our experience with a new course in cybersecurity. Other instructors made use of our work in developing their courses in cybersecurity.

(↑) (With Andrew Phillips, John Schultz, David Stahl, and Sarah Standard) Publish the article "Network Reconnaissance, Attack, and Defense Laboratories for an Introductory Cybersecurity Course." *ACM Inroads*, 4(3):52–64, 2013.

With this article, my co-authors and I shared our experience with laboratories for a course in cybersecurity. Other instructors made use of our work in developing their own labs.

(↑) (With Sanpawat Kantabutra) Publish the invited article "Survey of Clustering: Algorithms and Applications." Special issue of the *International Journal of Information Retrieval Research*, 3(2):1–29, 2013.

(↑) (With Allen Parrish and Andrew Phillips) Publish the article "Is It Time for ABET Cybersecurity Criteria?" *ACM Inroads,* 5(3):44–48, 2014.

This article laid the groundwork for developing ABET-accreditation Program Criteria for cybersecurity. We convinced the computing community as to its importance. Our continued work with the Cyber Education Project in getting that ABET-accreditation Program Criteria developed, approved, and implemented helped shape the development and content of cybersecurity curriculums throughout the world.

(↑) (With Geir Agnarsson and Sanpawat Kantabutra) Publish the article "The Complexity of Cyber Attacks in a New Layered-Security Model and the Maximum-Weight, Rooted-Subtree Problem," *Cybernetica,* 22(3):591–612, 2016.

(↑) (With Geir Agnarsson and Sanpawat Kantabutra) Publish the article "The Structure of Rooted Weighted Trees Modeling Layered Cybersecurity Systems," *Cybernetica,* 22(4):735–769, 2016.

Geir is my favorite collaborator. It's therefore appropriate that the last journal paper which I published was with him and my long-term collaborator Bobby. Geir is a brilliant mathematician, great problem solver, creative thinker, and excellent writer. He has great intuition. This final paper dealt with layered-security models and contained a lot of complex mathematics.

The essence of the paper is to determine the best-possible defensive strategy to protect a system in order to minimize the damage that can be done by a hacker. When a hacker breaks into a system, a separate (different) cost is paid for bypassing each security level. When a hacker breaks into disjoint regions of the system, various rewards and information are obtained.

We want to prevent hackers from getting into a game-over situation, where they end up having total control over a system. If that happens, the system becomes useless to its original owners. Our work provides insight into the structure of the types of systems that can be well defended from hackers, and conversely, those that are more vulnerable to attacks. This research gives insights into the designs necessary for more secure systems.

Chapter 42
Conference Papers

In many fields of study, conference papers aren't as prestigious to publish as journal papers. However, computer science is an exception. Due to the fast-paced and dynamic nature of the field, conference papers provide researchers with a venue for quickly disseminating new results. Conferences also give researchers a chance to gather, collaborate, brainstorm, and present their findings in front of peers. I met many of my collaborators at conferences. I had the great fortune to work with many excellent researchers.

Most of the bucket-list items here appeared in refereed/reviewed collections and conferences. For the ones appearing in conferences, either a co-author or I presented the paper at the conference. For the papers that I presented, in some cases I provided commentary in the chapter on presentations. A number of these preliminary works led to journal papers. They were discussed in the previous chapter. For these two reasons, I limit my commenting in this section.

(↑) (With David Notkin et al.) Publish the article "Experiences with Poker." ACM SIGPLAN Symposium on Parallel Programming: Experience with Applications, Languages, and Systems, New Haven, Connecticut, pages 10–20, 1988. *SIGPLAN NOTICES* 23(9):10–20, 1988.

David Notkin was a brilliant researcher, outstanding teacher, and mentor. He was generous with his time. While at the UW, I was fortunate to work with him. This paper was the first paper published that included my name. The paper had nothing to do with the card game Poker. Thank you and RIP, David.

(↑) Complete my dissertation: "The Complexity of Parallel Computations: Inherently Sequential Algorithms and P-Complete Problems." PhD Dissertation, UW, 1988.

I owe an enormous debt of gratitude to my PhD advisor Larry Ruzzo and to professors at the UW who served on my PhD-Dissertation Committee. They are: Richard Anderson, Larry Snyder, Pierre MacKay, and Richard Ladner. I learned a tremendous amount from these scientists.

(↑) (With Larry Snyder) Publish the article "Achieving Speedups for APL on an SIMD Parallel Computer." *APL Quote Quad,* 18(4):3–8, 1988.

Larry Snyder had a great writing style and a wonderful attitude toward publications. Collaborating with him on this paper taught me a tremendous amount.

(↑) Publish the article "The Parallel Complexity of Stack versus Queue Breadth-First Search." *Second IEEE Symposium on Parallel and Distributed Processing,* Dallas, Texas, pages 834–7, 1990.

(↑) Publish the article "Towards Understanding the Effective Parallelization of Sequential Algorithms."

SCCC International Conference on Computer Science, Santiago, Chile, pages 391–403, 1991.

(↑) (With Pilar de la Torre) Publish the article "Super Critical Tree Numbering and Optimal Tree Ranking are in NC." *IEEE Symposium on Parallel and Distributed Processing,* Dallas, Texas, pages 767–73, 1991.

(↑) (With Pilar de la Torre and Alex Schäffer) Publish the article "Optimal Edge Ranking of Trees in Polynomial Time (Extended Abstract)." *ACM-SIAM Symposium on Discrete Algorithms,* Austin, Texas, pages 138–144, 1993.

(↑) (With Jonathan Machta) Publish the article The Parallel Complexity of Algorithms for Pattern Formation Models. *Canada/France Conference on Parallel Computing,* Montreal, Canada. *Lecture Notes in Computer Science*, volume 805, Springer-Verlag, pages 23–34, 1994.

(↑) (With Jonathan Machta) Publish the article "The Parallel Complexity of Eden Growth, Solid-on-Solid Growth, and Ballistic Deposition." *European Symposium on Algorithms,* Utrecht, Netherlands. *Lecture Notes in Computer Science,* volume 855, Springer-Verlag, pages 436–447, 1994.

This title is one of my most interesting.

(↑) (With Carme Álvarez) Publish the article "A Compendium of Problems Complete for Symmetric Logarithmic Space." *Electronic Colloquium on Computational Complexity,* www.eccc.uni-trier.de/eccc, TR96-039, 25 pages, 1996.

(↑) (With Jonathan Machta) Publish the article "The Parallel Complexity of Randomized Fractals." *International Workshop on Parallel Algorithms for Irregularly Struc-*

tured Problems, Santa Barbara, California. *Lecture Notes in Computer Science,* volume 1117, Springer-Verlag, pages 351–6, 1996.

(↑) (With Jonathan Machta) Publish the article Parallel Computational Complexity and Logical Depth in Statistical Physics. *Workshop on Physics and Computation: PhysComp96,* New England Complex Systems Institute, Boston, Massachusetts, pages 201–7, 1996.

(↑) (With Kenneth Moriarty and Jonathan Machta) Publish the article "Parallel Computational Complexity in Statistical Physics." *International Conference on Complex Systems,* Nashua, New Hampshire. New England Complex Systems Institute, 1997.

(↑) (With Ellen Hepp) Publish the material "In-line/On-line: Class"—a classroom Web presentation for our book *In-line/Online: Fundamentals of the Internet and World Wide Web,* McGraw-Hill, 1998.

This cutting-edge website and the following one were two of the first of this nature and the most comprehensive ones accompanying any book at that time. They were used as models for other authors and were showcased by McGraw-Hill. Ellen and I programmed the entire (vast) websites on our own.

(↑) (With Ellen Hepp) Publish the material "In-line/On-line: Book"—a Web presentation supplementing our book *In-line/On-line: Fundamentals of the Internet and World Wide Web,* McGraw-Hill, 1998.

(↑) (With Rossella Petreschi) Publish the article "Computing Prüfer Codes Efficiently in Parallel." *Proceedings of the Discrete Mathematics and Theoretical Computer Science Symposium,* University of Auckland, New Zealand. Australian Computer Science Communications, Springer-Verlag, pages 21(3):202–216, 1999.

(↑) (With Geir Agnarsson and Magnus Halldórsson) Publish the abstract "On Chordal Graphs and Chromatic Polynomials." *Southeastern International Conference on Combinatorics, Graph Theory*, Boca Raton, Florida, 2000.

(↑) (With Magnus Halldórsson and Rossella Petreschi) Publish the article "On Computing Prüfer Codes and Their Corresponding Trees Optimally in Parallel (Extended Abstract)." *Proceedings of Journées de l'Informatique Messine,* Université de Metz, France, pages 125–130, 2000.

(↑) (With Charles Shipley and James Wogulis) Publish the article "Fast Sequential and Parallel Algorithms for Label Selection to Obtain Space Efficient Implementations in a Software Configuration Management System." *International Conference on Parallel Computing in Electrical Engineering,* Québec, Canada, pages 43–8, 2000.

I checked off this bucket-list item by publishing a paper with my Pomona College roommate Jimbo. He's an incredibly smart guy. While studying together at Pomona College, I learned a tremendous amount from him. He holds 25+ patents and spent most of his career at Google. I also got my colleague Chuck Shipley at AASU involved in conducting research. This title is one of the longest of my works.

(↑) (With H. James Hoover, Satoru Miyano, W. Larry Ruzzo, Shuji Shiraishi, and Takayoshi Shoudai) Digitally publish the "The Parallel Computation Project: Volume I: Fundamentals of Parallel Computation, Volume II: A Compendium of Problems Complete for P, and Volume III: A Compendium of Problems in the Class NC," 2000.

This website became an important one for researchers in parallel computation. It combined my work with Hoover and Ruzzo with a similar project originating in Japan. As noted earlier, I later went to work with Satoru Miyano at Tokyo University. I visited Takayoshi Shoudai at Kyushu University in Fukuoka.

(↑) (With Chris Williams) Digitally publish the material "Understanding Practical UNIX, Online Center," Franklin, Beedle & Associates, Inc., 2001.

The learning center that Chris Williams and I developed for this book was cutting edge at that time. It provided a host of additional activities and exercises to accompany my UNIX book. It included interactive quizzes and flash cards.

(↑) (With Ellen Hepp and Chris McCarthy) Digitally publish PowerPoint lecture notes supplementing the book *In-line/On-line: Fundamentals of the Internet and World Wide Web,* McGraw-Hill, 690 pages, 2001.

These were some of the first and most comprehensive lecture notes published by McGraw-Hill. They became the standard model for other authors. Many instructors taught their classes from these slides.

(↑) (With Ellen Hepp) Digitally publish the Online Learning Center to accompany *In-line/On-line: Fundamentals of the Internet and the World Wide Web,* McGraw-Hill, 2001.

(↑) (With Sergio De Agostino) Publish the article "Automata Theory," invited article, *Encyclopedia of Information Systems,* Academic Press, 47–63, 2003.

(↑) (With Daniel Liang) Publish the invited article "Object-Oriented Programming," *Encyclopedia of Information Systems,* Academic Press, 347–361, 2003.

Daniel Liang and I met as graduate students at a conference in the late 1980s. He later came to work for me at AASU in Savannah, Georgia. Daniel is a best-selling author of computer-programming books. With the publication of this article, we each checked off the bucket-list item of co-authoring a work.

(↑) Publish the article "Accurate and Efficient Accreditation Documentation Preparation." *Best Assessment Processes Symposium,* Rose-Hulman Institute of Technology, Terre Haute, Indiana, pages 45–52, 2003.

(↑) (With Ellen Hepp) Publish the invited article "The Internet," *Encyclopedia of Information Systems,* Academic Press, 667–81, 2003.

(↑) Publish the article "Leading a Self-Study Preparation." *Best Assessment Processes Symposium,* Rose-Hulman Institute of Technology, Terre Haute, Indiana, pages 47–54, 2004.

(↑) (With Sanpawat Kantabutra) Publish the article "Bottom-Up Hierarchical Clustering is CC-Complete." *Electronics, Computer, Telecommunications, and Information Technology Conference,* Chiang Rai, Thailand, pages 1264–7, 2007.

(↑) (With Sanpawat Kantabutra) Publish the invited article "A Mobility Model for Studying Wireless Communications," *International Conference for Interdisciplinary Mathematical & Statistical Techniques,* Shanghai, China, pages 37–8, 2007.

(↑) Publish the article "Utilizing an Advisory Industrial Board in the Accreditation Process." *Best Assessment Processes Symposium,* 9 pages, Atlanta, Georgia, 2008.

(↑) (With Geir Agnarsson and Sanpawat Kantabutra) Publish the article "The Graph Relabeling Problem and Its Variants." *International Conference in Electronics, Computer, Telecommunications, and Information Technology,* Krabi, Thailand, pages 49–52, 2008.

(↑) (With Geir Agnarsson and Sanpawat Kantabutra) Publish the article "The Complexity of the Evolution of Graph Labelings." *International Conference of Software Engineering, Artificial Intelligence, Networking, and Parallel-Distributed Computing,* Phuket, Thailand, pages 79–84, 2008.

(↑) Publish the invited article "Setting up and Maintaining a Strong Industrial Advisory Board," *Best Assessment Processes,* 9 pages, Indianapolis, Indiana, 2009.

(↑) Publish the article "Accreditation in Applied Science, Computing, Engineering, and Technology." *International Conference on Learning and Teaching,* 11 pages, Bangkok, Thailand, 2009.

(↑) (With David Cordes, Han Reichgelt, Jim Leone, Barbara Price, and Gayle Yaverbaum) Publish the article "Accreditation in Online and Hybrid Learning Environments." *ABET Symposium,* Las Vegas, Nevada, 2010.

(↑) Publish the article "ABET-Accreditation Timeline." *ABET Symposium,* Las Vegas, Nevada, 17 pages, 2010.

(↑) Publish the article "An Activity Profile Model and Dynamic-Matching Results for Social Networks Regarding Wellness Applications." *International Conference in*

Electronics, Computer, Telecommunications, and Information Technology, Chiang Mai, Thailand, 5 pages, 2010.

(↑) Publish the article "Wellness, Social Networking, and Algorithms." *International Computer Science and Engineering Conference,* 19 pages, Chiang Mai, Thailand, 2010.

(↑) Publish the invited article "Engaging Your Industrial Advisory Board," *ABET Academic Newsletter,* 2011.

(↑) (With Chris Brown et al.) Publish the article "Developing and Implementing an Institution-Wide Introductory Cybersecurity Class in Record Time." *Annual ACM Southeast Conference,* pages 95–100, Tuscaloosa, Alabama, 2012.

(↑) (With Chris Brown et al.) "Anatomy, Dissection, and Mechanics of an Introductory Cybersecurity Class's Curriculum at the United States Naval Academy." *Conference on Innovation and Technology in Computer Science Education,* pages 303–8, Haifa, Israel, 2012.

(↑) (With Andrew Phillips, John Schultz, David Stahl, and Sarah Standard) Publish the article "Network Reconnaissance, Attack, and Defense Laboratories for an Introductory Cybersecurity Course." *Annual ACM Southeast Conference,* 5 pages, Savannah, Georgia, 2013.

(↑) Publish the abstract "On a University-Wide Required Cybersecurity Course." In the *National Institute for Standards and Technology's Annual Shaping the Future of Cybersecurity Education Workshop,* Gaithersburg, Maryland, 2013.

(↑) (With Christopher Brown, Zachary Dannelly, Andrew Phillips, and Sarah Standard) Publish the article "Using a Message Board as a Teaching Tool in an Introductory Cybersecurity Course." *ACM Special Interest*

Group on Computer Science Education Conference, 308–13, Kansas City, Missouri, 2015.

I wanted to get my undergraduate student Zachary Dannelly involved in publishing a paper.

(↑) (With Geir Agnarsson and Sanpawat Kantabutra) Publish the article "The Complexity of Cyber Attacks in a New Layered-Security Model and the Maximum-Weight, Rooted-Subtree Problem," *Global Innovation and Knowledge Academy,* Valencia, Spain, appeared in *New Information and Communication Technologies for Knowledge Management Organizations,* 64–76, Springer International Publishing, 2015.

Chapter 43
Conclusions

In mountaineering and other activities, checklists are created to record achievements. For example, there are the Nuttalls—the 446 independent peaks in England and Wales that are 2,000+ feet high, all peaks 14,000+ feet high in Colorado, the seven summits, the highest peak in each African country, and so on. These and similar lists serve as lighthouses, guiding one to the next destination. They inspire. Such lists served as a compass for my life.

During the past two years, I gathered my lists together, organized them, and formed them into a bucket list. This process forced deep reflection. It inspired me. It added new items to my bucket list. It gave me (more) direction. I see a positive path forward. I need to get busy because there are so many things that I want to do. Checking off an item gives me pleasure. My true satisfaction and enjoyment though derive from participating in activities themselves and from creating long-lasting memories.

While reflecting on my life, I don't regret bucket-list items that I checked, but I do regret those I didn't. In some cases I waited too long. Other times I was unaware of an opportunity. Fear, bad timing, and costs limited me. I permanently deleted some bucket-list items (↓). I couldn't achieve them. It hurt. I felt disappointed. I felt sad. My losses motivate me to stay active. I learn from my mistakes.

I crossed 35 bucket-list items off from my 2,800+ items. With some missed opportunities, I never knew they wouldn't come again. I checked off 2,100+ items. I'm three-quarters of the way there. I have another 675+ to go. If I maintain good health, realistically I can check off another 15-20% of the remaining items on my list. Maybe I'm only dreaming. To live the dream, you must first dream it. I continue to dream.

To complete any category, by this I mean checking off all the bucket-list items in a given chapter, requires a huge amount of time and effort. It's certainly *not* easy to check off 90% of the items in any sublist, but once you do, the remaining 10% may require an equivalent amount of time and effort.[7] I saw this play out with US states. I visited 49 states and the District of Columbia by age 40, but it took me another 15 years before I finally made a special trip to North Dakota. Completing any category in its entirety is a special lifetime achievement.

I already traveled to more places than I can visit in the future. I won't be traveling another 3,200,000 miles in this lifetime. The moon is only 240,000 miles away. I need to be selective in what activities I choose to do and where I choose to travel. I can't make it to every destination on my bucket list. I'm okay with that. I won't get complacent. I won't stop trying.

I set some unrealistic goals. I'm not sure where my ambition came from. I naturally channeled my efforts into productive activities. Things I enjoyed. As an endurance athlete, I maintained a high-energy level. I was organized and a good planner. I tested and found out my limits. Once you taste success, you tend to believe in yourself more and take on greater challenges. Sup-

---

[7] As opposed to the more familiar 80-20 rule.

port and encouragement from others goes a long way, too, as does loving what you're doing.

I never had any extended down periods in my life due to illness, injury, or family-related issues. I was blessed with good genetics. My closest friends are all great, supportive, positive, and energetic people. I can honestly say that I wasn't bored in life. This look back has been healthy: to put things in context and perspective, to see where I spent my time, to help me lead a well-balanced life, and to make any necessary adjustments for the final phase. I'll keep dreaming and pressing forward.

I hope you're able to set and reach your goals. I hope this book illuminated your path. I hope you're inspired. Thanks for following along on my journey. Enjoy your journey!

When My Light Goes Out

I dove, caught, hit, kicked, swung, and biked.
I ran, threw, jumped, played tennis, and hiked.
Canoed, fished, kayaked, and swam at the lake.
Never stopped to count the candles on my cake.
Everything I knew, I did and I liked.

I love the mountains, nature, and trees.
I love the feeling of a warm, gentle breeze.
I learned and explained and taught and graded.
Through discovery and adventures life never felt jaded.
Thank you and please I said from my knees.

I saw the world because I liked to look.
My life's a gift I never mistook.
Rejoice with me friends as I say goodbye.
The trip's been wonderful so do not cry.
A gust and poof, there goes my book.

Books by Raymond Greenlaw

PALMARÈS (also available in electronic form).

The Thai Wife Story JOY (also available in electronic form), Book 1 of *The Thai Wife Series of Novels.*

The Thai Wife Story STAR (also available in electronic form), Book 2 of *The Thai Wife Series of Novels.*

Raymond's Checklist for Traveling in the USA (also available in electronic form), Book 1 of *Raymond's Checklist Series.*

Raymond's Checklist for Traveling in Thailand (also available in electronic form), Book 2 of *Raymond's Checklist Series.*

Raymond's Checklist for Traveling the World (also available in electronic form), Book 3 of *Raymond's Checklist Series.*

Raymond's Checklist for His Personal Bucket List, second edition (also available in electronic form), Book 4 of *Raymond's Checklist Series.*

Raymond's Checklist for Gear for a Long Hike, second edition (also available in electronic form), Book 5 of *Raymond's Checklist Series.*

Raymond's Checklist Cycling Gear, second edition (also available in electronic form), Book 6 of *Raymond's Checklist Series.*

The Hazards of Cycling in Thailand: Guidelines for Tourists, second edition (also available in electronic form).

Trapped in Thailand's Cave (also available in electronic form).

The Pacific Crest Trail: Its Fastest Hike, second edition (also available in electronic form).

Bob: My Dad, the Fisherman: A Father and Son's Relationship (also available in electronic form).

(With Saowaluk Rattanaudomsawat) *Essential Conversational Thai: Learn to Speak Thai Quickly, while Traveling in Thailand.*

You'll Never Walk Alone: Love Poems for My Sweetheart (also available in electronic form).

Poems of Raymond Greenlaw, 1986–2005 (also available in electronic form).

The Fastest Hike across Thailand (expected December 2021).

About the Author

Raymond "Wall" Greenlaw was born in Providence, Rhode Island, USA in 1961 to Roxy and Bob. Raymond has always enjoyed nature, big trees, lakes, mountains, and the sea. He writes about a wide range of topics and is the author of 35+ books.

www.ingramcontent.com/pod-product-compliance
Lightning Source LLC
Chambersburg PA
CBHW062145080426
42734CB00010B/1575